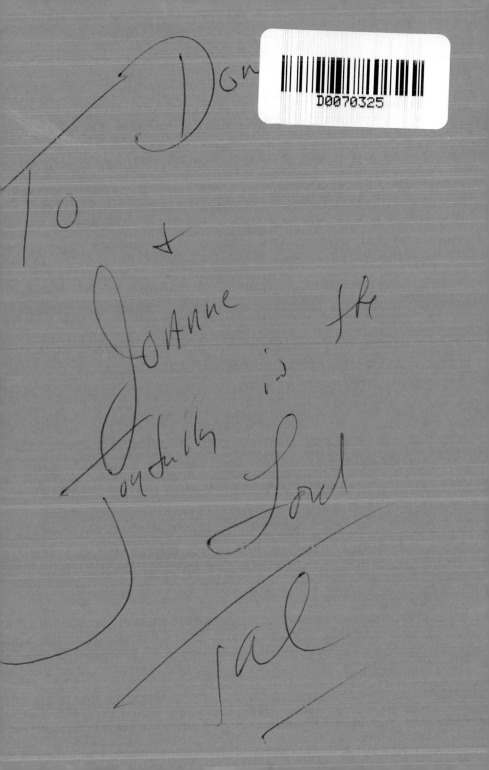

TAL D. BONHAM

BROADMAN PRESS
Nashville, Tennessee

© Copyright 1988 • Broadman Press
All Rights Reserved
4257-20
ISBN: 0-8054-5720-8
Dewey Decimal Classification: 248.4
Subject Headings: WIT AND HUMOR // CHRISTIAN LIFE
Library of Congress Catalog Number: 87-24999
Printed in the United States of America

Unless otherwise stated, all Scripture quotations are from the *New American Standard Bible*. Copyright © The Lockman Foundation, 1960, 1962, 1963, 1968, 1971, 1972, 1973, 1975, 1977. Used by permission.

Scripture quotations marked RSV are from the Revised Standard Version of the Bible, copyrighted 1946, 1952, © 1971, 1973.

Scripture quotations marked KJV are from the King James Version of the Bible.

Selections are reprinted from *The Healing Heart* by Norman Cousins, by permission of W. W. Norton & Company, Inc. Copyright © 1983 by Norman Cousins. Selections are reprinted from *The Smile Connection* by Esther Blumenfeld and Lynne Alpern with permission of Prentice-Hall, Inc., Englewood Cliffs, N.J., Copyright© 1986.

Library of Congress Cataloging-in-Publication Data

Bonham, Tal D., 1934-
  Humor, God's gift.

  Bibliography: p.
  Includes index.
  1. Wit and humor—Religious aspects. I. Title.
PN6149.R44B66 1988   202'.07   87-24999
ISBN 0-8054-5720-8

To Faye,
with whom I have
been in love and
in fun for almost
three decades

What They're Saying About
Humor: God's Gift
by Tal D. Bonham

CHARLES L. ALLEN: "a unique book . . . none like it
. . . it will bless all."

NORMAN VINCENT PEALE: "well-written, enjoyable,
and it gives fresh insight into the place of humor in the
Bible."

BILL MOYERS: "You have provided me laughter, joy,
and thought. Such trespass from the day's cares is all too
rare."

STEVE ALLEN: "An extensive bibliography, elaborate
footnotes (at the end of the book), a rich collection of
repeatable quotations, and a full index make this book
definitive in its field."

JERRY CLOWER: "Tal Bonham has written a book that
will be an aid to help all God's children giggle and grin
here and hereafter."

CALVIN MILLER: "You will laugh while you read this
book, but more important than that, you may decide that
laughter can be a life-style."

CAL SAMRA: "offers practical advice on how to develop
and use a wholesome and healing sense of humor, and to
triumph over life's problems with humor."

JIM SCULLY: "Tal Bonham not only writes about humor.
He incites it! . . . a chortlingly good compendium of the
funniest things ever said about laughter."

RUSTY AND LINDA WRIGHT: "a winner . . . It will warm
your heart, invigorate your mind, and lift your spirit."

EDWARD R. WALSH: "espouses that superlative truth
that the Supreme Being we worship is a God of life, love,
and laughter. For the *smileage* alone, it's worth the
price!"

Contents

Acknowledgments

I am deeply grateful to Robert Larremore who helped me wade through available material on this subject in several libraries. I also extend my gratitude to Chuck and Dottie Tommey who not only encouraged me on every hand but offered invaluable help in putting it all together. I am indebted to Peggy Harlan who did some preliminary typing on the manuscript. And to Mary Jo Freeman I owe a special word of appreciation for clerical assistance and for typing the majority of the manuscript; to Roger, her husband, I want to say a special thank you for your patience and advice; and thanks to Wesley, Melissa, and Aaron for your patience. To my wife, Faye, I am most grateful for allowing me to spend those many hours without interruption in the "dungeon study" at our home to write this book.

Foreword

by Steve Allen

It has probably never occurred to even most devout Christians to turn to the Bible as either a source for specific instances of humor or for evidence supporting the theological argument that God can be said to include humor among His own attributes. The connection has heretofore never occurred to me except as regards the one joke attributed to Jesus in which He says, "You are Peter, and upon this rock I will build My church." The humor did not, obviously, survive the translation into English, but it was there in the original Aramaic and other languages of the time simply because the name *Peter* means *rock*, as we see in such words as *petrified* or *petroleum*. According to Dr. Bonham, however, there is a great deal of scriptural support for the hypothesis that God is not only able to smile and laugh personally but has consciously bequeathed such comforting abilities to His human creatures.

The word *joy* is repeated in numerous instances in the Old and New Testaments; to Bonham it is self-evident that anyone experiencing rapturous enjoyment would express such emotion by the physical acts of smiling and laughter.

Granted that much, do we also find wit in the Bible? Dr. Bonham asserts that we do. "Two classes of people," he

11

says, "become the objects of the wise man's wit—the nagging woman and the lazy man." "It is better to live in a
corner of a roof, Than in a house shared with a contentious
woman" (Prov. 21:9). And note how similar to one of those
"Tonight Show" jokes in which Ed McMahon says "How
[adjective] was it?" is Proverbs 26:15. "The sluggard buries his hand in the dish; He is weary of bringing it to his
mouth again."

It strikes me that it isn't entirely inconsistent with Dr.
Bonham's theory that the Scriptures were written by the
wittiest people on earth: the Jews. Humor and wit are
certainly characteristic of ancient as well as modern Jewish literature. Would it not be unusual, therefore, if such
a lengthy collection of documents as the Bible contained
no humor at all?

Dr. Bonham, although he writes with a light, easy-to-
read style, has clearly done his homework and is not
merely sharing with us a personal hunch unsupported by
research. Nor is he the only Bible scholar to argue that the
Old Testament contains instances of jokes, riddles, proverbs, puns, irony, satire, and perhaps other forms of
humor as well, despite the fact that some of this has been
obscured by the process of translation.

The first time the word *laughter* appears in the Old
Testament is in the seventeenth chapter of Genesis
wherein we are told that when Abraham was advised his
over ninety-year-old wife was going to have a baby, he fell
on his face and laughed. Sarah had the same reaction
when she heard the news.

One refreshing aspect of the argument which Dr. Bonham raises is that the matter is of considerable interest
regardless of the reader's own perceptions about the
Bible. In other words, both those who believe that, even
as science, the Bible is more authoritative than any

avowedly scientific textbook ever written and those, on the other hand, who view it as only profoundly important religious documentation but in no sense divinely inspired, can take pleasure in addressing the question, Is there consciously intended humor in the Old and New Testaments and, if so, how much?

Dr. Bonham, of course, views the Bible with appropriate reverence as the inspired Word of God and cites examples of humor in both Testaments. Of special interest to Christians is an extensive study of Jesus' use of humor in His preaching, teaching, and interpersonal relationships. This book also draws on recent medical studies on humor and its now-acknowledged therapeutic value. You will read about "clowning around the hospital" and how humor can be used to counter pessimism, bitterness, worry, stress, and loneliness. There is much said here, too, about the possible place humor might have as one of the positive emotions for the prevention of suicide—especially among teenagers.

The author asks, "Who says good humor must be offensive humor?" taking issue with hostile, sexist, sick, and dirty jokes. He not only deals with these offensive uses of humor, but he shares practical suggestions and examples for developing a good sense of humor with one's spouse, children, fellow workers, or classmates.

An extensive bibliography, elaborate footnotes (at the end of the book), a rich collection of repeatable quotations, and a full index make this book definitive in its field.

Introduction

Will you celebrate humor and humorous laughter with me in the following pages? God has given you and me the unique gift of humor and I want us to be good stewards of His gift. I hope you will laugh with me generally throughout the whole book.

In these pages, I view the Bible with reverence as the inspired Word of God and cite many examples of humor in both the Old and New Testaments. You will find biblical references throughout the book.

I trust that the two chapters on the therapeutic value of humor will help many to overcome their pessimism, bitterness, worry, stress, and loneliness. If only one person could be better informed about the part humor might play in the prevention of suicide, it would have been worth it all!

I contend that, if you are ready to die, you are also ready to live and to laugh. Such preparation for the hereafter restores self-esteem, allows us to die laughing, and turns our speculations into certainties.

Is anyone out there as tired as I am of offensive humor? I register a negative word about such humor but not without also sharing some positive suggestions for developing a wholesome sense of humor in our homes, on the job, and at school.

14

I have also shared in these pages some helpful suggestions for collecting and using humor as a tool of communication on the platform and in the pulpit.

You will probably read and reread the final chapter which merely shares some humorous illustrations from some of the most unlikely places. I hope you will learn to celebrate humor to the point that you can laugh at death because you know why the reaper is so grim.

The "Quotable Quotations" are included in this book because few collections of quotations contain references to subjects related to humor.

Come now and celebrate with me!

Tal D. Bonham

1

The Laughter Factor

"If you ever need a place to sleep, just stop by my house anytime," Frank Sears had said to me on several occasions. He was a respected pastor in Oklahoma, and I was a struggling ministerial student working my way through college and preaching all over the state on Sundays. I thought of myself as a "young Billy Graham." However, as I look back over some of my sermon outlines from those days, I am sure those rural congregations had other opinions of their "supply preacher."

As I drove through Frank Sears's town late one evening, I decided to take him up on his offer. I watched as he shuffled sleeping children from bed to bed and finally found me a place to sleep for a few hours before driving on to a preaching engagement later that morning.

Several years later, the news reached me that Frank Sears, a victim of cancer, had lost both legs. He had returned from the hospital and was recuperating at home.

I should call and try to encourage him. But what would I say? How would I approach the subject of the loss of his legs? I started to dial the phone several times and hung up. I could think of nothing to say. Then, I let the phone ring. He must have been sitting nearby because he picked it up after only one ring.

"Shorty Sears speaking!" he boomed joyfully.

"Shorty Sears?" I asked.

"Yes, Shorty Sears. Surely you've heard about my surgery. In fact both legs had to be amputated," he stated.

"Yes, that's what I called about, Brother Sears, to see how you are feeling," I mumbled, hardly able to conceal my surprise at the way he had answered the telephone.

After visiting with my friend a few minutes, I hung up the phone and laughed. Laughed? At a man with no legs? Yes, I laughed and laughed and laughed. But why? What was the laughter factor?

A dear friend of mine is the elected leader of his denomination. Some say he is one of the greatest preachers in America. But he is blind. His faithful wife assists him in the office and walks close by his side wherever he goes.

When I first met him, I noticed that he had an infectious sense of humor.

"What do you do for relaxation?" he asked.

"Oh, I play a little golf," I said.

"Well, I would like to play you someday," he said.

I tried not to act surprised as I said, "Anytime!"

"I would like one concession," he continued, "to counter for my blindness."

"Anything you ask," I agreed.

"The only stipulation I have," he continued, "is that we play at night!"

I laughed. At a blind man? Not really. I laughed at his ability to make me laugh at his blindness. But what was the laughter factor?

Feeling Good All Over

Many interesting attempts have been made to define the laughter factor. Academically, laughter is simply defined as giving audible expression to an emotion by the expulsion of air from the lungs. Josh Billings added his own personal touch to that definition when he said, "Laughter is the sensation of feeling good all over, and showing it principally in one spot."[1]

Students of humorous laughter have isolated for us the various forms of humor into such categories as pun, parody, joke, quip, witticism, satire, and comedy. One does not have to be a serious student of the subject to know that humor makes us grin, smile, chortle, chirrup, giggle, titter, crow, cackle, shout, leap, roar, and burst into laughter. Those of us who have observed the behavior of one who is intoxicated, high on drugs, or afflicted with a certain mental or physical disorder are also aware of the fact that some laughter is not funny.

Robert Benchley was probably correct when he said, "Defining and analyzing humor is a pastime of humorless people."[2] One may use humor effectively, classify it systematically, and discover penetrating truths about it without really knowing why people laugh. It has been said that trying to define laughter is like dissecting a frog—in the process you might learn something about the anatomy of a frog, but it sure ruins the frog.

Thomas Hobbes defined laughter as "nothing else but sudden glory,"[3] and Wyndham Lewis said that laughter is simply "the mind sneezing."[4] Theologian Reinhold Niebuhr surmised that "laughter is a sane and healthy response to the innocent foibles of men; and even to some which are not so innocent."[5]

When asked to distinguish between a humorist and a comedian, Grady Nutt said, "Comedy is contrived, but humor is lived."[6] He went on to describe living humor as "the ability to laugh at a hammer-hit thumb after the nail has grown back!"[7]

If humor is lived, Kenneth Bird defined it properly when he said, "Humor is falling downstairs, if you do it in the act of warning your wife not to."[8] Irvin S. Cobb gave a living definition of humor when he described it as "tragedy standing on its head with its pants torn."[9] "Everything is funny as long as it is happening to somebody else," claimed Will Rogers.[10]

Through the years, it seems that humankind has demanded a more philosophical definition of the laughter factor. Quintillian, a first-century Roman scholar, said that no one had as yet explained adequately the meaning of humor. We are probably still waiting for that explanation. However, there have been three basic theories as to why people laugh.

Why Do We Laugh?

(1) *The Superiority Theory.* Plato surmised that laughter is an expression of one's feeling of superiority over someone else. "The laughable person is the one who thinks himself wealthier, better looking, more virtuous, or wiser than he really is."[11] Aristotle, agreeing with Plato, taught that laughter is basically a form of derision.

To say that all laughter is based upon a feeling of superiority is difficult to defend in light of the many cases of humorous and nonhumorous laughter that simply do not involve feelings of superiority. I for one am not ready to accept the theory that all laughter started from the roar of triumph in a prehistoric jungle. Such a theory opens Pandora's box for racist jokes, sick jokes, and all sorts of offensive humor. I can accept Romain Gary's definition of superiority much better: "Humor is an affirmation of dignity, a declaration of man's superiority to all that befalls him."[12]

(2) *The Incongruity Theory.* Immanuel Kant is generally considered the father of the incongruity theory of humor. It contends that humor is derived from the

unexpected or illogical. Thus humor is based on the assumption that we do live in an orderly universe. Kant illustrated his theory by telling the story of the heir of a rich relative who wished to arrange for an imposing funeral by hiring paid mourners. The incongruity? The more money he paid the mourners to look sad, the happier they looked![13]

Certainly the incongruities of life are often our best sources of humor. However, to say that all humor is derived from the unexpected and the illogical cannot be fully accepted.

(3) *The Relief Theory.* Some suggest that laughter is the release of psychic energy in an effort to escape from reason or prohibitions. While the superiority theory focuses on emotions involved in laughter, and the incongruity theory focuses on objects or ideas causing laughter, the relief theory deals with the biological function of laughter.

Sigmund Freud contended that we all store up psychic energy that is not needed. This surplus energy is discharged in laughter. However, Freud contended that humor is inevitably used for all sorts of psychological purposes—to degrade or intimidate, to disguise or compensate, and to express or deny a subconscious feeling.[14]

Some claim that this theory is evident in communities where there are high sex standards because many jokes are told there about sexual prohibitions. In the days of prohibition, many jokes were told about people who sought out bootleg liquor. In places where there are strict drug laws, a joke about drugs always seems to be funny to some people.

There is no doubt in my mind that humor is one of the best ways to relieve tension in any setting. I suspect that the use of humor by our presidents through the years is one of the best examples of such relief.

Oh, What a Relief!

Abraham Lincoln once said, "With the fearful strain that is on me night and day, if I did not laugh I should die."[15] The "fearful strain" of the presidency of the United States has been borne best by those who were able to laugh.[16]

In 1981 when President Ronald Reagan was shot in the chest by a would-be assassin, he reportedly said to his doctors, "I hope you're all Republicans!" That comment did more to relieve the strain on this nation than any of the broadcasts or news releases.

Many times the joke is on the president. President Gerald Ford was known for his ability to slip and fall on stairs, and to drive a golf ball into a crowd along the fairway.

Bill Moyers, while serving with President Lyndon Johnson, was often asked by the president to lead in prayer before meals. On one occasion, Moyers was sitting on the opposite end of the table from the president during the prayer.

"Speak up, Bill. I can't hear you!" Johnson suggested.

From the other end of the table, Moyers replied, "Mr. President, I was not speaking to you."

In 1944, President Roosevelt was accused of sending a destroyer to pick up his dog Fala from an Aleutian island. In a speech to the Teamsters Union, the President said, "Well, of course, I don't resent attacks, and my family doesn't resent attacks, but Fala does resent them. He hasn't been the same dog since."

President John F. Kennedy was often questioned about his Catholic beliefs in the 1960 presidential campaign. He responded, "Reporters have asked me my opinion about

the Pope's infallibility. So I asked my friend Cardinal
Spellman what I should say. Cardinal Spellman said, 'I
don't know what to tell you, Senator. All I know is that he
keeps calling me Spillman.' "

When accused of nepotism for appointing his brother
Robert as attorney general, President Kennedy replied,
"Bobby wants to practice law, and I thought he ought to
get a little experience first."

President Lyndon Johnson's humor was often coarse.
On one occasion he teased reporters visiting his ranch,
"Do you fellows know what a steer is? It's a bull that's lost
its social standing."

One of President Richard Nixon's more humorous mo-
ments occurred in London shortly after the 1968 election.
Prime Minister Harold Wilson had just appointed John
Freeman, former editor of *The New Statesman* (a journal
that had criticized candidate Nixon), as ambassador to the
United States.

With Mr. Freeman attending the dinner, there was a
great deal of tension. But Mr. Nixon managed to clear the
air when he said, "Everybody can relax now, because he's
the new ambassador and I'm the new statesman."

President Jimmy Carter once said to a White House
correspondents' dinner, "I'm not going to say anything
terribly important tonight, so you can all put your crayons
away."

President Dwight D. Eisenhower testified to the power
of humor to relieve tension when he said, "Laughter can
relieve tension, soothe the pain of disappointment, and
strengthen the spirit for the formidable tasks that always
lie ahead."[17]

Fun for Fun's Sake

Humor *does* relieve tension. However, if all laughter must be explained by the relief theory and all of its ramifications, it takes all of the fun out of it for me.

There is plenty of evidence to believe that humor often expresses hidden feelings and thoughts and that many use humor to express their own superiority while others use it to manipulate an audience. There is no doubt that humor has the power to reduce tension. But who says we have to agree that all laughter is caused by one or a combination of these three theories? And who among us is ready to admit that all humor is designed to degrade, intimidate, disguise, compensate, or express or deny subconscious feelings?

Humor is its only excuse for being! Laughter is a gift from God. I totally agree with Tom Mullen when he said, "To deny the validity of laughter for its own sake is to be the victim of a bad joke."[18]

If the superiority theory, incongruity theory, and relief theory are all there is to laughter and humor, the apparent conclusions are rather morbid. For one thing, this would mean that God has no sense of humor. John Morreall reasons that God cannot be surprised at anything because He knows the past, present, and future.[19] Since God is a changeless Being, nothing that happens could amuse Him. He would already know about all the possible incongruities of life, and He would not be able to experience the psychological shift that, according to some, is behind all laughter.

Another morbid conclusion of the three theories of laughter is that there's no fun just for fun's sake. Everything has hidden meaning. Tom Mullen began his book *Laughing Out Loud: and Other Religious Experiences* with an interesting story about an engineer, a psychologist, and a theologian who were on a hunting trip in northern Canada.[20]

They knocked on the door of an isolated cabin seeking shelter and rest. The cabin was not, at the moment, occupied, but the front door was unlocked. They entered the small, two-room cabin and noticed something quite unusual. A large potbellied, cast iron stove was suspended in midair by wires attached to the ceiling beams.

Why would a stove be elevated from the floor? Each of them began to look behind the phenomenon for "hidden meanings." The psychologist concluded, "It is obvious that this lonely trapper, isolated from humanity, has elevated his stove so he can curl up under it and vicariously experience a return to his mother's womb."

The engineer surmised, "The man is practicing laws of thermodynamics. By elevating his stove, he has discovered a way to distribute heat more evenly throughout the cabin."

But the theologian had a better explanation: "I'm sure that hanging his stove from the ceiling has a religious meaning. Fire lifted up has been a religious symbol for centuries."

The psychologist, the engineer, and theologian continued their debate for some time without really resolving the issue. Finally, when the trapper returned, they immediately asked him why he had hung his potbellied stove by wires from the ceiling.

His answer was rather simple: "Had plenty of wire, not much stovepipe!"

Laughter as God's Gift

I join Tom Mullen in deploring the modern preoccupation with examining life for "deeper meanings." It doesn't do much for humor.

Question: What's black and white and red all over?
Answer: A newspaper.

I first heard this riddle when I was a child and have laughed at it through the years with my own children.

However, Martha Wolfenstein psychoanalyzed this simple little riddle and just about ruined it for me. She claimed that the key word is *red*. Red signifies blushing and "black and white and red all over" becomes a naked person. The hair is black. The skin is white, and he or she turns red all over from the shame of being exposed.

Wolfenstein reconstructed the riddle: "Why is a naked person like a newspaper?" The newspaper is substituted for the naked person, and reading the newspaper symbolized peeking.[21] So, do you get the picture? It has something to do with peeking at a naked person. Horrors!

Question: Why do fire fighters wear red suspenders?
Answer: To hold up their trousers.

Wolfenstein saw in this riddle the combined themes of forbidden looking and exhibition, sex difference, and the danger of mutilation. I don't even want to bore you with how she arrived at such a ridiculous idea. The frog is hurting too much!

When I am asked by a teenager, "How can you tell when an elephant is in the telephone booth with you?" And I am told, "You can smell the peanuts on his breath!" I am going to laugh. I refuse to consider this little joke as a venting of antagonism toward elephants, a sense of superiority to pachyderms, or the possibility that this teenager has a deep fear of being run down by a herd of wild elephants. I'm just going to laugh—for the fun of it! Why look for deeper meanings?

The laughter factor is a vital part of this universe created by God. Fulton J. Sheen used to say, "Man is the only joker in the deck of nature." William Hazlit explained that mankind is the only animal that laughs and weeps because "he is the only animal that is struck with the difference between what things are and what they ought to be."[22]

Conrad Hyers asserted that laughter is a gift to humankind, noting that the most highly trained and domesticated animals neither get the point of a single pun or witticism nor devise any of their own.[23] Jackson Lee Ice asserted that mankind is "the most humorous-seeking, humor-making, and humor-giving species that has walked the earth."[24] Fulke Greville added that "man is the only creature endowed with the power of laughter; is he not also the only one that deserves to be laughed at?"[25]

Max Eastman, in his classic book *The Sense of Humor,* concluded that laughter is an innate part of humanity's creation. It is supported by the fact that children never need to be taught to laugh, but when not to laugh.[26]

Who can deny that God had a hand in laughter after reading the following anonymous description of a smile:

> It costs nothing, but creates much good. It enriches those who receive it without impoverishing those who give it away. It happens in a flash but the memory of it can last forever. No one is so rich that he can get along without it. No one is too poor to feel rich when receiving it. It creates happiness in the home, fosters goodwill in business, and is the countersign of friends. It is rest to the weary, daylight to the discouraged, sunshine to the sad, and nature's best antidote for trouble.
>
> Yet it cannot be bought, begged, borrowed, or stolen,

for it is something of no earthly good to anybody until it is given away willingly.

Humorous laughter must be a gift from God. Only God could bestow upon His creation something as enjoyable as humor that would release us from the unbearable responsibilities of life and preserve us from our pompousness.

Laughter is often our best alternative to crying, and all of us know that laughing people learn more than crying people. Those who have an unusual capacity for laughter also seem to have an unusual capacity for seriousness.

Laughter is the opposite of criticism. Criticism destroys relationships while laughter builds them. Someone has said, "A smile is a curve that straightens out a lot of things."

Laughter seems to be our sixth sense. The other five senses enhance the joys of life, but a sense of humor causes life to be enjoyable. Thomas Carlyle exclaimed: "How much lies in laughter: the cipher-key, wherewith we decipher the whole man!"[27]

The Best Sense of All

We have discussed laughter. Now, let us approach the subject of "a good sense of humor," which someone has described "as the best sense of all."

Most of us understand laughter. But what about the subject of humor? John E. Benson said, "Perhaps the best way to define humor is to describe it objectively without comment, and then hazard a guess or two."[28] Julius Gordon claimed that humor is essentially an expression of humaneness to be regarded as a form of "laughing-kindness."[29] Someone described a sense of humor as "instant intellect." Research has revealed that students who ranked high scholastically were not the most serious or sober minded, but were those who possessed a better sense of humor than the poorer students who tended to laugh indiscriminately.[30]

Paul King Jewett said, "Real wit is a flash of genius."[31] I suspect Charles R. Gruner would agree with this definition because he said, "It has been documented that laughter, along with a well-rounded sense of humor, is one of the surest signs of intelligence."[32]

Langston Hughes claimed that, "Humor is your own smile surprising you in your mirror"[33] while Gene Perret defined a sense of humor as three abilities: to see things as they are, recognize things as they are, and accept things as they are.[34]

William J. Tobin said, "Humor is anything—joke, jest, satire, quotable quote, startling fact or note—that makes people laugh or inspires them to react with a warm, knowing smile of appreciation."[35] But Grady Nutt expressed my feelings well when he said, "I think I could grow a new tooth by next Thursday easier than I can define humor."[36]

I don't plan to grow a new tooth by next Thursday. However, I would like to at least hazard a guess or two as to what we mean when we say that someone has a "good sense of humor."

(1) The "I'm funny" sense of humor. This is the one who laughs at that which I want her to laugh. In other words, she laughs at my jokes. I am not really describing this person's sense of humor but my ability to make this person laugh.

(2) The "it's funny" sense of humor. One has a "good sense of humor" who laughs at the same jokes, movies, cartoons, or situations at which I laugh. In other words, we see "eye to eye" on the same kind of humor. In this sense I am speaking more of the material that makes both of us laugh than I am of one's sense of humor.

(3) The "he's funny" sense of humor. This person is funny because he has a tremendous repertoire of jokes and funny stories. I am describing his ability to amuse a large segment of society, including myself.

(4) The "no respect" sense of humor. This person has a "good sense of humor" because she can "take a joke" or enjoy a joke at her own expense.

(5) The "more than funny" sense of humor. This person has a creative ability to produce that which causes laughter. Some people have a knack for being able to create stories, jokes, plays, and other material which cause us to laugh. Where would the great comedians be today without those who have the "more than funny" sense of humor?

(6) The "big picture" sense of humor. I am speaking of more than jokes and laughter. I am describing one who has his feet on the ground and his life anchored to something more stable than the ground. In short, I am speaking of one who is "at rest" with the Creator of humorous laughter.

Resting in God

The Christian life is described as entering the sabbath day's rest (Heb. 4:1-9). When one rests in God, one has found the basis on which to possess a "good sense of humor."

Martin Luther struggled for years with the legalistic expectations of his religion until he clearly understood that "The just shall live by faith" (Rom. 1:17, KJV), and that "man is justified by faith without the deeds of the law" (Rom. 3:28, KJV). When Martin Luther was able to trust God's grace rather than his own good works, he expressed his feelings in 1529 in that famous hymn: "A Mighty Fortress Is Our God." When we see God as all powerful and able to win our battles for us, we can rest in Him and truly possess a sense of well-being and a sense of humor.[37] Note the second stanza of Luther's hymn:

> Did we in our own strength confide,
> Our striving would be losing;
> Were not the right Man on our side,
> The Man of God's own choosing.
> Dost ask who that may be?
> Christ Jesus, it is He;
> Lord Sabaoth His name,
> From age to age the same,
> And He must win the battle.

What does all of this have to do with a sense of humor? Ask the jovial weatherman Willard Scott what makes him so happy, and he will give you this answer: "I'm happy and jocular because I believe in Jesus Christ and His teachings. . . . I believe in life after death. I know that my sins (and they have been many) have been forgiven."[38] We must conclude that a religion offering salvation, forgiveness, and eternal life cannot help but mold one's personality as well as one's outlook on life.

Who could number the thousands who have been blessed by the ministry of Norman Vincent Peale? His emphasis on the positive, humorous attitude has helped many people to recover from the emotional steamrollers of life. In his book *The Positive Power of Jesus Christ*, Peale told of his own relationship to Christ. When he was a young man in Cincinnati, Ohio, his father was preaching a series of revival meetings, but it never occurred to young Norman and his brother that they needed "saving." After all, they were the sons of a minister and felt that they had, by birth, simply inherited a relationship to the living God through Christ.

Peale described the experience that is the key to his positive approach to life's problems:

> Mother taught a Sunday School class for boys. She was a natural-born and highly gifted communicator. Besides, she knew boys very well and what would appeal to them. So her Sunday School talks were a bit about the Cincinnati Reds and a lot about the greatness of Jesus. She described His boyhood, young manhood, and, finally, how He went about doing good and helping people. She described graphically how He "set His face to go to Jerusalem," and the manly courage that was required to go to the Cross for our salvation.
>
> Her description of His endurance of suffering and pain as He carried the Cross really reached us, and we were thrilled and impressed when Pilate exclaimed, "Ecce homo!" (Behold the man). Mother made it read, "What a man!" So when she asked Bob and me to follow Him, we declared, "For now and always." At the same time she got over to us that there was sin in us from our belonging to the human race and that only the blood of Christ could wash it out and protect us from any more of it. We stood with others at the altar of the church, hand in hand, looking up at our father and publicly confessing Christ. My mother told me years later that Bob and I came to her that night and said we felt peace and joy in our hearts.[39]

Drake Levine said, "The ability to laugh is a measure of man's adjustment to his environment." Alan Watts said, "Humor is nothing other than perfect self-awareness." Even though Levine and Watts may not have adhered to my definition of a sense of humor, it is my firm conviction that we are able to adjust to our environment and possess self-awareness only when our humor is founded in peace with God.

At Peace with God

It would seem that peace of mind and a wholesome sense of humor go hand in hand. However, one may laugh and cause others to laugh, yet really not have peace of mind. Sometime in the last century, a prominent European physician was examining an elderly man who complained of several vague physical ailments. However, the physician could find nothing wrong with him and concluded that his imagined sickness might be serving as a mask for stress or depression.

Suddenly, the doctor thought of a solution to the man's problem. Joseph Girmaldi, the world's greatest clown, was in town for a performance that very evening.

"Why don't you go and see Girmaldi tonight?" the doctor suggested to his patient.

"But you don't understand, doctor," complained the distressed patient, "I *am* Girmaldi!"[40]

The Sociology Department of Duke University has isolated eight suggestions for those seeking peace of mind:[41]

(1) The absence of suspicion and resentment—nursing a grudge is a major factor in unhappiness.

(2) Not living in the past—an unwholesome preoccupation with old mistakes and failures leads to depression.

(3) Not wasting time and energy fighting conditions you cannot change—cooperate with life, instead of trying to run away from it.

(4) Force yourself to stay involved with the living world —resist the temptation to withdraw and become reclusive during periods of emotional stress.

(5) Refuse to indulge in self-pity when life hands you a raw deal—accept the fact that nobody gets through life without some sorrow and misfortune.

(6). Cultivate the old-fashioned virtues—love, honor, compassion, and loyalty.

(7) Don't expect too much of yourself—when there is too wide a gap between self-expectation and your ability to meet the goals you have set, feelings of inadequacy are inevitable.

(8) Find something bigger than yourself to believe in—self-centered, egotistical people score lowest in any test for measuring happiness.

How can we avoid resentment? Forget the past? Cooperate with life? Deal with depression? Bear our burdens? Develop compassion? Have a positive attitude?

Perhaps the last conclusion of the Duke University study holds the key—finding something bigger than ourselves to believe in. Finding peace with God is the ultimate way to true happiness and a genuine sense of humor.

Conclusion

What is the laughter factor? Why do people laugh? What does it mean to have "a good sense of humor?" Laughter is simply a gift from God to that part of His creation which He chose to create "in His image." To be "in fun" is to be human. Some of our laughter may be traceable to feelings of superiority, incongruous situations, and the release of tension. But who says that all laughter must have "hidden meanings"?

The real laughter factor involves much more than being "in fun." It also involves being "at peace" with the Creator of laughter. Salvation, forgiveness, and eternal life are the real laughter factors.

At this point, the skeptic might ask, "Does God have a sense of humor?" Hopefully, the next chapter will answer that question with a resounding, "YES!"

2

Yes, God Has a Sense of Humor

"I noticed that you use humor in your preaching," a man observed rather judgmentally after a service in which I had spoken.

"Yes, I do. I find it both helpful to me and to those who are listening."

As he squared off like a boxer about to land a knockout blow on the nose of his opponent he asked, "How do you get around the apostle Paul?"

"Get around the apostle Paul?" I asked. "What do you mean?"

"Well," he continued, "Paul said in Ephesians 5:4 that Christians should not engage in jesting!"

This encounter reminded me of a story I had heard many years ago about a little girl who had become a Christian and was baptized in a country church on Easter Sunday morning. That afternoon she ran through the house singing and dancing.

Her sour grandfather rebuked her with these words, "You ought to be ashamed of yourself! Just joined the church and you're singing and dancing on the Lord's Day!"

Crushed by her grandfather's attitude, the child strolled out to the barn, climbed up on the corral fence, and stared at an old mule standing there with a sad, droopy look on his long face.

As she reached over and patted the mule sympathetically, she said, "Don't cry, old mule. I guess you've just got the same kind of religion that Grandpa has!"

Wanted—More Happy Saints

It never occurred to me that I would ever have to "get around" the Bible to justify the use of humor in communicating biblical truth. However, I have learned that some use this verse in Paul's Letter to the Ephesians as their sole proof text to squelch a godly sense of humor.

It is always helpful to read a verse of Scripture in its context. Ephesians 5:4 is a part of that great passage where Paul challenged Christians to be "imitators of God." The full passage reads as follows:

> Therefore be imitators of God, as beloved children; and walk in love, just as Christ also loved you, and gave Himself up for us, an offering and a sacrifice to God as a fragrant aroma. But do not let immorality or any impurity or greed even be named among you, as is proper among saints; and there must be no filthiness and silly talk, or coarse jesting, which are not fitting, but rather giving of thanks (Eph. 5:1-8).

Those who first read these words would be familiar with the Greek custom of training orators. Teachers of rhetoric in those days declared that good oratory was taught by theory, imitation, and practice. The major training, however, was considered the imitation of the great orators of the past.

Paul was simply making a plea for Christians to reproduce God's attitudes of love, forgiveness, kindness, mercy, and purity. It is totally inconceivable that one who is bent on imitating God would be devoid of a sense of humor.

Three interesting words in this verse help us understand the meaning of the passage often used to paint a somber picture of our loving God.

(1) "Filthiness" denotes indecency and obscenity. The ancient world to which the apostle Paul spoke regarded sexual immorality so lightly that it was considered no sin at all. In fact, in places like Corinth, the great temples were staffed by hundreds of priestesses who were "sacred prostitutes" and whose earnings were used for the upkeep of the pagan temples. The Greeks saw nothing wrong with building a temple to the gods with the proceeds from prostitution. No wonder Paul coupled idolatry with promiscuity in this passage!

(2) "Silly talk" translates a Greek word which is used only in this verse in the entire New Testament. The word *morologia* comes from two words—*moros* which means "foolish" or "moronic" and *lego*, "to speak." In other words, it means to "talk like a fool." But note the context again. To talk like a fool for what purpose? Answer—to cause others to think lightly of sexual immorality.

(3) "Coarse jesting" is used only in this verse of Scripture. The Greek word, *eutrapelia*, comes from the verb *trepo*, which means "to turn," and the adverb *eu*, meaning "well or good." To engage in this kind of jesting implied getting laughs by turning good words and phrases into that which was sexually immoral. It involved innuendos which made light of purity and godliness while encouraging immorality.

Paul was not prohibiting Christians from enjoying wholesome humor or using it to communicate biblical truth. He was prohibiting the use of gross, tasteless humor which spotlighted and encouraged moral impurity. Those who are "lights" in a dark world dare not stoop to that level.

Rusty and Linda Wright, coauthors of *Secrets of Successful Humor,* are often called on to speak to student groups and professional gatherings. Combining their delightful sense of humor with keen insights into interpersonal and group dynamics, the Wrights also train professionals to develop more effective communication skills.

Rusty was being interviewed recently on a radio talk show which allowed listeners to call in and ask questions. One well-meaning Christian lady called to reprimand Rusty for using humor in church and for his assumption that God has a sense of humor. Her main argument was, "I thought laughter was the result of the fall, and if man had not sinned, there would be no laughter on earth."

Far out, to say the least! However, many people are offended at the mere thought that the Bible includes humorous material or might support a tasteful and appropriate use of humor. Of course, the writer of Ecclesiastes warns against the reckless use of humor: "For as the crackling of thorn bushes under a pot, So is the laughter of the fool" (Eccl. 7:6). But elsewhere in that same book of the Bible we find: "To every thing there is a season, and a time to every purpose under the heaven: . . . A time to weep, and a time to laugh" (Eccl. 3:1,4, KJV).

In his autobiography, *Count It All Joy,* Grady Wilson included a chapter entitled "Laughing All the Way to Heaven." He claimed that he was tempted to name this chapter "Red Faces on the Way to Paradise." Wilson, a lifetime associate of Billy Graham, called for humorless Christians to reexamine their hearts. "After all, Christians are going to rejoice throughout eternity." In one sense," he concluded, "they're the only people who have a legitimate reason to laugh for the sheer joy of it."[1]

Humor's Divine Origin

Seriously, does God really have a sense of humor? It is my firm conviction that our God is a God of laughter, merriment, and joy, as well as a God of righteousness, judgment, and love. We can observe His humor by looking at His nature, His creation of human beings in His own image, and His created world. We can read about His humor in the Bible. And, finally, we can experience His humor in Christ—the final revelation of Himself to us.

What about the nature and attributes of God? Can we, without reservation, claim that God actually has a sense of humor? Some theologians have asserted that even though God is not frequently thought of as possessing a sense of humor, we must attribute it to Him because He is "perfect personality."[2] God is omnipotent, omniscient, and omnipresent. Why should we not allow the possibility of His unlimited sense of humor and His ability to enjoy laughter, to laugh, and to be amused?

Jackson Lee Ice asked another pertinent question: "If we attribute the powers of creativity, thought, feeling, desire, love, hate, and will to God, why not the power of mirth?"[3] Cal Samra concluded, "God is a God of love and a God of peace and a God of joy; God also must be a God of fun."[4]

Conrad Hyers claimed that one of the best-kept secrets in the annals of theology is that "human beings are endowed by their Creator with the capacity to laugh and see the humour in things."[5]

Most theologians agree with the scriptural teaching that God created human beings in His own image (Gen. 1:26-27). Neither do they deny that mysterious capability called "a sense of humor" with which God has endowed every human being. To the deep theological question, "Does God have a sense of humor?" Ice replied, "He made you and me—that must be evidence of something."[6]

When we think seriously about the nature of God, we conclude that He *does* have a sense of humor. As we observe His image in us as human beings, we reach the same conclusion. A. T. Pierson aptly asserted, "If God had not meant us to laugh, He would not have put 250 muscles in the human face, which are all brought into exercise only in a hearty laugh; and He would not have given to man alone, of all animals, a true laughing faculty."[7]

But what of the other creatures in our world? Do we see divine humor in them too? Grady Nutt assumed, "If God didn't have a sense of humor, the ostrich would put his head somewhere else when he got upset and nervous." Nutt also observed that the ostrich "does look strange, and I know God gets tickled every time he hides."[8]

George Buttrick said, "No somber God could have made a bullfrog or a giraffe."[9] Abraham Lincoln asserted that God must have meant for us to laugh, "Else He would not have made so many mules, parrots, monkeys, and human beings."[10]

The assumption that God has a sense of humor is best illustrated in the Scriptures. In my opinion, there are some absolutes in this life based on the nature of God and revealed in the Bible. Abraham Lincoln was right when he observed, "I believe the Bible is the best gift God has ever given to man." Patrick Henry went a step further when he said, "The Bible is worth all other books which have ever been printed."

Sir Isaac Newton echoed his faith in the Scriptures by

saying, "There are more sure marks of authenticity in the Bible than in any profane history."

The Bible—A Happy Book

I am firmly convinced that the Bible gives us answers for our moral, social, ethical, and personal dilemmas! I not only believe in the authority and inspiration of the Scriptures, I also accept the Bible as the primary, complete, trustworthy, and authoritative foundation for belief and action.

In my opinion, obedience to the Word of God is the most convincing affirmation of belief in the God who speaks through the Bible.

As Marcian Strange said, "The Bible's sense of humor can be accepted as an echo of the divine laughter."[11] When I find so much about laughter, joy, happiness, and humor in the Bible, I must assert emphatically, "Yes! God Does Have a Sense of Humor."

I do not wish to leave the impression that humor is the dominant characteristic of the Bible. However, I do believe that humor is more theologically significant than most scholars have admitted through the years. "Humor has been excluded, not by the Bible," claimed Conrad Hyers, "but by our assumptions concerning it."[12]

A casual reading of the Old and New Testaments will reveal many interesting references to happiness, blessedness, delight, and exultation. I share here only a few:[13]

Old Testament

Job 5:17: "Behold, how happy is the man whom God reproves,
So do not despise the discipline of the Almighty."

Psalm 36:8: "They drink their fill of the abundance of Thy house;

And Thou dost give them to drink of the river of Thy
delights."

Psalm 40:8: "I delight to do Thy will, O my God;
Thy Law is within my heart."

Psalm 128:1: "How blessed is everyone who fears the
Lord,
Who walks in His ways."

Psalm 144:15b: "How blessed are the people whose
God is the Lord!"

Proverbs 3:13: "How blessed is the man who finds
wisdom,
And the man who gains understanding."

Proverbs 14:21: "Happy is he who is gracious to the
poor."

Proverbs 16:20: "He who gives attention to the word
shall find good,
And blessed is he who trusts in the Lord."

Proverbs 29:18: "Where there is no vision, the people
are unrestrained,
But happy is he who keeps the law."

Ecclesiastes 2:26: "For to a person who is good in His
sight He has given wisdom and knowledge and joy,
while to the sinner He has given the task of gathering
and collecting so that he may give to one who is good
in God's sight. This too is vanity and striving after
wind."

New Testament

Romans 5:2: "Through whom also we have obtained our
introduction by faith into this grace in which we stand;
and we exult in hope of the glory of God."

Philippians 4:7: "The peace of God, which surpasses all comprehension, shall guard your hearts and your minds in Christ Jesus."

1 Peter 3:14: "Even if you should suffer for the sake of righteousness, you are blessed. And do not fear their intimidation, and do not be troubled."

A casual reading of the Bible will also reveal several refrences to joy, rejoicing, laughing, gladness, and even shouting for joy. Again, here are a few of these:

Old Testament

Deuteronomy 12:18e: "You shall rejoice before the Lord your God in all your undertakings."

1 Chronicles 16:27: "Splendor and majesty are before Him;
Strength and joy are in His place."

Job 8:21: "He will yet fill your mouth with laughter,
And your lips with shouting."

Psalm 5:11: "But let all who take refuge in Thee be glad,
Let them ever sing for joy;
And mayest Thou shelter them,
That those who love Thy name may exult in Thee."

Psalm 13:5: "I have trusted in Thy lovingkindness;
My heart shall rejoice in Thy salvation."

Psalm 19:8: "The precepts of the Lord are right, rejoicing the heart;
The commandment of the Lord is pure, enlightening the eyes."

Psalm 30:5: "For His anger is but for a moment,
His favor is for a lifetime;
Weeping may last for the night,
But a shout of joy comes in the morning."

Psalm 32:11: "Be glad in the Lord and rejoice you righteous ones,
And shout for joy all you who are upright in heart."

Psalm 100:1: "Shout joyfully to the Lord, all the earth."

Proverbs 15:15: "All the days of the afflicted are bad,
But a cheerful heart has a continual feast."

Proverbs 15:30: "Bright eyes gladden the heart;
Good news puts fat on the bones."

Proverbs 17:22: "A joyful heart is good medicine,
But a broken spirit dries up the bones."

Isaiah 12:3: "Therefore you will joyously draw water
From the springs of salvation."

Jeremiah 33:11: "The voice of joy and the voice of gladness, the voice of the bridegroom and the voice of the bride, the voice of those who say,
'Give thanks to the Lord of hosts,
For the Lord is good,
For His lovingkindness is everlasting.' "

New Testament

Matthew 25:21: "His master said to him, 'Well done, good and faithful slave; you were faithful with a few things, I will put you in charge of many things, enter into the joy of your master.' "

Luke 2:10: "The angel said to them, 'Do not be afraid; for behold, I bring you good news of a great joy which shall be for all the people.' "

Luke 6:23: "Be glad in that day, and leap for joy, for behold, your reward is great in heaven; for in the same way their fathers used to treat the prophets."

Luke 10:20: "Nevertheless do not rejoice in this, that the spirits are subject to you, but rejoice that your names are recorded in heaven."

Luke 15:7: "I tell you that in the same way, there will be more joy in heaven over one sinner who repents, than over ninety-nine righteous persons who need no repentance."

John 15:11: "These things I have spoken to you, that My joy may be in you, and that your joy may be made full."

John 17:13: "But now I come to Thee; and these things I speak in the world, that they may have My joy made full in themselves."

Acts 13:52: "The disciples were continually filled with joy and with the Holy Spirit."

Romans 5:2: "Through whom also we have obtained our introduction by faith into this grace in which we stand; and we exult in hope of the glory of God."

Galatians 5:22: "The fruit of the Spirit is love, joy, peace, patience, kindness, goodness, faithfulness."

Philippians 4:4: "Rejoice in the Lord always; again I will say, rejoice!"

James 1:2: "Consider it all joy, my brethren, when you encounter various trials."

1 John 1:4: "These things we write, so that our joy may be complete."

Divine Truth in Comic Form

Divine truth can be expressed in comic form. If we fail to recognize either the truth or the form, the grimness is in us—not in God or His Word. Perhaps one of the best illustrations of divine truth in comic form is found in Proverbs. Who can read some of these Proverbs without a smile or laugh? Two classes of people become the objects of the wise man's wit—the nagging woman and the lazy man. Ladies first:

As a ring of gold in a swine's snout,
So is a beautiful woman who lacks discretion (11:22).

It is better to live in a corner of a roof,
Than in a house shared with a contentious woman
(21:9).

It is better to live in a desert land,
Than with a contentious and vexing woman (21:19).

A constant dripping on a day of steady rain
And a contentious woman are alike;
He who would restrain her restrains the wind,
And grasps oil with his right hand (27:15-16).

The Hebrew writer of the Proverbs was no male
chauvinist. Here are some choice bits of wisdom about
lazy men:

The sluggard buries his hand in the dish,
And will not even bring it back to his mouth (19:24).

The sluggard says, "There is a lion outside;
I shall be slain in the streets!" (22:13).

As the door turns on its hinges,
so does the sluggard on his bed (26:14).

The sluggard buries his hand in the dish;
He is weary of bringing it to his mouth again (26:15).

Don't miss the point of the Book of Proverbs. The Hebrew writer spotlighted the nagging woman and the lazy
man and used comic form to do so. However, he also sang
the praises of the woman who brings refreshment, joy,
and invigoration to her husband (5:15-19). One of the
most enlightening passages in Proverbs is the discussion
of the resourceful, independent, and God-fearing woman
(31:10-31). The writer of Proverbs also commended the
hardworking man (27:23-27). The nagging woman and

the lazy man are exceptions in the Hebrew wisdom tradition, and they are made to appear ridiculous by the use of humorous expressions.

And who can keep a straight face when they read in the Song of Solomon some of his descriptions of his beloved?

> To me, my darling, you are like
> My mare among the chariots of Pharaoh (1:9).
>
> Your hair is like a flock of goats
> That have descended from Mount Gilead (4:1).
>
> Your nose is like the tower of Lebanon,
> Which faces toward Damascus (7:4).

Much of the humor in the Old Testament is lost to the modern mind in translations. However, biblical scholars assure us that the Old Testament is filled with jokes, humor, riddles, proverbs, puns, irony, and satire. Many scholars believe that the Hebrew Scriptures are filled with a "sense of playfulness," especially with the language. Eugene Fisher observed, "Often the point of a passage depends on the reader's appreciation of an outrageous pun. Satire, gentle wit, and even farce abound in almost every book."[14]

It seems only fitting to discuss biblical humor in the context of humorous personalities. Some believe that the best humor is to be found in the quirks, foibles, and excesses of fellow human beings. If that is true, the Bible is full of good illustrations of humor in its best form.

Adam, Sarah, and Jacob

1. Adam and Eve. There is really nothing funny about the fall. But, for the first time in the Bible, we see the old tendency to "pass the buck" to someone else. Adam actually told God that his sin was not his fault but "the woman (whom, I must remind You, *You* gave me) made me do it."

Eve responded, "Don't look at me." And she concluded, "The serpent tempted me to eat the fruit" (Genesis 3:12 *ff*, author's paraphrase).

2. *Sarah and Abraham.* The first time the word *laughter* appears in the Bible is when Abraham fell on his face and laughed (Gen. 17:17). And why shouldn't he laugh? His wife was over ninety years of age, he was pushing one hundred, and God had just announced that they would have another child! His wife, strong-willed Sarah, had the same reaction when she learned the news (Gen. 18:12).

Sarah, listening at the tent door, could not hold back the laughter when she heard the news and was surprised when the Lord asked Abraham, "Why did Sarah laugh?"

But Sarah, out of fear, denied that she laughed while God asserted, "No, but you did laugh" (Gen. 18:13-15).

After the birth of the unexpected child, Sarah exclaimed, "God has made laughter for me; everyone who hears will laugh with me" (Gen. 21:6).

The more you think about Sarah, the more you want to laugh with her. I once heard Grady Nutt say, "There she is, over ninety years of age, craving pizza before it was invented! Can you imagine the scene when the doctor brought out the lab scroll and made his announcement? 'I'm what!' "

David Redding let his imagination run wild about Sarah:

> Imagine old Aunt Sadie down at the nursing home being given a careful checkup for possible malignancy because of increasing abdominal extension. And the x-rays reveal instead a perfectly live fetus. I would love to see the doc-

tor's face. Wouldn't such an event break up a nursing home? How embarrassing![15]

Abraham and Sarah named their son Isaac—the Hebrew word for "laughter" or "he laughs." From Isaac's line came our Savior who brings joy and laughter not only to the Sarahs of the world but to all those who believe in Him.

3. *Jacob.* Jacob, the trickster, affords an interesting study of one of the most complex personalities in the Bible. You cannot help but admire him for his persistence and energy. However, you cannot help but be amused by his trickery.

Jacob labored long and hard physically and mentally over his wives and his sheep (Gen. 29—31). His struggles with Laban are appropriately summarized when the Scriptures assert, "Jacob saw the attitude of Laban, and behold, it was not friendly toward him as formerly" (Gen. 31:2).

Some have even assumed that there is much to laugh about in Jacob's wrestling match with the Lord (Gen. 32:24-28). Jacob, who gave every evidence of being arrogant and self-centered, was probably nicknamed "supplanter" or "heel grabber." But after his fight with God, he walked away with a constant limp and was renamed "Israel." The meaning of Jacob's new name was "God persists" or "rules." As someone has suggested, it might be translated, "God won the wrestling match!"

Jonah and Balaam

4. *Jonah.* God lost no time in telling Jonah what He wanted him to do—go to Nineveh and pronounce judgment upon the city (Jonah 1:1 *ff.*). Jonah wasted no time in doing exactly what *he* wanted to do. Without a word,

Jonah took off in the opposite direction and did not stop until he came to the port of Joppa where he took a ship down to Tarshish (Jonah 1:3).

In the midst of a great storm at sea, lots were cast, and the sailors decided that Jonah was the cause of the storm. So Jonah suggested that the sailors throw him into the sea. Reluctantly, they followed his instructions and cast Jonah into the whitecaps.

The rest of the story is known by every child who has ever attended Sunday School—God provided a large fish to rescue Jonah and after three days to vomit him up onto the shore. God had gotten Jonah's attention! Jonah went on to the city of Nineveh and prophesied that it would be destroyed within forty days. The people began to repent by the hundreds.

God honored Nineveh's repentance and spared the city. In essence Jonah had an argument with God to the effect that God knew exactly how it was going to turn out in the first place, and that's why Jonah went to Tarshish instead of Nineveh (Jonah 4:2).

So grumpy Jonah sat down under a temporary booth to protect him from the sun just to see what was going to happen next. God gave him a little shade by providing a fast-growing vine which soon died. Again Jonah lost his temper with God and complained "Death is better to me than life" (4:8). The last three verses of this little, four-chapter book teach a lesson that we only hope Jonah learned:

> Then God said to Jonah, "Do you have good reason to be angry about the plant?" And he said, "I have good reason to be angry, even to death."
>
> Then the Lord said, "You had compassion on the plant for which you did not work, and which you did not cause

to grow, which came up overnight and perished overnight.

"And should I not have compassion on Nineveh, the great city in which there are more than 120,000 persons who do not know the difference between their right and left hand, as well as many animals?" (4:9-11).

Recent studies have revealed that the ancient reader of Jonah's story may have found an extra laugh that we miss when we read it.[16] Ancient Nineveh was often identified as a fish around which a line was drawn denoting its city walls. The humor? If Jonah would not go to the city-enclosed fish, he would himself become a fish-enclosed Jonah!

5. *Balaam and His Donkey.* If you can read the story about Balaam's donkey without bursting out in laughter, you have more self-control than I have (Num. 22:21-30). On three different occasions the helpful little donkey tried to avoid the fearful spectacle of the angel of the Lord, seen only by the donkey, who stood ready to slay Balaam.

On the first encounter, the donkey dashed into the field only to be beaten by Balaam. Then, she ran down a "narrow path of the vineyards, with a wall" on either side, bumping Balaam's foot against the wall. Again, she received a beating at the hands of her master. Then, upon seeing the angel of the Lord, she turned onto another path "where there was no way to turn to the right hand or to the left." The poor little beast finally lay down, defeated by the whole situation, and took her third thrashing by Balaam.

Then the donkey spoke! After a friendly argument between Balaam and his donkey, the angel of the Lord revealed himself to Balaam. The humor? Some donkeys are smarter than human beings when it comes to recognizing God's direction for their lives!

6. *Other Ironic Situations.* There are several other examples of humor in the Old Testament. Gideon led a small band of faithful warriors to defeat a mighty army of the Midianites (Judg. 7:19-23). Elijah confronted the false prophets and priests of Baal by ironically accusing their gods of being asleep (1 Kings 18:27). Wicked Haman begged for his life from Queen Esther whom he had tried to destroy, while being hanged on the very gallows he had built for her uncle, Mordecai (see Esther 7:8-12).

Cruel, but human, laughter is in order in the victory song of Deborah and Barak after the defeat of Sisera (Judg. 5:1-31). Sisera's mother looked out the window, wondering why her son's victorious chariot had been delayed. She surmised that the delay had been caused by the time involved in dividing up the spoils—"a maiden, two maidens for every warrior" (Judg. 5:29 *ff.*).

The words are intensely ironic since, at that very moment, Sisera lay dead of a tent peg driven through his head into the ground, by "a maiden," Jael, the wife of Heber the Kenite (Judg. 4:21).

Larry M. Taylor concluded that "there are some five-hundred puns or word plays in the Old Testament and two-hundred more in the New Testament." Most of these are understood only by scholars who are proficient in the original languages of the Old and New Testaments. We will have to take their word for it.[17]

Peter and Paul

7. *Peter.* In human personalities such as Simon Peter we are readily aware of the humor. One cannot help but admire and, at the same time, often laugh at Simon Peter.

He felt inclined to make a speech and take charge of the

arrangements at the transfiguration (Matt. 17:4). When
the soldiers came to take Jesus to the cross, Peter drew his
sword and announced that he was ready to take on the
entire Temple guard (John 18:10). Peter was unique in
that he was one of the few persons known to have
rebuked the Lord Himself and thereby received a coun-
terrebuke (Matt. 16:22). When Simon Peter realized that
the risen Lord was standing on the shore in the dawn, he
was the only disciple to leap overboard and swim to shore
while the others stayed in the boat (John 21:7). Linton
concluded that Simon Peter was "often in error, but
never in doubt; and when right, gloriously right!"[18]

At Caesarea Philippi Jesus asked His disciples, "Who do
people say that the Son of Man is?" (Matt. 16:13).

The disciples reported that people were saying He
could be John the Baptist, Elijah, Jeremiah, or one of the
other prophets.

And then, Jesus pointedly asked, "But who do you say
that I am?" (Matt. 16:15). Peter answered, "Thou art the
Christ, the Son of the living God."

After affirming Simon's confession as being divinely inspired, Jesus renamed Simon Peter when He said, "I also
say to you that you are Peter, and upon this rock I will
build My church" (Matt. 16:18).

The word for Peter meant "rock." But the rock upon
which Jesus announced He would build His church was
like the thick strata of rock on which Caesarea Philippi
stood. He would build His church on Peter's confession
that He really is who He said He was—the Christ, the Son
of the living God!

In the process, Jesus would give Simon a nickname that
he and his fellow disciples would never forget—Rocky!
The disciples must have roared with laughter. Simon's
name was changed to Rocky! The man who denied Jesus

three times? Who sank when he tried to walk on the water? Who followed Jesus at a distance prior to His crucifixion?

Jesus would nickname Simon "Rocky," and he would later prove to match that name! For, you see, warts and all, Peter knew the bottom line well—"Thou art the Christ, the Son of the living God!"

Another humorous story involving Simon Peter is related to his experience of being released from jail (Acts 12:1-17). He hurried to Jerusalem to the home of Mary, the mother of John Mark. He knocked at the door and identified himself to a girl named Rhoda. She was so excited that she forgot to unlock the door, left Peter standing there, and ran back joyfully to announce to the crowd that Simon Peter was out of jail. Peter kept on knocking at the door, was finally heard, and allowed to enter the house. (What a way to treat the "Rock")

8. *Paul.* In the writings of Paul, instances of humor are infrequent. However, his watchword in all of his epistles seems to be, "rejoice in the Lord always; again I will say rejoice" (Phil. 4:4). He encouraged Christians to show mercy and to give of their financial means with hilarity when he said that "God loves a cheerful giver" (2 Cor. 9:7; see Rom. 12:8).

Paul often employed an effective use of irony, particularly in defense of himself (2 Cor. 10:1 ff; 11:1,16-21). He made good use of irony in defending himself before Ananias in Acts 23:2-5.

In writing to the Corinthians, Paul delighted in telling of visits to the best jails in the Roman Empire, and his escape at Damascus where he was lowered over the city walls in a basket (2 Cor. 11:32-33). How unapostolic could he get?

As Paul wrote to the Corinthians he literally celebrated

the "foolishness" of the cross. That God, in Christ, would suffer the death of the cross is foolishness to the world. "God has chosen the foolish things of the world to shame the wise, . . . and the base things of the world and the despised, . . . the things that are not, that He might nullify the things that are" (1 Cor. 1:27-28).

Followers of Christ were invited by Paul to enter into God's great sense of humor and be known as "fools for Christ's sake" (1 Cor. 4:10). But ego-diluting ink was in his pen as he drew a contrast between being a fool for Christ's sake and the arrogance of the Corinthians.

God's Laughter—Sad and Glad

We cannot leave the subject of a godly sense of humor without a discussion of two often-misunderstood verses in the Psalms:

> He who sits in the heavens laughs,
> The Lord scoffs at them [the rebellious] (2:4).
> The Lord laughs at him [the wicked];
> For He sees his day is coming (37:13).

Why did the psalmist write that God sits in the heavens and laughs? Does God possess a sadistic delight in seeing the wicked perish? Not at all! God is described as laughing because the psalmist understood the absurdity of human puny attempts to play God and to deliver ourselves from God's divine claim upon us. It is tragically hilarious to the mind of God that human beings, who owe God everything, are willing to pay Him nothing—not even the admission of His existence.

While the psalmist painted a picture of God's laughter at our neglect of Him and the typical "I'm-the-captain-of-my-soul" attitude, Jesus painted another picture of God's laughter in Luke 15. He shared three parables after being criticized by the religious leaders for eating with "sinners." His parables are about a lost sheep, a lost coin, and a lost son.

In the first story, a shepherd found that one of his sheep was missing. He left ninety-nine others to go out and find the lost sheep. Upon finding the sheep, he exclaimed to his neighbors, "Rejoice with me, for I have found my sheep which was lost!" (v. 6). Jesus concluded, "I tell you that in the same way, there will be more joy in heaven over one sinner who repents, than over ninety-nine righteous persons who need no repentance" (Luke 15:7).

The second story is about a woman who lost one of her ten precious silver coins. After frantically sweeping her house by lamplight and finding her coin, she announced to her neighbors, "Rejoice with me, for I've found the coin which I had lost!" (v. 9). Jesus concluded again, "In the same way, I tell you, there is joy in the presence of the angels of God over one sinner who repents" (Luke 15:10).

Then he told the story of the prodigal son (Luke 15:11-24). A young man leaves his father's house, goes into a far country, wastes all of his money, "bottoms out," and finally decides to return to his father's home. When he comes home to his waiting father, there is rejoicing, the "fatted calf" is killed, and everyone is encouraged to rejoice because the prodigal son has returned.

But the prodigal son's elder brother returns from the field and expresses sheer displeasure over the feast celebrating the return of his brother (Luke 15:25-30). The father consoles the faithful son upon the return of his brother with the words, "We had to be merry and rejoice, for this brother of yours which was dead has begun to live, and was lost and has been found" (Luke 15:32).

The laughter of God in the Psalms is sad because of the rebellion and lostness of those created in His image. But the laughter of God described in Luke 15 is that of joy because some people choose to repent and be recreated through Jesus Christ. "Therefore if any man is in Christ, he is a new creature; the old things passed away; behold, new things have come" (2 Cor. 5:17).

Yes, God laughs! And blessed are those who get the joke!

Drawing a Picture of God

"What are you drawing?" a little girl in kindergarten class asked the boy at her table.

"I'm drawing a picture of God," he announced proudly.

"But no one knows what God looks like!" she observed.

"They will now!" the young fellow proclaimed.

We have allowed others to draw their pictures of God, and some have come up with a frown. Our theories about God and the possibility of His sense of humor have been philosophical, literary, psychological, sociological, physiological, and linguistic. Where have all the theologians gone when it comes to a discussion of holy laughter?

Let us conclude that the God who has the power of creativity, thought, feeling, desire, love, hatred of sin, and will, also possesses the power of mirth. Since we who have been created "in His image" naturally possess a sense of humor, how can we deny our Creator the possibility of an unlimited ability to enjoy laughter, to laugh, and to be amused?

The Bible draws its picture of God and He has a smile on His face. God's incomparable Book is addressed to a fallen world where "even in laughter the heart is sad" (Prov. 14:13, RSV). However, its urgent proclamation of salvation by grace through faith in Christ is good news! As we read further we find its pages smiling back at us and hear our Lord promising us, "Blessed are you who weep now, for you shall laugh" (Luke 6:21*b*).

Two little boys were talking about God when one of them said, "I don't know much about God, but I know something about Jesus."

"Yeah, what do you know about Jesus?" his friend asked.

"Well, the main thing I know about Jesus," the boy commented, "is that He is about the best picture of God that anybody ever took."

Conclusion

We affirm God's sense of humor in His nature, His creation, His image in us, and His Word. However, the best picture of God's humor is to be found in Christ. The Bible declares, "How blessed is the man who finds wisdom" (Prov. 3:13). The same Bible also declares that the fear or reverance of God is the beginning of true knowledge (Prov. 1:7). The apostle Paul called Jesus the "wisdom from God" (1 Cor. 1:30) and declared that in Jesus all the treasures of wisdom and knowledge are hidden (Col. 2:3).

It is a firm conviction and assumption of this study that God has revealed His nature and His will through Jesus Christ:

> God, after He spoke long ago to the fathers in the prophets in many portions and in many ways, in these last days has spoken to us in His Son, whom He appointed heir of all things, through whom also He made the world (Heb. 1:1-2).

Therefore, if we really want to understand God's sense of humor to its fullest, then we must understand how Jesus used humor. That brings us to the next chapter.

3

Jesus: the Master Humorist

I was an unmarried, seminary-student pastor. The church house was a small, white-frame building on top of a hill located in a rural community. The parsonage was located down the hill facing Main Street. Between the church and the parsonage sat the one and only "outhouse."

I never quite became accustomed to making the trek from the parsonage up the hill to the outdoor bathroom. I could imagine that the eyes of every citizen in our little town were fixed on me.

It rained heavily that spring. When that happens, the dirt in that part of Oklahoma tends to "shift." I noticed one day that the hole over which the outhouse was sitting seemed to be caving in from the back. Not being mechanically minded and knowing that our church couldn't afford to launch a major building program, I said nothing about it.

Then one day I noticed the outhouse was beginning to lean backward. I thought, *Well, if there is any danger, surely the deacons will see that it is repaired.* What happened one Sunday evening proved that I and the deacons had waited too long!

Just before the evening service, I made my way to the outhouse, opened the door, and slammed it behind me. I

felt the building toppling back. As I sat down, I felt like
the pilot of a plane making its climb into the clouds.

Crack!

The outhouse fell on its back. I managed to unlatch the
door and open it as quietly as possible. When I looked out
I saw one of our elderly members standing nearby waiting
his turn to use the outhouse. As he turned and walked
away laughing, Mr. Gordon said, "Pastor, you shouldn't
use that thing! It's dangerous!"

I really didn't want to attend church that evening. I
waited until the song service had begun and walked down
a side aisle. I wondered, *Does anyone know?*

Yes, they knew! Mr. Gordon had been an excellent in-
formant! By the time I reached the platform during the
first stanza of a hymn, one could hear snickering all over
the house. I think it was the first service in which I remember every member of the congregation smiling during the announcements.

When it was time to preach, I knew I was a dead duck!
No one would hear a serious word I might say. I decided
to change my sermon topic for the evening.

Knowing that most of them had already peeked out the
window to see the plight of the outhouse, I said, "I know
what all of you are thinking about tonight."

"I had planned to preach on another subject," I continued, "but I think I'll preach on Tal's Touching Tale of
the Tilted Toilet Told in Terse Trepidation!"

The Laughing Christ

They claim you could hear the laughter all over town.
I spent that evening sharing with my small congregation
the joys of the Christian life and the dangers of taking
ourselves too seriously. I told them that Jesus and His

disciples laughed often, and we should be able to laugh too—even at church and, if need be, at ourselves.

Have you ever thought of Jesus as throwing back His head and engaging in a good, hearty laugh? Can you imagine Jesus telling a joke? Or a ripple of laughter in the crowd while He spoke? And can you hear Him saying, "That reminds me of a funny thing that happened in Nazareth when I was a boy"?

Many of our Lord's greatest admirers and greatest critics fail to visualize Jesus with a smile on His face. Because of this, Elton Trueblood wrote, "The widespread failure to recognize and to appreciate the humor of Christ is one of the most amazing aspects of the era named for Him."[1] However, Gaines S. Dobbins claimed that "Christ's best gifts are first of all Himself, and then His gifts of salvation, happiness, love, and good humor."[2]

Why do we fail to recognize the humor of Christ? Simply because we somehow miss it as we read the New Testament. And why do we fail to appreciate His humor? Because we fail to understand that which we do catch as we read the New Testament. Why do we miss the humor of Christ? Mainly because we view Him strictly in a theological sense.

The world is not asking, "Did He laugh?" but the world is asking, "Who is this Jesus?" Is He really who He said He was? Or was He just a good man? A great teacher? An insightful prophet? If indeed God revealed Himself to us through Christ, what is the nature of that revelation? It goes without saying: we must give the world an answer to the question of Jesus' identity.

Our Eternal Contemporary

Who is Jesus? Simon Peter answered that question on the day of Pentecost when he said, "Therefore let all the house of Israel know for certain that God has made Him both Lord and Christ—this Jesus whom you crucified" (Acts 2:36). His name is not a mantle thrown lightly over His shoulder but a perfectly fitting garment. "Christ" is His heavenly name. "Jesus" is His earthly name. "Lord" is His personal name to the believer.

Who is Jesus? After His resurrection, doubting Thomas answered that question when he fell on his knees and cried, "My Lord and My God!" (John 20:28). Paul answered that question when he said, "God was in Christ reconciling the world to Himself" (2 Cor. 5:19).

Who is Jesus? The best answer to that question actually came from Jesus Himself. In John 8:58 He said, "Truly, truly, I say to you, before Abraham was born, I am." He had no beginning, and He will have no ending. He is our eternal contemporary!

In John's Gospel, Jesus made seven other claims about Himself:

(1) He is the Bread of life (John 6:35). Just as bread, the staff of life, is an absolute physical necessity, knowing Jesus Christ is an absolute spiritual necessity.

(2) He is the Light of the world (John 8:12). Jesus is our only hope for light to dispel the darkness of sin.

(3) He is the Door of the sheepfold (John 10:9). Jesus is the only entrance into the kingdom of God and the only protector for the kingdom citizen.

(4) He is the Good Shepherd (John 10:11). He has laid down His life for His sheep; they hear His voice and follow Him.

(5) He is the Resurrection and the Life (John 11:25). He is not only our assurance of abundant life here on earth but our assurance of life after death in heaven.

(6) He is the Way, the Truth, and the Life (John 14:6).

He is the only way to God, the embodiment of all truth, and the only way to live life here and now.

(7) He is the true Vine (John 15:1). As the believer abides in Him, everything in life and death seems to fit together and have meaning.

From the Cradle to the Cross

We often miss the humor of Christ because of the centrality of the cross. Because He came to die, we seldom associate humor with Christ. He was a man of compassion who called His disciples to deny themselves, take up the cross daily, and follow Him.

It is difficult for some to comprehend that Jesus possessed both compassion and a sense of humor at the same time. Without a doubt, the crucifixion of our Lord overshadows His humor. The fact that He came to die for our sins is far more important than the fact that He also taught us how to laugh. However, He *did* teach us how to laugh.

Jesus moved from the cradle to the cross. The devil tempted Him in the wilderness of temptation to take a shortcut around the cross (Matt. 4:1-11). But He endured the temptation and walked on toward the death of the cross. When Peter suggested that He bypass the cross, He said, "Get thee behind me Satan!" (Matt. 16:23).

Cal Samra made an interesting observation about the devil: "If the devil is always grave, solemn, and mirthless, one would suppose that it would be blasphemy to suggest that Jesus had the same qualities."[3]

Many people miss the humor of Christ because He just seems to be serious throughout the New Testament. Nowhere does it say that "Jesus laughed" or "Jesus joked with His disciples" or "Jesus smiled" or "Jesus giggled." Therefore, we simply assume that He did not do these things.

Some are quick to point out that the Scriptures do say "Jesus wept," "Jesus was moved with compassion," and "Jesus was a man of sorrows." However, because the Gospels fail to mention the fact that Jesus smiled and laughed is no reason to believe that He was a perpetual sad sack.

The New Testament records only thirty-five days of His entire thirty-three years—an average of about one out of every thirty days of His three year-ministry. And, even at that, only fragments of these days are usually chronicled by the Gospel writers.[4] John ended his Gospel by saying, "There are also many other things which Jesus did, which if they were written in detail, I suppose that even the world itself could not contain the books which were written" (John 21:25).

Even though the shadow of the Cross enveloped our Lord and His disciples with solemnity, we can still see the picture of optimism and serenity on the face of Jesus. He attended a wedding in Cana where, to relieve the embarrassment of the host at a lack of sufficient refreshments, He performed His first miracle. He resorted often to the home of Mary, Martha, and Lazarus to relax and enjoy Himself. Jesus must have possessed a keen sense of relaxed humor, else children certainly would not have been drawn to Him, and women would not have spoken to Him.

Humphrey Osmond claimed that Jesus had an excellent sense of humor and pungent wit. "If he hadn't, he could not have made such a favorable impression on publicans and sinners, and such an unfavorable impression on the religious establishment."[5]

Traveling from Then to Now

We often miss the humor of Christ simply because humor does not travel well from century to century. Les-

lie B. Flynn claimed that "psychological re-orientation to
the first century scene may be required before we can
enter into some of Jesus' humor."[6]

Occasionally, Jesus made use of a play on words operating from the principle of the known to the unknown. For
instance, He invited Peter and Andrew to become His
followers by saying, "Follow Me, and I will make you
fishers of men" (Matt. 4:19).

The play on words is the idea of fishing for fish as over
against fishing for men. Those who had been catching fish
were told, "From now on you will be catching men"
(Luke 5:10). Such a play on words would probably need
further explanation to the average twentieth-century
congregation. However, His disciples caught the joke in
the first century: a fisherman catches live fish that die, but
a Christian witness captures men who are dead in sin but
become spiritually alive in Christ!

Imagine this scenario: you observe a man walking down
the street with a huge pole protruding out of one eye
socket. Needless to say, he has his hands full balancing the
long pole like a circus acrobat balancing a pole with another acrobat sitting on top of it. Coming toward him is
another man who has a small speck of sawdust in his eye.

The man with the pole in his eye points to the fellow
with the speck of sawdust in his eye and exclaims, "I see
you've got something in your eye! You'd better get off this
busy street with your vision impaired like that. Don't
even think of crossing the street here because you probably can't even tell when the light changes to green!

"Here," says the man with the pole protruding out of
his eye, "let me help you get that speck of sawdust out of
your eye."

He asks his friend to lie down on a sidewalk bench while
he props his pole up on the back of the bench in order to

remove the speck of sawdust. As he works, he continues his critical tirade of such a stupid act as walking down a busy street unable to see out of one eye because of a sliver of sawdust.

Did that story really turn you on? Probably not! However, in the first century when Jesus said these words to the disciples, I am sure they laughed:

Why do you look at the speck [stubble, splinter, shaft, small dry thing] in your brother's eye, but do not notice the log [spar of timber, piece of lumber, pole] that is in your own eye? Or how can you say to your brother, "Let me take the speck out of your eye," and behold, the log is in your own eye? You hypocrite, first take the log out of your own eye, and then you will see clearly enough to take the speck out of your brother's eye (Matt. 7:3-5).

Did you get the point? Jesus is talking about the censorious attitude of those who are always able to find fault with others while failing to see their own faults.

Spare me another scenario: you are driving down a busy highway and see the flashing lights of a policeman's motorcycle leading a funeral procession. You pull over to the side of the road and reverently wait for the procession to pass. As ten or twelve cars pass with their lights on, you begin to study the expressions on the faces of those in the cars.

The first car contains a couple of ministers who officiated at the funeral. The next car is the hearse which contains the casket of the deceased. You glance at the driver of the hearse and look away. Then, unable to believe your eyes, you look back again at an unbelievable sight. The driver of the hearse is a dead man!

Because humor fails to travel well from the first century to the twentieth century, that scenario probably did not

register very high on your Richter scale of laughter. When
Jesus said, "Let the dead bury their dead" (Matt. 8:22,
KJV), the play on words inferred that many people who
are spiritually dead take a great deal of interest in seeing
that the physically dead are properly buried without ever
giving any thought whatsoever to their own need for spiritual vitality. In other words, they are dead and don't
know it!

Another reason that we often miss the humor of Jesus
is that we misinterpret some of His teachings. What did
He mean when He said, "I say to you, that every careless
word that men shall speak, they shall render account for
it in the day of judgment" (Matt. 12:36)?

Some people automatically associate the words *idle* or
careless with "humor." While much of our humor is idle
and careless, we are not to suppose that Jesus prohibited
the telling of wholesome jokes and boisterous laughter
just for laughter's sake.

It always helps to interpret Jesus' words in the context
in which they were first spoken. What then is the context
of this unusual admonition of our Lord?

The Pharisees had just made a very stupid and careless
statement. When they learned that Jesus had healed a
demon-possessed man, who was both blind and dumb,
they felt that they must make some sort of comment.
They vented their jealousy by making a dramatic accusa-
tion with no forethought whatsoever—they claimed that
Jesus had performed this miracle by the power of Satan!

Jesus proceeded to show the Pharisees that if He had
cast out demons by the power of Satan, then Satan was
"divided against himself" (Matt. 12:26). After a few words
about the danger of attributing the works of the Holy
Spirit to Satan, Jesus then warned the Pharisees about the
use of idle or careless words.

Most idle or careless words being spoken today are those related to the divinity of Jesus Christ. Either Jesus is who He said He was or, in the minds of those who deny Him, He is a fake. We may actually say more idle words by the way we live, our lack of commitment, or our theological bias against Jesus Christ than we actually do with our mouths. But by no stretch of the imagination can we surmise that Jesus taught that it was wrong to laugh or to be "in fun."

The Smiling Christ in Art

Another reason we miss the humor of Christ is that most of the artistic renderings of Christ pictured Him as somber and serious. Country humorist Minnie Pearl, who has always associated Jesus with happiness, has an interesting word to say about the solemn images of Jesus portrayed in religious paintings:

> I don't agree with the image many Christians have of Christ as the sad, tragic man depicted in most religious paintings. You can't tell me He didn't laugh, or that He wasn't happy. I think He had a great sense of humor. If He had walked along the Sea of Galilee with a look of doom on His face I don't believe for a minute all those people would have followed Him. I think they found such joy in His presence they were willing to leave everything behind to go with Him. I'm certain He knew the value of humor and the power of a smile.[7]

We are deeply indebted to Cal Samra in *The Joyful Christ* for his meticulous study of the different portraits of Christ through the years.[8] We are also indebted to Samra for sharing many of the modern images of "joy and laughter" now being painted and drawn of Christ. Among my favorite renderings of the happy Jesus is *Christ: the Es-*

sence of Life, Light, Love, and Laughter[9] by Joyce Martin
who pictures the usual long-haired, bearded Christ with
His bright teeth showing through a wide smile.

Another, *The Smiling Christ*[10] by Lawrence Zink, pictures a side view of a short-haired, bearded Jesus with a
distinct smile on His face. *The Smiling Christ*[11] by
Frances Hook reveals a distinct grin with wrinkles around
the eyes of the bearded face. Frances Hook has also drawn
another picture, *Christ, My Friend,*[12] showing Him smiling at a child which He tenderly holds in His arms.

My favorite is a color screen-print adaptation by Ralph
Kozak of an original drawing by Willis Wheatley entitled
Jesus Laughing.[13] It is a picture of Jesus with traditionally
long hair and beard, his head thrown back enjoying a
gusty laugh.

Because of the popularity of these new drawings and
Samra's book, a whole new organization has grown up,
complete with its own monthly publication: *The Joyful
Noiseletter.* The publication of "The Fellowship of Merry
Christians" includes articles, stories, and jokes related to
humor and religion.[14]

James R. Cameron has shared some interesting insights
regarding the sad pictures which we have seen of Jesus for
so many years.

> It has been said that for nineteen centuries Christen-
> dom has gazed into His shining face and felt that all things
> work together for good. But, too often, His face has been
> portrayed as stricken with grief, exciting the pity and pain
> of men.[15]

Sharing Good News with a Laugh

There is one other reason why we often miss the humor
of Christ—because of the urgency of sharing His gospel

with such a needy world. Some evangelical Christians have trouble justifying humor with the task of evangelizing the world with the gospel of Jesus Christ.

In his book *Master Principles of Evangelism,* Delos Miles shared a chapter based on the thesis that Jesus used humor in His evangelism.[16] Miles gave the following illustrations:

(1) The Canaanite woman whose daughter was demon possessed, and Jesus ironically used the word *dog* to describe the woman (Matt. 15:21-28).

(2) The case of Zaccheus, a man of wealth and short in stature, who climbed up a tree to see Jesus and was asked to come down and take Jesus to his home for a meal (Luke 19:1-10).

(3) The banter between Jesus and the scribes on the occasion of the four men who brought one of their friends to Him on a stretcher, broke up the roof of a house, and let the patient down through the hole in the roof to receive healing (Mark 2:1-12).

(4) The visit to the home of Simon the Pharisee who was critical of a woman who had come to have her sins forgiven; she used expensive perfume to anoint the feet of Jesus (Luke 7:36-50).

(5) The case of the woman taken in the act of adultery, especially involving the irony of the statement, "Let him who is without sin among you be the first to throw a stone at her" (John 8:1-11, RSV).

(6) The Jewish ruler by the name of Nicodemus who used the cloak of darkness to come to Jesus to hear about the new birth (John 3:4-12).

(7) The case of Nathaniel who wondered, "Can any good thing come out of Nazareth?" (John 1:45-51).

(8) The case of the Samaritan woman at the well who confused spiritual water with physical water, recognized

that Jesus knew about her adulterous life-style, and ran to
the city yelling, "Come, see a man who told me all the
things that I have done" (John 4:1-29).

It has been my privilege through the years to know
some of the most effective evangelists and pastors of this
generation in several denominations. Without exception,
these great evangelists and evangelistic pastors have possessed a deep compassion for the salvation of the lost and,
at the same time, an infectious sense of humor!

I have found that some of the most compassionate pastors and evangelists are fond of telling jokes and enjoy a
healthy sense of humor. They have the uncanny ability to
lace deeply biblical sermons with appropriate humor.
Here is one of those stories that they tell on themselves!

The evangelist for a country church high up in the
mountains was out visiting prospective members one day.
He had spotted a house up in a mountain range that required at least a two-mile walk from the mailbox.

Out of breath from climbing the hill, he arrived at the
front porch. He discovered a man rocking back and forth
lazily on the porch.

"Howdy, friend, my name is Evangelist Jones. What's
yours?"

"Calloway's the name. What can I do for ye?"

The minister continued, "Well, I just came up here to
talk to you about some things and ask you a few questions."

"Shoot!" replied the mountaineer.

"Well, the first thing I want to know, Mr. Calloway, is,
have you made peace with God?"

"Peace with God?" questioned Calloway. "Me and God
ain't never had no argument!"

"No, no, no, you don't understand, Mr. Calloway. Are
you a Christian?"

"Nah, I ain't no Christian, preacher; I just told you my

name is Calloway. The Christians live four mountains up the road."

"Mr. Calloway, I'm having a hard time getting through to you. What I really want to know is this—are you lost?"

"Nah, I ain't lost. I've been living here in these parts all my life. I know these mountains like the back of my hand."

"Mr. Calloway, what I really want to know is, are you ready for the judgment day?"

"Judgment Day? When's it going to be?"

The young minister replied, "Well, Mr. Calloway, it could be today, or it could be tomorrow."

"Well, land sakes alive, parson, don't tell my wife. She'll want to go both days!"[17]

I contend that, from the beginning of His life to the end of His life on earth, Jesus was surrounded by and caused joy, happiness, merriment, gladness, rejoicing, delight, and laughter. Isaiah's prophecy of the coming of the Messiah included a prophecy of "good news" and "gladness:"

The Spirit of the Lord God is upon me,
Because the Lord has anointed me
To bring good news to the afflicted;
He has sent me to bind up the brokenhearted,
To proclaim liberty to captives,
And freedom to prisoners;
To proclaim the favorable year of the Lord,
And the day of vengeance of our God;
To comfort all who mourn,
To grant those who mourn in Zion,
Giving them a garland instead of ashes,
The oil of gladness instead of mourning,
The mantle of praise instead of a spirit of fainting.
So they will be called oaks of righteousness,
The planting of the Lord, that He may be glorified
(Isa. 61:1-3).

Upon hearing that she would bear the Christ child Mary exclaimed, "My soul exalts the Lord,/And my spirit has rejoiced in God my Savior" (Luke 1:46-47). The angel announced the birth of Jesus to the shepherds as "good news of great joy" (Luke 2:10). When the Wise Men saw the star that marked His birth, "they rejoiced exceedingly with great joy" (Matt. 2:10).

Chad Walsh saw the birth of Christ in a stable as "touching but also funny, suggesting a farce in which a presidential candidate is assigned to a disreputable motel in the red-light district of a city, and there receives the visitation of the TV cameramen and commentators."[18]

Happiness—More than an Attitude

Robert H. Schuller claims that knowing Jesus and following His teachings constitute the secret of real happiness for anyone in this world. "If you have a medical problem, see your physician," he advised. "If your problem is an unhappy spirit, then I have a spiritual Doctor that I recommend. His name is Jesus Christ."[19]

Along that same line of thought, happy weatherman Willard Scott wonders, "How many half-sick people are walking around who only need one medicine to get well: a shot of 'Doctor Jesus.' " Scott contends that Jesus Christ "was the one person in all of history who showed us all how we could get the most out of life."[20]

Jesus knew and taught others the secret of real happiness. Carl Henry claims that "the best known fact about Jesus Christ is that He gave the Sermon on the Mount."[21] The Sermon on the Mount (found in Matthew 5—7 and Luke 6:20-49) has been more widely discussed than any other piece of literature of equal length.

Our Lord's Sermon on the Mount has been acclaimed as "the most searching and powerful utterance we possess on what concerns the moral life."[22] It has been given such titles as "The Inaugural Message of the King," "The Magna Charta of the Kingdom," "The Manifesto of the King," and "The Manifesto of the Kingdom."

Other than His Golden Rule, I suspect the Beatitudes of our Lord are quoted more than any of His teachings in the Sermon on the Mount:

> Blessed are the poor in spirit: for theirs is the kingdom of heaven.
> Blessed are they that mourn: for they shall be comforted.
> Blessed are the meek: for they shall inherit the earth.
> Blessed are they which do hunger and thirst after righteousness: for they shall be filled.
> Blessed are the merciful: for they shall obtain mercy.
> Blessed are the pure in heart: for they shall see God.
> Blessed are the peacemakers: for they shall be called children of God.
> Blessed are they which are persecuted for righteousness' sake: for theirs is the kingdom of heaven.
> Blessed are ye, when men shall revile you, and persecute you, and shall say all manner of evil against you falsely, for my sake.
> Rejoice, and be exceeding glad: for great is your reward in heaven: for so persecuted they the prophets which were before you (Matt. 5:3-12, KJV).

"Christ in Tuxedo" was the title of a blasphemous comedy produced on a Russian stage several years ago.[23] A distinguished Russian actor played the leading role to a packed house. The stage depicted a church altar upon which bottles of vodka, wine, and beer were proudly displayed. Actresses dressed as nuns played cards on the floor around the altar.

The scene called for the actor to read a few verses from

the Beatitudes, remove his oriental gown, and don a tuxedo and top hat.

A strained silence fell upon the audience as the actor opened the New Testament in his hand. He read slowly and loudly, "Blessed are the poor in spirit: for theirs is the kingdom of heaven. Blessed are they that mourn: for they shall be comforted."

Then, the script called for him to say, "Give me my tuxedo and top hat!" But he paused, remained silent for an instant, and stood as though he were paralyzed. His body began to shake from head to toe.

Fascinated by Jesus' words, the actor continued to read loudly from the fifth chapter of Matthew: "Blessed are the meek: for they shall inherit the earth. Blessed are they which hunger and thirst after righteousness: for they shall be filled . . ." and on he read.

When he had finished reading the entire fifth chapter of the Gospel of Matthew, no one in the audience had moved. Backstage the prompter and other actors shouted and stamped their feet to remind the actor that he had forgotten his blasphemous monologue.

Lifting his head heavenward, the actor did not blaspheme but prayed aloud, "Jesus, remember me when You come into Your Kingdom." He had more to say but the curtain was lowered.

Within a few minutes, an announcement was made that the actor had become suddenly ill and the show was canceled. No official explanation of the incident was ever given. But some knew that the Word of God had conquered again!

In the Beatitudes, Jesus speaks of an inner peace and happiness which does not necessarily depend upon the external circumstances of one's life. He uses the word *blessed* nine times to describe this unusual Christian trait.

It means more than the word *happy*, which comes from the root *hap* meaning "by chance." True happiness is not by chance, nor is it dependent upon luck.

The Greek word for *blessed* (*makarios*) had been used for centuries to describe the island of Cyprus. This "blessed island" was considered self-contained. The soil was fertile, and the climate was good. Natural resources were so adequate that those who lived there never had to look elsewhere for provisions.

"Blessed" describes the self-contained person who is truly happy. Our happiness in Christ never depends on what happens *to* us but what has happened *in* us. We find our happiness in Christ instead of in a newer car, a larger bank account, a newer boat, or a house full of furniture.

Oh, the blessedness of one who has found Christ! He or she is to be congratulated!

• Congratulations, Christian: you have found the secret of happiness in realizing your spiritual helplessness! Like the beggar who depends upon others for his needs, you have realized that your greatest needs are met in Christ. You are "poor in spirit."

• Congratulations, Christian: you cannot successfully sin. Because the Holy Spirit lives within you, sin brings conviction and confession. You are truly happy because you are among those who "mourn."

• Congratulations, Christian: you are God controlled! Like a wild animal who is brought under the control of its master, you have let your impulses, passions, instincts, thoughts, and actions come under the control of Jesus Christ. You are not weak but "meek."

• Congratulations, Christian: the closer you get to God, the more sinful you feel, and the further you get from God, the more satisfied you are! You grow closer to God because you maintain a holy dissatisfaction with yourself.

You are among those who "hunger and thirst after righteousness."

• Congratulations, Christian: you have learned to acti-
vate love! You have learned the opposite of being selfish
and self-centered because you are "merciful" toward your
fellow humans.

• Congratulations, Christian: you have had a personal
encounter with Jesus Christ, known as the new birth, in
which the Holy Spirit has cleansed you and made you
"pure in heart"!

• Congratulations, Christian: you are actively engaged
in the most important project on earth: making peace
between rebellious people and our loving Heavenly Father! You are not just a peace lover or peace keeper but
a "peacemaker."

• Congratulations, Christian: for living the Christian
life without compromise for "all who desire to live godly
in Christ Jesus will be persecuted" (2 Tim. 3:12)! What a
joy to be numbered among those who are "persecuted for
righteousness' sake"!

A casual reading of the Gospels reveals that joy and
happiness surrounded the public ministry of our Lord.
Here are a few examples:

> And the seventy returned with joy, saying, "Lord, even
> the demons are subject to us in Your name."
> "Nevertheless do not rejoice in this, that the spirits are
> subject to you, but rejoice that your names are recorded
> in heaven" (Luke 10:17,20).

> At that very time He rejoiced greatly in the Holy Spirit,
> and said, "I praise Thee, O Father, Lord of heaven and
> earth, that Thou didst hide these things from the wise and
> intelligent and didst reveal them to babes. Yes, Father, for
> thus it was well-pleasing in Thy sight" (Luke 10:21).

As He said this, all His opponents were being humiliated; and the entire multitude was rejoicing over all the
glorious things being done by Him (Luke 13:17).

He hurried and came down, and received Him gladly
(Luke 19:6).

As He was now approaching, near the descent of the
Mount of Olives, the whole multitude of the disciples
began to praise God joyfully with a loud voice for all the
miracles which they had seen (Luke 19:37)

The humor of Jesus Christ seemed to be directed in one
of three directions. He laughed with His disciples. He
laughed and led others to laugh at hypocrisy and religious
haughtiness, and He laughed at the absurdity of those
who reject His good news of salvation by grace.

Laughing with Fellow Believers

According to David Augsburger, Jesus made three
strange promises to His disciples: "They would be absolutely fearless, they would be in frequent trouble, and
they would be absurdly happy."[24]

Jesus was fond of giving nicknames to His disciples (as
we have already seen in the case of Simon Peter in the
first chapter). As He named His twelve disciples, He gave
the brothers James and John the nickname of "Sons of
Thunder" (Mark 3:17). There seems to be good reason for
such a nickname because it was James and John who later
wanted to call down fire from heaven to consume the
Samaritans because they would not receive Christ (Luke
9:54). This nickname for the two brothers was never mentioned again in the New Testament. Why did Jesus give
them such a name in the first place? Perhaps it was indica-
tive of the freedom, friendship, and common joy which
Jesus shared with His disciples.

Have you heard about the fellow who purchased a new fluorescent lamp to give more light on his desk at work? His secretary noticed that he did something very strange the first day he brought the lamp into the office.

He wrapped the cord around the lamp and gently placed it in a drawer of the credenza near his desk. Every morning before he started to work, the businessman would open the drawer, switch on the light that was not even plugged in, close the drawer, and go on about his work.

Stupid? Jesus said, "Nor do men light a lamp, and put it under the peck-measure, but on the lampstand; and it gives light to all who are in the house" (Matt. 5:15). In other words, the silent witness of many Christians is about as effective as that man's fluorescent lamp in the drawer of his credenza!

Our Lord used some humorous jibes when He spoke to His disciples about the subject of worry (Matt. 6:25-34). Can you imagine a small sparrow throwing seed to the wind, cultivating young plants, harvesting the crop, and putting it into the barn? How ridiculous! Yet, we are of much more value to God than the sparrows, and God takes care of us just like He takes care of them. "Look at the birds of the air, that they do not sow, neither do they reap, nor gather into barns, and yet your Heavenly Father feeds them. Are you not worth much more than they?" (Matt. 6:26).

Can you imagine someone worrying an extra year onto his life? "Which of you by being anxious can add a single cubit to his life's span?" (Matt. 6:27).

Can you imagine a beautiful lily primping? She is ever so careful to comb back each petal, worrying about how she might look to others. "Why are you anxious about clothing? Observe how the lilies of the field grow; they do not toil nor do they spin, yet I say to you that even Solomon is all his glory did not clothe himself like one of these" (Matt. 6:28-29).

Instead of worrying about food, clothing, shelter, and status, Jesus challenges us to make God's will and Christlikeness the priorities of our lives, and He promises that "all these things shall be added to you" (Matt. 6:33).

Jesus told a story about a nobleman who called ten of his servants together and gave each of them the same amount of money and asked them to "do business with this until I come back" (Luke 19:11-27). A report was given by three of the servants—one increased his money by tenfold and one by fivefold. However, the third servant kept his money put away in a "handkerchief" (Luke 19:-20); the servant justified his laziness by claiming that he was afraid to do business with the money because he might lose it, and such a loss would cause his master to be quite displeased with him. Whereupon, the nobleman took his money and gave it to the man who had increased his by tenfold.

The humor is found in the "handkerchief," a common word used in that day for the sweat rag, used for wiping perspiration from one's face while working. But there was no sweat on one rag! The servant had neither gained nor lost. Neither had he worked! But he had found an ingenious way to use the sweat rag—wrap the money in it! Perhaps one of the servant's arguments for his laziness was going to be, "I couldn't work anyway because I had used my sweat rag to keep the money safely."

It somewhat reminds us of the two men out fishing on Sunday morning. At the sound of the church bells in the distance, one said to the other, "Gosh! It's Sunday morning, and we are out here fishing instead of going to church."

"I couldn't go to church anyway," his friend replied, "my wife is sick today."

Our Lord set an example of humility by washing His disciples' feet at His Last Supper with them (John 13:4-10). The whole story took on an amusing turn as Peter refused to have his feet washed by Jesus, believing it was below the dignity of the Messiah. Jesus told Peter to present his feet for washing or their friendship was over. Peter then went to the opposite extreme and asked Jesus to wash not only his feet but his whole body. Jesus reminded Peter that he had probably taken a bath recently, so there was no need to wash his whole body but to please expose his feet.

The interaction is quite amusing when we reconstruct the story: Peter misunderstands and refuses to cooperate . . . Jesus makes a tongue-in-cheek threat . . . Peter overreacts . . . Jesus calls him back to reality. The Last Supper might have lasted all night if Jesus had taken as much time to wash the other disciples' feet.

Laughing at Religion

Yuri B. Boryev claimed that, "a bullet does not care who stops it, but laughter always hones in on scoundrels."[25] The scoundrels on which Jesus concentrated were often the Pharisees and scribes. Jesus often described these religious leaders as "hypocrites." This word comes from the Greek play and describes the false face used by the Greek actor. It would allow one actor to play several parts in the same play. This playacting kind of religion is spoken of extensively in Matthew 6:1-18.

Jesus warned His disciples to "Beware of practicing your righteousness before men to be noticed by them" (Matt. 6:1). The Greek word *thethani*, translated "to be noticed by," is the word from which we get our word *theatre.* Do you get the picture of the kind of religion at which Jesus poked fun?

When it came to giving alms, He warned His disciples not to "sound a trumpet before you, as the hypocrites do in the synagogues and the streets, that they may be honored by men" (Matt. 6:2). Perhaps Jesus had reference to the metal, trumpet-shaped offering plates and the Pharisaic practice of throwing coins in the top of the trumpets and listening to them clank all the way around the sides and fall loudly to the bottom.

Again, our Lord cautioned His disciples about praying "in order to be seen by men" (Matt. 6:5) and fasting "so that you may not be seen fasting by men" (Matt. 6:18). Praying to be heard and fasting to appear righteous to others is about as bad as stopping the traffic on the two main thoroughfares of your city and yelling as you kneel down in the street, "I'm about to pray now!"

The key to serving our Lord is found in that humorous play on words when He said, "But when you give alms, do not let your left hand know what your right hand is doing" (Matt. 6:3). In other words, don't even remind yourself, much less others, of the good you do in Jesus' name. You can never do enough!

Leslie B. Flynn called our attention to the fact that clowns often cause us to laugh because of their grotesquely patched clothes. When Jesus' disciples were criticized for their failure to fast as John's disciples had done, our Lord indicated that it would be as unreasonable for His disciples to fast while He was present with them as it would be to cut out a piece of new cloth to patch a hole in an old garment. Not only would the old garment look funny, but the new cloth would have a hole in it as well (Luke 5:36).

Our Lord was the master of the one liner. For instance,

there is His amusing description of wolves dressed in sheep's wool (Matt. 7:15). He described the religious leaders of His day as blind people leading other blind people as both guide and follower promptly fell into the same hole (Matt. 15:14). It is pathetic but a little funny when Jesus spoke of religious leaders who are able to predict the weather but cannot read the signs of the times (Matt. 16:3).

We catch the pathos and irony in our Lord's words when He was about to be stoned: "I showed you many good works from the Father; for which of them are you stoning Me?" (John 10:32). His irony is obvious when He called Herod a "fox" (Luke 13:32) and when He called Gentile rulers "benefactors" (Luke 22:25).

Jesus laughed at haughtiness. He pictured a pompous man who attended a feast and took the seat of greatest honor only to be asked by the Host to move to a less-important chair when someone more highly honored came to the party (Luke 14:8-11).

Flynn commented "Inasmuch as a principle factor in humor is the ridiculous or absurd, wit served as an excellent vehicle to expose the inconsistencies of religious hypocrites," and "Since humor sometimes spotlights truth, the Master Pedagogue would naturally use it."[26]

Laughing at Indifference

Jesus' humor was often directed toward the indifferent. Would you build a house whose only foundation was sand? When rains came, your house would wash away. Yet people build their lives on the shifting sands of their own speculations and beliefs instead of obeying the teachings of our Lord (Matt. 7:24-27).

A wealthy man had invited at least three people to a great feast. The invitation had been general. However, when the feast was ready, he sent his messenger to the homes of the three guests only to receive three unusual excuses (Luke 14:16-24).

One man claimed that he had closed the deal on a piece of property and he had to go see it. At night? It would be impossible for him to see his land at night in the darkness.

The second man had bought five yoke of oxen and wanted to be excused from the dinner, so he could take them to the field for a test of their ability. That's like buying an expensive, luxury car sight unseen and then taking a test drive!

The third man excused himself because he had just gotten married. How unreasonable! What better place to celebrate their marriage than at a dinner?

Jesus used these flimsy excuses to show how unreasonable it is for anyone ever to reject God's great invitation to salvation in Christ. But Jesus never encourages anyone to rush into Christian discipleship. He told another story of a man who started to build a tower without sitting down to make his plans and count the cost. He ended up with nothing but a foundation and the laughter of his neighbors (Luke 14:27-30).

Jesus said it was easier for a camel to go through the eye of a needle than for a rich man to enter the kingdom of God (Matt. 19:24-26). There have been many attempts to water down the preposterous elements of this statement. However, we must let it stand as Jesus said it. Can you see a camel with its big hump trying to squirm its way through the eye of a needle? Can you see how difficult it is for those who are blessed with unlimited material blessings to simply humble themselves before the Cross and invite Jesus Christ into their lives?

That must be the same camel of which Jesus spoke when He said the Pharisees would strain out a gnat and swallow a camel (Matt. 23:24). All insects were considered quite unclean by the righteous Pharisees. They would ceremoniously strain their water to be sure no insects were found before they drank it. However, their legalistic religion had its blind spots. They were as ridiculous as a man who meticulously strained out a gnat and then swallowed a camel.

Do you get the picture? He turns up his bucket to drink. First, the long, hairy neck of a camel goes down . . . then the two loose humps . . . then the lanky legs . . . then the broad caloused knees . . . then the flat padded feet—so he strained out the gnat but swallowed the camel! Could anyone ever forget the absurdity of a legalistic religion with such a mental picture?

Allow me one more scenario: a family is getting ready for an exciting vacation. The car is packed the night before. The itinerary has been well prepared. The alarm clock has been set. At the crack of dawn, the husband, wife, and three children awake, dress, and excitedly run to the car. But the car is out of gas!

Jesus told such a ridiculous story about five foolish virgins who went out to meet a procession on its way to a wedding feast (Matt. 25:1-3). The groom would lead the procession to the wedding feast, but they would have to wait until he came for them. They took their lamps, but they took no oil for their lamps.

As the groom tarried, they fell asleep with five other wise virgins who had brought both lamps and oil. When the bridegroom finally came, the foolish virgins were denied the privilege of becoming a part of the procession to the marriage feast because they had no oil. How funny, yet how sad! And how foolish of anyone to neglect preparing for the coming of Christ!

Gary Webster concluded that an "attentive reading of

the gospel record reveals that Jesus certainly would have a well-developed sense of humor." "In fact," Webster contended, "He employed humor in such a variety of ways and upon so large a scale that it can be regarded as a major element in His recorded teachings."[27] Elton Trueblood concluded that there are at least thirty humorous passages in the Synoptic Gospels alone.[28] We have only touched the surface of a vast array of our Lord's teachings containing humorous elements.

Easter—The Last Laugh!

I mentioned earlier that Jesus' ministry started on the festive occasion of a wedding feast. Some believed it ended on a bloody cross on Good Friday. But Easter Sunday was coming! On that day, death was swallowed up in victory. Since that day, those of us who follow the risen Christ are able to thumb our noses at death and ask, "Where is your sting?"

They laughed at Jesus throughout His public ministry. When He declared that He was the prophet of whom Isaiah spoke, they laughed and asked, "Is not this the carpenter's son?" (Matt. 13:55). On the way to the cross, they chided, "He saved others; himself he cannot save" (Matt. 27: 42, KJV). They blindfolded Him, beat Him, and then asked Him to prophesy who struck Him. They stripped Him, put a scarlet robe on His back, placed a crown of thorns on His head, put a reed in His hand, and knelt down before His feet mocking Him with the words, "Hail, King of the Jews!" (Matt. 27:29, KJV).

Soldiers around the cross, considering Him only a petty rebel, laughingly nailed the legend over His head, "This Is Jesus, the King of the Jews" (Matt. 27:37). Even the Gentiles mocked Him as He hung on the cross and reminded Him that He had promised to rebuild the Temple in three days after its destruction. They all laughed at His cross.

But Sunday came! God had the last laugh!

On the evening before His crucifixion, Jesus had encouraged His disciples by saying, "These things I have spoken to you, that My joy may be in you, and that your joy may be made full" (John 15:11).

On another occasion He had said to His disciples, "Be of good cheer; I have overcome the world" (John 16:33, KJV). After His death, burial, and resurrection, His disciples were scattered to proclaim the good news of the gospel. The typical reaction to the gospel is found in Samaria: "There was great joy in that city" (Acts 8:8, KJV). No wonder the watchword of the apostle Paul was: "Rejoice in the Lord always; again I will say rejoice!" (Phil. 4:4).

Conclusion

Jesus *was* the master Humorist. So, in the words of Grady Nutt:

> In your reading of the gospels of Jesus Christ
>   let Him chuckle occasionally
>   let Him smile frequently
>   let Him laugh a lot
>   let Him get the two-by-four
>   out of your eye
>   and show you a clear day . . .
>   may you see
>   forever![29]

So . . . God has a sense of humor. With such a divine stamp, surely the gift of humor has been given for the physical and emotional benefit of those created in His "image."

4

The Physical Healing Power of Humor

It has been said that, like snowflakes, no two heart attacks are alike. I didn't know what to expect. I certainly wasn't expecting to be awakened in the middle of the night by a sharp pain between my shoulders and a burning sensation in my throat.

When I called my doctor and explained the symptoms, he said, "You'd better come in for an EKG!"

As Faye drove me to the doctor's office nearby, the pain became more severe. "If I pass out, just take me on to the emergency entrance at Riverside Hospital," I explained.

After the EKG, my doctor announced, "Well, you're having one!"

They transported me to the emergency room of the hospital about three blocks away. A few days before I had read that 50 percent of those who have heart attacks die within twenty-four hours. What a time for my mind to recall *that* statistic!

I awoke in a coronary intensive care room to the "beep, beep" of a machine nearby. As I glanced around the room at the tubes, lines, and monitors I realized that the pain had not yet subsided.

Had it been twenty-four hours? Would I be one of the 50 percent who lives or one of the 50 percent who dies? Because of my strong faith in Christ who is "the resurrection and the life," I was not worried. However, I could not help but wonder as I drifted back to sleep, *Will I awake here or hereafter?*

The room was full of nurses and interns when I awoke. I glanced at the clock on the wall and realized that, indeed, it was approaching twenty-four hours after the heart attack. One of the young interns standing at the foot of my bed anxiously asked, "How do you feel?"

"I feel like the monkey that kissed the skunk!" I replied.

"The monkey that kissed the skunk!" exclaimed the young doctor. "Are you having more pain?"

"What is the nature of your discomfort?" another asked.

"Do you know what the monkey said when he kissed the skunk?" I asked the doctors and nurses.

"No, what did he say?" they asked as they lined my bed.

"He said, 'I probably haven't had all of this I need, but I've had about all I can stand!' " I replied.

Laughter's Healing Music

The roar of laughter from my room may not have been appreciated by the other patients nearby. However, I can honestly say that it was healing music to my ears and, I trust, to my heart.

In the ensuing hours, the pain subsided, some of the tubes were removed, and I was moved to a "normal room" in the hospital. With the combination of a good doctor, a well-equipped hospital, and the prayers of many friends, my recovery was swift and successful. However, I'll always believe that the ability to laugh when we are hurting is most helpful in the healing process.

For centuries, great minds have hinted of a connection between humor and health. Shakespeare said, "A light heart lives long."[1] Carl Sandburg claimed that "the right laughter is medicine to weary bones."[2] "If I had no sense of humor," conceded Mahatma Gandhi, "I would have long ago committed suicide."[3]

Theologian Henry Ward Beecher defined mirth as "God's medicine.' "[4] Max Beerbohm hinted at the therapeutic value of humor when he said, "Strange, when you come to think of it, that of the countless folk who have lived before our time on this planet, not one is known in history or in legend as having died of laughter."[5]

Lawrence Sterne came even closer to connecting laughter and good health when he said, "Every time a man smiles—but much more so when he laughs—it adds something to this fragment of life."[6]

What does humor add to this fragment of life? We have heard such statements through the years as, "A hearty laugh is better than an ulcer any day of the week!"[7] But, until recent years, the medical profession has not been willing to "go out on a limb" and admit that a sense of humor and good health are closely related. According to Claudia M. Dewane, the American Medical Association has concluded "that laughter has a preventative as well as a curative value in regard to health and illness; and studies have shown that laughter aids digestion and stimulates the endocrinological system."[8]

Laurence J. Peter, the author of *The Peter Principle*, claimed with coauthor Bill Dana in the *Laughter Prescription* that, "Laughter may not cure, but at the very least it reduces pain, diffuses trouble, has no bad side effects— and it's free!"[9]

In the very popular and helpful book given to many who experience heart attacks—*Type A Behavior and Your Heart*—the authors conceded that the behavior pattern of most Type A persons is not crippled beyond repair. They contended that most Type A persons still retain a sense of humor, and "this is a priceless aid to recovery."[10]

In the sequel to this helpful book: *Treating Type A Behavior—and Your Heart,* another well-thought-out medical conclusion is made: Type A heart patients can help fend off future heart attacks by learning to ease up and conduct themselves like the milder-mannered Type B's.[11] The authors of the newer book contended that one of the most difficult accomplishments for the Type A person is to learn to smile. As Type A persons learn to slow down their driving, speak kindly to their families, and develop a sense of humor, they can move into the Type B category.[12]

Unhealthy Laughter

Raymond Moody reminded us that all laughter is not therapeutic. Certain types of laughter are everything but funny because they are the results of lesions of the brain. These "disorders of mirth" are found in patients with such diseases as pseudobulbar palsy, kuru, epilepsy, and the presenile dementias (Alzheimer's disease).

"Similarly," Moody contended, "today one can recognize that there is something wrong and inappropriate about the mirth of patients with hysteria, schizophrenia, or mania, even though science is not aware of any brain lesions or changes associated with these conditions."[13] He said that, "the schizophrenic laughs at things the majority of humanity recognizes as sad." And "the laughter of a victim of pseudobulbar palsy occurs even when nothing has taken place which the rest of us commonly accept as being funny."[14]

Poisoning or intoxication by a number of drugs or chemical substances can result in excessive, uncontrolled, or inappropriate laughter, Moody insisted.[15] Those acutely intoxicated with alcohol or drugs often go through distinct stages. At first they seem happy-go-lucky and jovial.

Then they are clownish—"albeit the kind of clownishness that they usually regret the next day, when the party is over."[16] Then, they become sad, despondent, and despairing; they sometimes grow belligerent or angry, and may even provoke a fight. Finally, they collapse into an unresponsive state and lose consciousness. Many doctors have used a memory device to memorize this sequence: "jocose, morose, bellicose, comatose."[17]

Certainly no doctor would claim that all laughter has therapeutic value. But who these days has not heard of the healing power of humor in the life of Norman Cousins? His twin battles with a crippling, irreversible disease in 1964[18] and a heart attack in 1980[19] have been most inspiring and helpful to thousands of people who have learned about them.

Internal Jogging

Cousins, who considers laughter a "form of internal jogging,"[20] is said to have laughed his way back to good health in 1964 by watching old films of humorous television shows and movies. "Ten minutes of genuine belly laughter," he claimed "had an anesthetic effect and would give me at least two hours of pain-free sleep."[21] He checked out of the hospital into a hotel room "which, happily, would cost about one-third as much as the hospital" and continued on a swift road to recovery.

Cousins later conceded that laughter is simply "a metaphor for the entire range of positive emotions." He considers that range of positive therapeutic emotions to include hope, faith, love, will to live, cheerfulness, humor, creativity, playfulness, confidence, and great expectations. "Since negative emotions can set the stage for illness," he concluded, "it seemed to me reasonable to believe that the positive emotions might help set the stage for recovery."[22]

These positive emotions also saw Cousins through a serious heart attack in 1980. In *The Healing Heart*, he dealt with the problem of panic and helplessness which is produced by any serious illness—especially heart ailments which cause more deaths in the United States than any other disease.

Dr. Bernard Lown, professor of cardiology at Harvard University School of Public Health, admitted that much of the panic and helplessness experienced by patients could be relieved by physicians and nurses. He told the story of a conversation with a sad-faced patient on one occasion.

When he asked the reason for his somber attitude, the man replied, "Doc, I don't think I'm going to make it."

"Why not?" the doctor asked.

The patient groaned, "Well, the intern told me that I have a massive anterior wall infarct; the resident said I had a transmural heart attack; the cardiology fellow indicated that I experienced an occlusion of a major coronary artery; while the attending physician called it a coronary thrombosis; and the nurses advised me not to ask questions. How can anyone survive so much heart damage?"

Lown concluded, "We physicians invariably mean well; not infrequently we do ill and justify our ill-doing by our well-meaning."[23]

Dr. Omar Fareed described the scene at the hospital on the day that Norman Cousins was admitted with his heart attack:

Imagine the scene in the emergency room of the UCLA Hospital. Dean Sherman Mellinkoff, of the UCLA School of Medicine, and several of the school's top cardiologists are awaiting the arrival by ambulance of a patient who has just had a heart attack. The telephoned report from the paramedics is alarming; it says that the patient is coughing up blood, an ominous indication of congestive heart failure.

The swinging doors to the emergency room open wide and a rolling stretcher comes through. The patient sits up, waves, grins, and says, "Gentlemen, I want you to know that you're looking at the darndest healing machine that's ever been wheeled into this hospital."[24]

Dr. Fareed summarized the essence of Cousins' personality, philosophy of life, and approach to illness and healing as follows:

(1) There is the absence of panic despite grave danger.
(2) The confidence in the ability of the human body to fight back even under extreme circumstances of illness or injury.
(3) The irrepressible good humor that creates an auspicious environment for both healing and treatment.[25]

The Norman Cousins Prescription

Illness is not generally thought to be a laughing matter. However, it is rapidly becoming viewed through medical eyes as deserving a good laugh. Raymond Moody, a medical doctor who has been investigating the therapeutic value of humor for many years, tells an interesting story in *Laugh After Laugh: the Healing Power of Humor*.[26]

One of his patients complained of constant headaches, insomnia, and the inability to say no to the unreasonable demands of others. With no formal education, the only job he could acquire was in the intolerable setting of a cookie factory. While the doctor continued to encourage him to seek further training in order to get a better job, the man insisted that his job had nothing to do with his health.

On one occasion, the cookie maker told of a new foreman who had experienced dissatisfaction with the number of cookies being produced in the factory and demanded an increase. Moody's patient had protested mildly that the wrapping machine just would not function fast enough to produce more cookies. But the new boss, determined to produce more cookies, ordered an increase in cookie production.

Just as the man had predicted, the wrapping machine went haywire and cookies went flying everywhere. There he stood helpless before his boss who publicly humiliated him even though he was the only person in the building who had predicted the cookie invasion.

As his patient related the story, Moody recalled imagining the situation. Then he did something he had always been taught never to do. Even though he was biting the inside of his cheeks to prevent it, he felt the corners of his mouth begin to form into a smile.

Amazingly, his patient responded with a smile, and the two of them burst into peals of laughter. Moody actually believes that this event started the healing process in the man's life that caused him to enter a training program and obtain a more gratifying job.

Norman Cousins's experience of using humor to aid the healing process proves the truth of Sir William Osler's statement: "It is much more important to know what sort of patient has a disease than to know what sort of disease a patient has."[27]

Can the patient deal with panic? Does the patient understand the biochemical effects of negative emotions? If Norman Cousins is correct, people do become ill as a result of such negative forces as panic, fear, suppressed rage, exasperation, frustration, and depression. If Cousins is correct, negative and positive emotions can affect hormonal flow, heart functions, and the constriction of blood vessels. Even though Cousins makes no attempt to posit a universal prescription and claims that what worked for him may not work for others, he shares six vital conclusions and convictions:[28]

(1) The conquest of panic is an essential part of any recovery process from a serious illness. There is a tendency, especially in a prolonged illness, to expect the worst and, thereby, become depressed and panicky. Cousins claims that confidence, deep purpose, joyousness, laughter, and the will to live are good conditioning agents, and their value should never be underestimated. These increase the value of the medical treatment we receive.

(2) The body's drive to recuperate may not work under all circumstances, but it works often enough to demand our confidence and special efforts. Cousins, at least, has proven that the human body is capable of more than one titanic regenerative effort in one lifetime.

(3) A sharing of responsibility with one's physician is in the best interest of both physician and patient. After his two bouts over which he became victorious, Cousins joined the faculty of a medical school and studied even more closely the relationship of the physician and the patient. He concluded that the physician brings his or her trained knowledge while the patient brings a healing system that needs to be freed to do its job.

(4) There are times when intervention in the form of medicine or surgery is absolutely necessary, but the nourishment of one's body and mind are always essential to good health.

(5) Surgery may sometimes be required to save one's life, but a second or third opinion need not be regarded as a lack of confidence in one's physician who made the original recommendation. Cousins believes that, in many

cases related primarily to heart attacks or coronary disease, the heart is capable of "making its own bypass."

(6) Medical treatment should seek not just to repair damage and restore vital balances but to enhance the quality of one's life and to help the patient to overcome feelings of hopelessness and helplessness. If the physician is to be fully effective in these directions, the patient must be a responsive and appreciative partner.

Taking Humor Medicine

An increasing number in the medical profession are beginning to recognize the physical healing power of humor. Raymond Moody also gave his disclaimer in his statement, "I am not proposing that doctors become comedians. Nor am I recommending that laughter replace the medical techniques that we already have. I propose only that it could be used to supplement them."[29]

There is a growing number of institutions now using humor to supplement medical techniques. A Missouri state prison rehabilitates inmates with a laugh-a-day program. A veterans administration hospital in Los Angeles prescribes that discharged patients laugh fifteen minutes a day. In several retirement homes, elderly residents take regular humor "medicine"—funny books, poems, cartoons, movies, and performances by stand-up comedians.[30]

Norman Cousins was called upon to develop a laughter program at a veterans administration hospital to brighten the mood of cancer patients. He entered a room that was used for reading and social functions that had been rearranged especially for his meeting with about six or seven rows of chairs to accommodate forty to fifty patients. His host introduced him to the patients, told them a little bit of his experience with humor and informed them that he had come to "make them laugh."

Cousins spoke to them about recent studies which show that attitudes play an important part in one's effort to combat illness. He emphasized, as he always does, that laughter is only one of the many positive emotions which help one deal with adversity and noted again the need for faith, love, the will to live, creativity, and playfulness. Even though laughter may not produce biochemical changes, Cousins explained, "It tends to block deep feelings of apprehension and panic that all too frequently accompany serious illness." He also reminded them that laughter "frees the body of the constricting effects of the negative emotions that in turn may impair the healing system."[31]

He then asked if the cancer patients would join him in an experiment. He asked for a volunteer who enjoyed hearty laughter and who could almost laugh on cue. A tall, sandy-haired man on the front row named Bill stepped forward. Cousins told some of his favorite stories. The room rocked with laughter, and the response of the patients was reinforced by Bill's thunderous laughter.

After Cousins played a cassette laugh track, the cancer patients were "on a toboggan that had reached the steepest part of the hill and continued to accelerate." This runaway laughter continued for about ten minutes. Some of the patients could hardly stay in their chairs. It was so contagious that Cousins found himself "rolling in the aisles." After about ten minutes, Cousins asked the patients how they felt. Some claimed that their pain had receded.

Cousins concluded his initial meeting at the VA hospital by suggesting that the members of this group develop a program for creating "an upbeat atmosphere." He suggested that they might take turns accepting the responsibility for staging one-act plays, showing videotapes, and using audiotapes of stand-up comics. He encouraged them to watch funny motion pictures and to use their own imagination to create a humorous atmosphere among themselves.

When Cousins returned to the VA hospital several weeks later, he was surprised at how the patients had arranged their own programs for laughter. They were not sitting in rows but in a large circle along with the doctors and nurses. The patients were sharing with each other. One patient shared a letter from his nephew who had been admitted to medical school and wrote, "I'm going to come up with answers. Just hang in there." The room resounded with applause.

Another patient reported that he had heard from a friend he had not seen in over twenty years. More applause. Other upbeat testimonies were shared, each followed by applause. Then they indicated that it was Cousins's turn to share something funny. After Cousins shared the following story, he received a standing ovation from the patients:

> I went to the telephone to call the office and promptly lost a dime when an operator came on and asked for a quarter. It was a recording. I put in another dime, got a live operator, told her what happened, and she said the phone company would be glad to send me the dime if I would give her my name and address. It seemed absurd that the phone company would spend 20 cents in stamps, to say nothing of personnel expense, just to refund a dime —and I said so. I also pressed the coin-return lever.
>
> At that point, all the innards of the machine opened up and quarters and dimes tumbled out in magnificent and overflowing profusion.

"Operator," I asked, "are you still there?"

"Yes."

"Operator, something quite remarkable has just happened. All I did was press the coin-return lever and the machine is giving me all its earnings. There must be more than three dollars in coins here and the flow hasn't stopped."

"Sir," she said, "will you please put the money back in the box?"

"Operator," I said, "if you will give me your name and address I'll be glad to mail it to you."[32]

The staff physicians at the VA hospital have been impressed with the change in the general mood and the average improvement in the condition of their patients. This program has continued successfully at that hospital, and many others have introduced the laughter program.

Laughter's Limitations

Cousins concluded his report of the laughter program in the VA hospital with some disclaimers. "I didn't want people to think that getting over a serious illness was no more complicated than having a good laugh."[33] He explained that he had used laughter to illustrate the importance of all the positive emotions, laughter being the most vigorous and the one that most readily captured popular attention. He also wanted to make sure that the physician-patient relationship is most vital in establishing positive attitudes and aiding the healing process. "Certainly the last thing in the world I wanted to do was to give people the idea that they could hah-hah their way out of all their problems."[34]

Dr. Bernard Lown, Professor of Cardiology at Harvard University School of Public Health, wrote the introduction to Norman Cousins's *The Healing Heart.* Even though no comment was made about it, this Bible verse appeared at the top of the introduction: "A merry heart doeth good like a medicine: but a broken spirit drieth the bones" (Prov. 17:22, KJV). If we are to surmise that men of Dr. Lown's stature believe this verse, perhaps there is a bright future for the healing power of humor.

When we enter the hospital, we face intense fear and anxiety. We are prodded, poked, dressed, undressed, and told every few minutes to open our mouths or close our mouths. Every bit of humor helps when it comes to spending time in a hospital. If you have ever been there, perhaps you can identify with this little bit of verse:

The Gown with the Split Down the Back

I was sittin' here mindin' my business,
Kinda lettin' my mind go slack,
When in comes a nurse with a bright, sunny smile.
And a gown that was split down the back.

"Take a Shower," she said, "and get ready,
And then jump into this sack."
What she was really talkin' about
Was the gown with the split down the back.

"They're coming to do some tests," she said.
They're gonna stretch me out on a rack,
With nothin' twist me and the cold, cruel world,
But a gown that's split down the back!

It comes only to the knees in front,
In the sides there is also a lack,
But by far the greatest shortcoming
Is that bloomin' split down the back.

Whoever designed this garment,
For humor had a great knack.
But I fail to see anything funny
'Bout a gown that's split down the back.

I hear them coming to get me,
The wheels going clickety-clack.
I'll ride through the halls on a table,
In a gown with a split down the back.

When I get to Heaven it'll make me no odds
If my robe is white, red, or black.
The only thing I will ask is, "Please,
Give me one with no split down the back."[35]

Clowning Around the Hospital

One of the most unusual testimonials for the healing power of humor is the revival of the clowning ministry in several denominations. Raymond Moody told an encouraging story of the ministry of a clown who visited a ninety-five-year-old man with severe depression. Because he had not eaten, talked, or responded in any way, the patient's doctors thought he would soon die.

A clown visited his room and within thirty minutes had the patient laughing and talking and eating. He lived a few more years, and the clown maintained communication with him during that time.[36]

"Clownseling" clinics are beginning to catch on in some parts of the country. The therapist becomes a clown along with the patient, allowing both of them to stand back and look objectively at the problems of the patient.[37]

While most clowning ministries are aimed at physical and emotional healing, at least one ministry begun in recent years has an evangelistic appeal. Since 1980, the Sunday School Board of the Southern Baptist Convention has sponsored a clown seminar which has grown rapidly.

The director of the seminars gave this report of the evangelistic effectiveness as well as the therapeutic value of the ministry:

Last year when we returned from our first day's clowning on the streets of Nashville to our sharing session, many of the people new to clowning were in tears. They had discovered a whole new Christian experience through clowning. Because of the joy they had seen on people's faces, they knew that they could witness to people and do so effectively.[38]

Nurses for Laughter, based in Portland, Oregon, seeks to inform nurses of the legitimate use of laughter in health care and of misconceptions about its use.[39]

Debbie Liber, leader of the organization, finds that patients welcome humor in the hospital room. "One day," she recalled, "we decided to have a professional cap day. But instead of wearing nurses caps, we wore our regular white uniforms with all kinds of hats, like construction hats and baseball caps, and the patients had a lot of fun.[40]

Conclusion

I am not a physician. I make no claim to a vast knowledge of medical data. I have simply tried to share in this chapter what I have observed about the physical healing power of humor. I am not dispensing laughter prescriptions to anyone who is physically ill. However, there is too much evidence in the Bible and everyday experience to deny that, as one of the positive emotions, humor has a healing effect.

Neither am I recommending that every pastor don a clown costume and hit the hallways of the hospitals. However, for many years I have believed the Scriptures which teach that a "merry heart doeth good like a medicine." I have seen too many people lose hope and their sense of humor and die. I have also observed how quickly some with a "merry heart" overcame the same ailments and lived.

Neither do I want to discount the power of prayer in healing. Whether God uses laughter, medicine, or a combination of both, our healing is still divine. It is my firm conviction that God often chooses to perform the miracle of healing in one's life as an answer to prayer. At other times, however, I have observed how some who are never healed have borne an unusual Christian testimony through their illness—even to the grave! I will share more of a biblical approach to both physical and emotional healing in the next chapter.

5

The Emotional Healing Power of Humor

Depression!

I secretly wondered if my wife would ever laugh again.

The doctor said that her deep depression and withdrawal had been caused by a chain of disappointing events coupled with some physical problems and emotional "hang-ups" carried from childhood. She had lost over twenty pounds and spent most of her time in bed. For more than a year, doctors were unable to find the proper medication or treatment to bring her out of those dark days.

"I am recommending that she be admitted to a hospital," her doctor announced. After three weeks of treatment and counseling by a team of able psychologists, I could see a flicker of a smile.

As we drove home from the hospital that day she looked into a mirror and exclaimed, "Yuk, I look like a witch!"

"A visit to the beauty shop will do wonders for you," I suggested. "But if you insist," I said, "I'll tell your friends when they call that you've emerged successfully from the hospital except for one problem."

"And what is that?" she asked.

"I'll tell them that you think you're a witch and that you ride a broomstick around the house!"

She laughed. "Why don't you?" she asked.

"Are you serious?"

"Yes, maybe it'll break the ice a little bit. People never seem to know just what to say to someone with emotional problems," she explained.

Later that evening, one of her friends called and asked if she and another friend might come over to see Faye.

"Come right on over," I said.

"Well, how is she?" asked her friend. "Are there any aftereffects?"

"Only one," I explained deliberately and compassionately. "You see, she recovered well from the treatments except for periodic spells when she thinks she's a witch."

"She thinks she's a witch!" her friend yelled into the phone.

"Yes, from time to time, she'll jump up, run to the kitchen, get the broom, and ride it across the room. It doesn't last long. I suggest, if she has a spell while you are here, that you just remain calm and act as though nothing is happening."

Later in the evening, Faye's friends came laden with gifts of perfume and, thankfully, much food. I could tell that it was difficult for Faye to talk about her stay in the hospital. Then, I noticed a gleam in her eye as she got up from the sofa in the den and walked to the kitchen.

She was going to do it!

Her friends were sitting with their backs to the kitchen, and I was facing them. As Faye mounted her broom, she smiled at me like a child about to take the lid off the cookie jar to steal a cookie.

"Giddy up!" she called as she rode the broom from the kitchen, made a *U* turn in the den in front of her friends, and galloped back to the refrigerator. Their eyes followed every stride as she deposited her faithful steed in the kitchen corner. They kept talking about something else, but their eyes and their minds were focused on Faye and her broom.

When she returned to the sofa, her friends were strangely silent and seemed to have nothing more to say. When we finally explained our little plan to break the ice, we all laughed boisterously and enjoyed a delightful evening of conversation thereafter.

Faye would laugh again!

Many had prayed fervently for her victory over depression. We had claimed the biblical promise that, "God causes all things to work together for good to those who love God, to those who are called according to His purpose. . . . to become conformed to the image of His son" (Rom. 8:28-29).

Faye's doctors had done their work well. All of these factors had placed her on the road to recovery. But laughter had made the trip more bearable and, at times, enjoyable. We had experienced the emotional benefits of humor!

It was during those long hours of waiting, praying, and hoping that I decided to go to my files of many years and produce a book of clean jokes. After her stay in the hospital, I asked Faye to help me with the book. At first, it was difficult for her to laugh, but gradually she regained her sense of humor and jumped into the project of *The Treasury of Clean Jokes,* the first of several such books that we would produce in the ensuing years.

Since her bout with depression, Faye has developed a sense of humor that far exceeds that of previous years. She and I both believe that her increased sense of humor has been a major factor in overcoming subsequent depression.

Surviving Emotional Steamrollers

Erma Bombeck claims to be a great believer in the premise that humor heals. "I have nothing to back it up physically," she admits, "but emotionally I have file drawers of pure testimonials."[1] Emily Hardy said, "You can survive almost any emotional steamroller if you can hold onto your sense of humor."[2]

Bil Keane defined laughter as the "safety valve of the mind." He said, "There is no better way to keep emotionally stable than by laughing or creating laughs."[3] Henry Ward Beecher, a minister from another generation, said, "A man without mirth is like a wagon without springs—he is jolted by every pebble in the road."[4]

That humor and emotional stability go hand in hand is now being claimed by ministers, psychologists, physicians, and other professionals. B. M. Foss said, "Laughter is a defense against neurosis, humor is a defense against psychosis."[5] Martin Grotjahn said almost the same thing in another way: "Witty people may be neurotic, but they're not as likely to be psychotic."[6]

But why are laughter and a sense of humor so closely associated with emotional stability? In the first place, laughter is an emotional response. In fact, Steve Allen claimed that "humor takes many forms because it is based on an emotional response to many kinds of experiences."[7] Such an emotional response makes one exclaim, "It felt so good to laugh!" Or one might also say, "I needed a good laugh!"

Esther Blumenfeld and Lynne Alpern concluded, "Laughter is a positive emotion. And as long as we can choose to laugh, it means we affirm life—no matter how burdensome it might become."[8]

Not only is laughter associated with emotional stability

because it represents a positive emotional response, it also calls for self-abandonment. Chad Walsh said, "By laughter we acknowledge the human condition and get outside the solitary prison of the self."[9]

David Shapiro claimed that paranoid people never laugh. They may act like they are laughing, but they really do not genuinely laugh because they do not really feel amused. The reason? "Because laughing always involves a certain degree of self-abandonment."[10]

Cop-out or Cope?

Humor and emotional stability also go hand in hand because humor is a tremendous tool for coping. Thus, Steve Allen claimed, "without laughter, life on our planet would be intolerable."[11] Blumenfeld and Alpern explain the coping power of laughter when they claim, "Psychologically, seeing the funny side of life helps you maintain your balance while trying to cope with daily irritations."[12]

The parents of a sixteen-year-old boy were frustrated beyond words when they learned that their son, who had been on drugs for over a year, was rushed from school to the hospital suffering from a "bad trip." Weeks dragged into months. The young man lay in the hospital with no one knowing just how seriously his brain had been affected by the drugs.

One evening, the family physician stopped by to give a report to the parents. "Until a few days ago," he said, "I felt we were going to have to face the inevitable and accept that Peter never again would be normal. But now I'm sure we're past the crisis. I visited him in the hospital this afternoon—and for the first time I got him to laugh."[13]

It is no surprise that many doctors, psychiatrists, and psychologists are using humor in the counseling process.

Mary Ann Wall claims that counseling has had the traditional reputation of being "so heavy" that there is no place for laughter. "Often," she notes, "a client comes away more depressed, and so does the counselor."[14]

There are, of course, some risks in using humor in therapy. But Marianne Roncoli believes that the greatest risk of all is that the counselor is "appearing imperfect, fallible, and human." But, on the other hand, Roncoli believes that humor in therapy "also gives the patient license to behave imperfectly, fallibly and humanly."[15]

Recognizing one's imperfection often helps in overcoming depression. Minirth and Meier believe, "Many individuals improve as soon as they learn no one is perfect (not even they) and as they begin to laugh at their own perfectionistic demands or other shortcomings."[16] Furthermore, Tom Walsh would conclude, "You cannot be depressed, or anxious, or angry when you're laughing."[17]

Mary Ann Wall echoed the same sentiments when she said, "It is my contention that you can't stay depressed long if you are laughing."[18]

Humor and Suicide

Perhaps the most depressing outcome of depression in our society is the prevalence of suicide. When Abe Burrows defined humor as "a way to keep from killing myself,"[19] few realized what a prophetic statement he had made. Suicide among American teenagers has nearly tripled over the past two decades, making it the second leading cause of death among the nation's youth.[20] Suicide is also among the top ten causes of death for those over 65. Recent studies of suicidal behavior on the college campus have led to the conclusion that suicide is a serious public health problem and, in the college setting, ranks as the second or third leading cause of death.[21]

"Cluster suicides" and "copycat suicides" have attracted our attention in recent years. Psychologists have cited increased child abuse, the fear of a nuclear holocaust, drug and alcohol dependency, family problems, and the pressure to succeed as being possible causes for suicidal behavior among teenagers.

A recent study by the Duke University Center for the Study of Aging and Human Development warns that today's baby boomers might experience even greater incidents of suicide beyond the year 2000. More competitive job markets, increased social stress, delayed marriage (and therefore delayed establishment of intimate relationships), fewer children (and therefore a small social network), frequent divorce, and feelings of alienation are listed as possible reasons for the predicted surge in suicide among the baby boomers as they begin to turn sixty-five.[22]

In their research on current trends of youthful suicide, Michael L. Peck and Robert E. Litman linked teenage suicide with unhappiness in the home. Nearly two thirds of those who took their lives as adolescents were discovered by the Peck and Litman study to be on poor terms with their families and nearly 90 percent felt that their families did not understand them. Surprisingly, a large number of this group (42 percent) was reported to have been in physical fights with other persons, and an equally large number reported to have engaged in physical fights with persons in their own families.

The American Association of Suicidology has concluded, "It should be pointed out that suicidal youth, regardless of the specific trigger factor, all have one thing in common: a nagging lack of optimism, lack of hope about their future and an enormous sense of unhappiness."[23]

A fifteen-year-old boy wrote the following poem two

years before he committed suicide. Note the total absence of humor.

To Santa Claus and Little Sisters

Once . . . he wrote a poem.
And called it "Chops."
Because that was the name of his dog,
    and that's what it was all about.
And the teacher gave him an "A"
And a gold star.
And his mother hung it on the kitchen door,
    and read it to all his aunts . . .
Once . . . he wrote another poem.
And he called it "Question Marked Innocence."
Because that was the name of his grief
    and that's what it was all about.
And the professor gave him an "A"
And a strange and steady look.
And his mother never hung it on the kitchen door,
    because he never let her see it . . .
Once, at 3 a.m. . . . he tried another poem . . .
And he called it absolutely nothing,
    because that's what it was all about.
And he gave himself an "A"
And a slash on each damp wrist,
And hung it on the bathroom door
    because he couldn't reach the kitchen.[24]

One wonders how many suicides could be prevented both among youth and senior adults if we could learn to laugh in our homes. I do not want to leave the impression that laughter is the major deterrent to suicide. However, it has to be one of the major "positive emotions," along with faith, hope, love, the will to live, and creativity, which work against suicidal tendencies.

If, indeed, laughter tends to block deep feelings of apprehension and panic which frequently accompany physical illness, could it also be an emotional healer as well? According to Norman Cousins, laughter "helps free the body of the constricting effects of the negative emotions that in turn may impair the healing system,"[25] If that be true, could laughter also help free the suicidal person from the stress that leads to self-destruction?

Panacea for Pessimism

Cal Samra called attention to the fact that psychologists are now discovering truths that have surprisingly been built into the traditions of the church for centuries.[26] Does the Bible have anything to say about emotional stability? George Vlahos went so far as to say, "Everything in the psychotherapeutic world can be traced to the Bible. And there was no greater psychiatrist than Jesus Christ."[27]

The Bible sheds much light on factors which lead to emotional instability—pessimism, bitterness, worry, and loneliness.

It is now fashionable to be pessimistic. That is the conclusion of Michael Korda, who said, "It's as if the entire country, having suddenly lost faith in everything from paper money to social security . . . has turned into a nation of old-fashioned European pessimists."[28]

Our preoccupation with collectibles, the popularity of flea markets, and the philosophy of "buy gold and bury it in the garden" are indications of a pessimistic attitude that has gradually slipped up on our nation. Our passion for sports and fitness reminds Korda of Germany in the 1920s and early 1930s when hordes of people turned to hiking, sunbathing, and "the worship of the body beautiful" in an effort to divert their attention from German politics and the family next door.

Psychologist Jay S. Lindsay thinks national pessimism can be countered with positive thoughts that are supported by the Bible. According to Lindsay, the ultimate basis for being able to approach life positively is our relationship to God through Jesus Christ. "In that relationship is all the security in the world and all the reason one could want for being able to think positively," he concluded.[29] Lindsay encouraged us to accentuate the positive and shared four practical suggestions:

(1) Identify your negative feelings such as anxiety, anger, jealousy, distrust, and discern if surface feelings are caused by deeper feelings.

(2) Identify negative and irrational thoughts that contribute to negative feelings and list these on one side of an index card.

(3) For each negative, irrational thought, write on the reverse side of the card a positive, rational counter thought and a supporting Bible reference.

(4) Carry the card with you, and whenever a negative or irrational thought occurs, flip the card and focus on the positive rational counter thought and supporting Bible reference.

Beating Bitterness

But what does humor have to do with bitterness? Tom Mullen described humor as "a survival mechanism" which enables us to "forgive and remember that we can't forgive and forget." He also claimed that "The ability to laugh in a world like ours is an act of faith, a declaration of belief in a God who can be trusted."[30]

An unforgiving spirit and the inability to forget the harm done to one by others constitutes one of the greatest deterrents to a healthy self-image and to a sense of humor. When a little boy was asked to define forgiveness, he said,

"It is the odor that flowers give when they are trampled upon." All of us need the forgiving breath of God in our lives. But Jesus taught us to go a step further: "Forgive us our debts, as we also have forgiven our debtors" (Matt. 6:12).

How do we forgive others? We forgive others when we seek to understand them. True forgiveness looks behind what one does. It concludes, "They know not what they do."

We forgive others when we forget what others have done to us. There is never any record that Jesus recalled the harm done to Him—not even after His resurrection. We have no record of His sitting around the campfire discussing His ill treatment at the hands of the Romans. Instead of talking about His troubles, He came to His disciples with, "Peace I give unto you" (John 14:27, KJV).

Two little boys returned to their separate homes after a fight. One declared to his mother, "I will never speak to him again as long as I live!" The next day the mother observed both boys playing together as usual as though nothing had happened the day before. When she questioned her son about his vow never again to speak to his friend, he answered, "Me and Johnny is good forgetters."

We forgive others when we learn to love the unlovely. Christian love does not depend upon what one is, what one does to us, nor what one does for us. How unlovely was the crowd around the cross! Some of them actually got a thrill out of seeing people die and rejoiced in the bloodcurdling cries of condemned criminals upon the cross. But Jesus said, "Father, forgive them" (Luke 23:34, KJV).

Tantamount to forgiving is to experience God's forgiveness. When you receive Christ, you die to self. You realize how unworthy you are of God's forgiveness. You cry out

with the psalmist, "If Thou, Lord, shouldst mark iniqui-
ties,/O Lord, who could stand?" (Ps. 130:3). A person who
knows Christ realizes that salvation is by grace through
faith. "For by grace you have been saved through faith;
and that not of yourselves, it is the gift of God; not as a
result of works, that no one should boast" (Eph. 2:8-9).
How then can we be less gracious to others than God has
been to us?

Winning Over Worry

Blumenfeld and Alpern claim that "anxiety over real
problems is real, but self-induced worry about what hasn't
happened is fabricated."[31] Their evaluation of worry reminds me of the story about the nervous clock.

Like any good clock, it had been ticking away for years,
two ticks per second every day. But one day the clock
began to worry about its responsibilities—all those ticks it
had to tick. It had to tick 120 ticks a minute, 7,200 ticks
an hour, 172,000 ticks per day, 1,209,600 ticks per week!

"That's 62 million ticks a year!" the clock cried, and
promptly had a nervous breakdown.

The sick clock went to a psychiatrist and explained its
troubles. "All those ticks—I don't see how I can stand it!"

The psychiatrist said, "Wait a minute. How many ticks
must you tick at a time?"

"Oh, I just tick one tick at a time," the clock replied.

"You go home," the doctor said, "and think about ticking only one tick. And until you have ticked that tick,
don't even think about the next tick."

That clock describes many if not most of us. How can
we learn to tick one tick at a time and win the battle over
worry and depression? Does the Bible have answers? The
Bible gives us four great challenges regarding worry:

(1) Realize the Harm. Worry hurts us spiritually. The

Bible teaches, "The one who does not believe God has made Him a liar" (1 John 5:10). God's Word has made some great promises which are denied by worry: "I will never desert you, nor will I ever forsake you" (Heb. 13:5); "He cares for you" (1 Pet. 5:7); "My God shall supply all your needs according to His riches in glory in Christ Jesus" (Phil. 4:19); "I can do all things through Him who strengthens me" (Phil. 4:13). If we do not believe these promises from God's Book we are, in essence, calling God a liar and stunting our own spiritual growth.

Worry hurts us physically. The physical body of the Christian is described as God's temple. "Do you not know that you are a temple of God, and that the Spirit of God dwells in you?" (1 Cor. 3:16); "And because you are sons, God has sent forth the Spirit of His Son into our hearts" (Gal. 4:6).

According to many physicians, fear, worry, hate, selfishness, and the inability to adjust to the world of reality may cause one to become ill—thus harming God's temple! Gary Schwartz said, "Those people who view daily hassles as frustrating and respond most often with anger are more likely to succumb to all kinds of physical diseases."[32]

(2) Recognize the Uselessness. When we worry, we devaluate ourselves. Jesus said, "Look at the birds of the air, that they do not sow, neither do they reap, nor gather into barns, and yet your heavenly Father feeds them. Are you not worth much more than they?" (Matt. 6:26). We are human beings made in the image of God. Why then should we worry?

No one ever became taller or older by worrying. This is why Jesus asked, "Which of you by being anxious can add a single cubit to his life's span?" (Matt. 6:27).

Worrying blinds us to the blessings of God.

Why are you anxious about clothing? Observe how the lilies of the field grow; they do not toil nor do they spin, yet I say to you that even Solomon is all his glory did not clothe himself like one of these. But if God so arrays the grass of the field, which is alive today and tomorrow is thrown into the furnace, will He not much more do so for you, O men of little faith? (Matt. 6:28-30).

When we worry, we trample the beauties of the earth under our feet and forget that the same God who adorns the lily can also make something beautiful of our lives as well.

(3) Establish Priorities. When we elevate the will of God above everything else in our lives, we learn to trust instead of worry. "But seek first His kingdom and His righteousness; and all these things shall be added to you" (Matt. 6:33). How does one find the will (kingdom) of God?

• By earnest prayer.

In the same way the Spirit also helps our weakness; for we do not know how to pray as we should, but the Spirit Himself intercedes for us with groanings too deep for words; and He who searches the hearts knows what the mind of the Spirit is, because He intercedes for the saints according to the will of God (Rom. 8:26-27).

• By following the leadership of the Holy Spirit: "For if you are living according to the flesh, you must die; but if by the Spirit you are putting to death the deeds of the body, you will live" (Rom. 8:13).

• By having faith that God will cause everything to fit together in one's life: "We know that God causes all things to work together for good to those who love God, to those who are called according to His purpose" (Rom. 8:28).

(4) Live in the Now. Don't live in tomorrow. The New Testament places an emphasis on the now. Jesus asked,

"Do you *now* believe?" (John 16:31, author's italics). John exclaimed, "Beloved *now* we *are* the children of God, and it has not appeared as yet what we shall be" (1 John 3:2, author's italics). *Today* is the watchword for those who will do the will of God: *"Today* if you hear His voice,/Do not harden your hearts" (Heb. 4:7, author's italics). Today is the tomorrow you worried about yesterday!

Don't live in yesterday. We cannot live with yesterday's sorrows nor yesterday's sins. We are promised that "If we confess our sins, He is faithful and righteous to forgive us our sins and to cleanse us from all unrighteousness" (1 John 1:9). We cannot keep reliving yesterday's success. If we spend today merely recounting the successes of yesterday, we cannot succeed today.

Harvey Firestone, Jr., reportedly said that "Today is the first day of the rest of your life," and concluded, "So, it's no use fussing about the past because you can't do anything about it. But you have today, and today is when everything that's going to happen from now on begins."

Licking Loneliness

Loneliness has become an epidemic in our country. It is usually defined as "absence of companionship or society." One doctor, who defines loneliness as "pain turned inward," has concluded that the rise of human loneliness may be one of the most serious sources of disease in the twentieth century.

A growing number of social scientists and mental health professionals are now studying contemporary American loneliness. Some of the greatest contributing factors to loneliness in our society are the emphasis on the acquisition of material possessions and the desire for status. These materialistic goals discourage Americans from forming and maintaining relationships which tend to relieve loneliness.

More people live alone today than ever before—almost one fourth of our population. In this group are a large number of people under forty who, for a variety of reasons, have chosen not to marry. Others who live alone are divorced, separated, or widowed. Experts estimate that for every married couple in some cities, there is a single adult.

Loneliness among children and teenagers has caused a great deal of concern among child psychiatrists. A contributing factor to loneliness among children and teenagers is the broken home which causes so many children to be raised without both parents. Loneliness among youth may also be a contributing factor to the increase of teenage suicide.

Ordinary people cope with loneliness in ordinary ways. They depend on the radio and television for company. For companionship, they turn to soap operas that offer the illusion of involvement in other people's lives. Some people take tranquilizers and go to bed; others read, go to a movie, or purchase items which they really do not need.

We, as believers in Christ, have found an answer to loneliness—practicing the presence of God! Every human being on the face of this earth lives in the presence of a holy, righteous, and loving God. This is a convicting truth because of our sins. But it is also a comforting truth because of our needs.

Life is full of shadows. But shadows are made because of the shining of the sun. In Christ, we have found the light that dispels the darkness of loneliness.

Turning Stress into Success

Some are lonely while others are stressful. The circumstances of life produce a great deal of stress these days. Over one-hundred years ago, Robert Louis Stevenson shared some suggestions for those who "think themselves sick."[33]

(1) Make up your mind to be happy—learn to find pleasure in simple things.

(2) Make the best of circumstances. No one has everything, and everyone has something of sorrow.

(3) Don't take yourself too seriously.

(4) Don't let criticism worry you: you can't please everybody.

(5) Don't let your neighbors set your standards: be yourself.

(6) Do things you enjoy doing but stay out of debt.

(7) Don't borrow trouble. Imaginary things are harder to bear than actual ones.

(8) Since hate poisons the soul, do not cherish enmities and grudges. Avoid people who make you unhappy.

(9) Have many interests. If you can't travel, read about places.

(10) Don't hold postmortems or spend time brooding over sorrows and mistakes.

(11) Don't be the one who never gets over things.

(12) Keep busy at something. A very busy person never has time to be unhappy.

Prior to Stevenson, however, the Scriptures spoke on the subject. In fact, James, the half brother of our Lord, wrote in the epistle named for him, "Consider it all joy, my brethren, when you encounter various trials" (Jas. 1:2).

When stress comes, most of us ask, "Why? Why? Why?" Some cry, "How can I live with this?" Some, like Job's wife say, "Curse God and die!" (2:9). Others merely grin and bear their adversities. But those who know Christ can "Consider it all joy" (Jas. 1:2).

But we are not left hanging on this unusual challenge. There are reasons why the true believer in Christ can find joy in adverse circumstances and turn stress into success.

• Consider your stress to be joy because, in this experience, you or someone else may gain an unshakable faith in God: "Knowing that the testing of your faith produces endurance" (Jas. 1:3). As those who know not Christ observe the Christian's way of bearing his burdens, they often turn to Christ. Some find that God certainly does give them strength for the hour and their faith grows tremendously!

• Consider your stress to be joy because, through this experience, you or someone else may learn the power of prayer: "But if any of you lacks wisdom, let him ask of God, who gives to all men generously and without reproach, and it will be given to him. But let him ask in faith without any doubting, for the one who doubts is like the surf of the sea driven and tossed by the wind" (Jas. 1:5-6).

• Consider your stress to be joy because through this experience, you or someone else may find the meaning of life at its best: "Blessed is a man who perseveres under trial; for once he has been approved, he will receive the crown of life, which the Lord has promised to those who love Him" (Jas. 1:12).

To receive the "crown of life" is to understand life as it really is. Actually, life is rather simple. We live for a few years. We die. We stand before God in a day of judgment. We spend eternity either in heaven or hell. Only when one faces life "in Christ," does one really understand life at its best.

We Christians are given the unusual privilege of considering "it all joy" when our lives are filled with stress. We may never know, this side of eternity, how God uses adversity to bring us closer to Him. But we can be assured that He will do just that, and we can even laugh about it!

Conclusion

I have simply tried to be an observer in this chapter. I do not claim to be a psychologist or psychiatrist, but many well-trained persons in these fields have called our attention to the emotional healing power of humor. I have tried to share their observations and document them with what I have seen in life and found in the Bible.

An elderly minister friend of mine has one of the most sparkling, delightful personalities of anyone I have ever known. Until recently I thought he had always been that way.

Many years ago, however, he experienced "burnout" before we had ever discovered a name for it. He told of making the long trip to a large city to visit a psychiatrist about his problem. After finally being squeezed into the doctor's busy schedule, the minister was informed on the second visit that his doctor would be unable to see him again.

"I see you have a good sense of humor," the doctor observed. "Go home and use it! Use it every day. Laugh at your tensions, smile at your frustrations, and be willing to laugh at yourself. If you do, you won't need to see me again."

A strange prescription indeed! But in this case it worked, for my friend has remained healthy and happy for over three decades. Though humor is seldom the only prescription needed, it must be allowed to take its rightful place among those positive emotions that produce emotional stability.

In these last two chapters, we have discussed humor only as it relates to the life situations of physical and emotional illness. These are earthbound problems. How does humor relate to eternal matters? I shall attempt to answer that question in the next chapter.

6

Laughter and the Hereafter

"Want to buy a paper, mister?" I asked.

"Yes son, I'll take a paper," he said as he fumbled in his pocket for a nickel.

"Come on in and sit a spell," he said as I followed him through the door and sat down in the front of Claude Chandler's appliance store. As he gave me a cold drink he asked, "Where do you live?"

"I just live a block down the street at 604 1/2 Frisco," I said.

"Over the tire store?" he asked.

"Yes," I explained, "We live in one of those apartments."

"Do you have a dog?" Claude asked.

"Yes, his name is Lucky," I said. "And that apartment we live in is so small that we've had to teach Lucky to wag his tail up and down!"

Claude slapped his knee and roared with laughter. Then he said, "Did you hear about the dog that ran into a saw and cut off his nose?"

"No, I haven't heard that one," I said, "What happened?"

"Well, the kid went to school and told all of his friends that his dog had cut off his nose," Claude continued. "The teacher asked, 'How does the dog smell?' The kid said, 'Not very good!' "

It wasn't a very funny joke, but that was the beginning of a long and enjoyable friendship with Claude Chandler. He invited me to church, told me of Christ, and encouraged me to give serious consideration to becoming a Christian. He was always joking, but he was always serious. I became a regular attender at the First Baptist Church in Clinton, Oklahoma, where Claude was an active member.

As I sold newspapers after school each day, I would try to work both sides of the street and end up at Claude's store for a visit and the latest joke. He would always greet me the same way: "Come on in and sit a spell." When I became a Christian and was baptized, Claude Chandler was one of the first people down the aisle with "the right hand of church fellowship."

"You are wanted in the church office," my Sunday School teacher announced after class one Sunday, several years after I had become a member.

"The church office?" I asked. "What have I done wrong?" I had heard those words at school. Was I about to flunk Sunday School? Was Claude's wife, our church secretary, going to inform me that I would have to repeat a grade?

Mrs. Chandler informed me that someone, who wished to remain anonymous, had given me a scholarship to youth camp at Falls Creek Baptist Assembly. During that week at Falls Creek, at the age of seventeen, I made a commitment to the ministry that has led to over three-and-a-half decades of Christian service.

Periodically during the next year, Claude would invite me to come to his Sunday School class and speak. He surmised, "It will give you a little practice. If you can preach to that bunch, you can preach anywhere."

It was Judge J. Z. Barker's Bible class. I never really knew exactly what position Claude held in this large class of businessmen. However, every Sunday morning prior to the Bible lesson, Claude would greet the class and share some humorous stories. At times, he would read several jokes that he had collected during the week.

What am I doing here? I thought on the first Sunday of "practice preaching." Sitting there in the class that day were the mayor and several of our "city fathers." Needless to say, it was quite an unnerving experience for their former paperboy to stand before men of this caliber. However, after Claude had finished with them, all minds were clear and my knees had stopped knocking.

Through the years, Claude and Mrs. Chandler would write letters of encouragement—especially during college and seminary. They would always enclose some jokes. They assured me of their prayers and encouraged me to "keep laughing."

Dying with a Smile

Some thirty years after that first encounter in Claude's store I went by his home to visit. Cancer had dealt its treacherous blow to Claude's body. He knew and I knew that his days were numbered. I don't think he really felt like it, but he had asked Mrs. Chandler to move him from the bed into a chair.

"Come on in and sit a spell," he said in a coarse, weak voice. He wanted me to read the Bible and pray with him. Then, he just wanted to sit there and "shoot the breeze" until he got too tired to talk any longer.

After we had finished reading the Bible and praying,

Claude said, "Well, as you can see, I am getting old. I'm down, but I'm not out. At least, I can still hear well."

His eyes lit up as he asked, "Have you heard about the three older men who were walking down the street?"

"No, I haven't heard that one," I replied.

"One of them said, 'Windy today, isn't it?' Another one said, 'No, I think it's Thursday.' The third man said, 'I am, too. Let's go and get a cold drink.'"

He could hardly wait to finish laughing at that story to tell me another one. This time, it was about elderly women.

"These three ladies were sitting in a retirement home talking about how forgetful they were becoming," he continued. "One of them said, 'I'm getting so forgetful. When I awake in the morning, I can't remember where I put my teeth the night before.' The second lady said, 'I am getting forgetful, too. In fact, I often get up in the morning and forget where I put my glasses.' The third one said, as she leaned over to knock on the table, 'I'm the same age as you ladies, but I don't forget anything—knock on wood.' Then she turned to the door and said to no one, 'Just come right on in!'"

As I left Claude's house that day, he waved from his chair with a smile and said, "I'll see you later." I knew what he meant. Claude Chandler died in a few weeks, but he died laughing at what had killed him.

Claude Chandler died laughing here on earth because he had made adequate arrangements for the hereafter. Most studies about humor, however, deal only with matters related to our existence here on earth and have nothing to say about the hereafter.

Will Rogers said, "We're all here for a spell; get all the good laughs you can."[1] I totally agree with that philosophy. We're not going to get out of this world alive, so I think we should enjoy it as much as possible while we are here.

But there's more! Fred Allen said, "If one comes to the end of life with nothing but a collection of jokes, he has nothing to sustain him but the echo of forgotten laughter."[2]

Mel Brooks defined humor as "just another defense against the universe."[3] One of Groucho Marx's closest friends said, "I never heard him laugh out loud, never even at jokes or comedians he enjoyed."[4] Just before his death, Peter Sellers's fourth wife said, "His mind is in a constant state of turmoil."[5]

Even though one laughs and makes others laugh, laughter, at best, is only earthbound. Laughter on earth is certainly good for the body and mind.

Faith and Laughter

But what about the hereafter? Where does faith fit in? Conrad Hyers said, "Faith without laughter leads to dogmatism and self-righteousness," and "laughter without faith leads to cynicism."[6] Jules H. Masserman described one without a system of belief as "rudderless, adrift in a sea of chaos" and "unable to achieve happiness."[7]

Alfred North Whitehead said that he had always noticed "that deeply and truly religious persons are very fond of a joke," and he admitted "I am suspicious of those who are not."[8] "A sour religion is the devil's religion,"[9] according to John Wesley. Billy Sunday added, "If you have no joy in your religion, there's a leak in your Christianity somewhere."[10]

Gerald Kennedy was right when he said: "Joy and laughter are the products of faith."[11] David Augsburger pointed out that laughter is closely akin to praise and is the natural response to joy. He concluded that "a good soul-stirring laugh is near to a prayer."[12]

It is my firm conviction that faith and humor go hand in hand. I will go even further than that and affirm that genuine humor is based on one's relationship to God. Robert Thomas Haverluck observed that, for the humorist, the possibility of faith is always in the books. However, he admitted that the humorist will not open the Book for us (referring to the Bible). "He simply holds before us the truth of laughter on earth that may find its consummation in the eternity of heaven."[13]

Fred Layman has accurately observed that "when humor is joined to faith, it may also be one of the expressions of Christian joy, pointing to the ultimate eschatological joy."[14] The Bible calls that "ultimate" joy heaven!

Elton Trueblood claimed that the humor of those who are followers of Christ is not just a way of "denying the tears" here on earth, "but rather a way of affirming something which is deeper than tears."[15]

Being Funny Forever

Peter Berger described heaven where "man will remain funny forever."[16] When one is right with God through Christ and believes that when death comes, there is something far brighter, more joyful, and more fulfilling than this life on earth, there is legitimate reason for laughter. This is why R. Leonard Small would describe joy as the "standard that flies on the battlements of the heart when the King is in residence."[17]

Nelvin Vos described "the juxtaposition of the derisive scornful laughter of the Inferno with the delightful joy of Paradise." Then he concluded, "Either way, laughter reveals that one's relationship to God is the biggest laugh of all."[18] While most people on earth still laugh at the cross and scoff at "butchershop theology," heaven's laugh will be the last laugh.

But what does the hereafter have to do with a healthy sense of humor? Henry Cormier said, "Christian humor, in the following of Christ, is based on a realistic optimism, a hearty good sense, considerable knowledge of self, of others, of God."[19] It is at the point of "knowledge of self" that I wish to speak further.

If we understand the vast difference between the here and the hereafter, and if we are certain of our relationship to God which has adequately prepared us for death and the afterlife, our self-esteem is considerably improved. A strong self-concept provides the inner security needed to withstand stress or rejection and helps us overcome the fear of failure. It goes without saying that greater self-confidence will improve one's sense of humor.

A Gallup Poll, commissioned in 1982 to examine the self-esteem of the average American, revealed that only one third of us possess a strong self-esteem.[20] The poll concluded that those who possess healthy self-concepts are distinguished by several outstanding characteristics:

(1) They are morally and ethically sensitive and generous in giving.

(2) They are highly productive in their jobs, and they are far freer from the abuse of chemicals and alcohol.

(3) They are more actively involved in society's problems.

(4) They view success not in a materialistic way but in terms of relationships.

(5) They have stronger families and marriages, and they are more successful in interpersonal relationships.

(6) They handle stress more successfully and live healthier lives.

Restoring Self-esteem

Why do two out of three Americans lack a healthy view of themselves? Rusty and Linda Wright suggested four main reasons: guilt, fear of death and circumstances, problems of interpersonal relationships, and lack of meaning.[21] When these needs are met, one's self-esteem is restored and a healthy sense of humor is possible.

1. Guilt: Some feel guilty because they have failed to achieve the moral, ethical, social, or vocational standards that they have imposed upon themselves, or others have imposed upon them. However, some people feel guilty because they *are* guilty.

Guilt feelings may lead to anxiety, rebellion, several neurotic and psychotic disorders, and even depression. Feelings of worthlessness and self-hate can cause some to punish themselves and even commit suicide.

Regardless of the reasons for guilt feelings, one's guilt can be erased when one comes into a personal relationship with God through Jesus Christ. Peace and relief from guilt come when one realizes that his or her sins are moved "as far as the east is from the west" (Ps. 103:12). In fact, God assures us that when we confess our sins, He remembers them no more (Heb. 10:17). "He not only wipes the slate clean: He throws it away."[22]

Much of the guilt and resulting unhappiness in our country today is related to our materialistic goals and pursuits. Please understand from where I am coming! This is not a treatise against capitalism. It is a plea for us to see this material world as only the antechamber to eternity.

It is a matter of ups and downs for those whose lives revolve around this material world. One investment analyst confided, "The hardest thing to do now is to develop a proper balance between gloom and hope." When you ask, "How are you doing?" many people answer, "Well, pretty well, *under* the circumstances!" The follower of Jesus, however, never lives "under the circumstances."

Jesus said, "Do not lay up for yourselves treasures upon earth" (Matt. 6:19). An earthly treasure is that in which one finds hope and joy here on earth.

Money is an earthly treasure for many, yet the Bible says, "The love of money is a root of all sorts of evil" (1 Tim. 6:10).

Earthly possessions become treasures for some. In our unending task "to keep up with the Joneses" it is good for us to hear again the words of our Lord when He said, "For not even when one has an abundance does his life consist of his possessions" (Luke 12:15).

Status is an earthly treasure for many people. Someone has said, "We Americans spend money that we don't have to buy things which we do not need to keep up with people whom we really do not like." Jesus said, "Seek ye first the kingdom of God, and His righteousness; and all these things shall be added unto you" (Matt. 6:33, KJV).

Financial problems are often the order of the day. But God's Word teaches that "godliness actually is a means of great gain, when accompanied by contentment. For we have brought nothing into the world, so we cannot take anything out of it either" (1 Tim. 6:6-7).

Our Lord challenged us to lay up "treasures in heaven" —to find our main joy, satisfaction, and meaning in life in our relationship to Him. When our treasures are heavenly, we can say with Paul, "I have learned to be content in whatever circumstances I am" (Phil. 4:11). One cannot be "in fun" who feels guilty. When guilt is legitimately erased and self-esteem is restored, we are able to experience laughter at its best.

The Ultimate Put-down

2. Fear of Death and Circumstances: It is generally agreed among philosophers, theologians, psychiatrists, psychologists, and physicians that the greatest fear of all is the fear of death.

The psalmist wrote as though he knew of our fears:

Fret not yourself because of evil doers,
Be not envious toward wrongdoers.
For they will wither quickly like the grass,
And fade like the green herb. Trust in the Lord, and
do good;
Dwell in the land and cultivate faithfulness.
Delight yourself in the Lord;
And He will give you the desires of your heart. Commit
your way to the Lord,
Trust also in Him, and He will do it.
And He will bring forth your righteousness as the light,
And your judgment as the noonday.
Rest in the Lord and wait patiently for Him;
Fret not yourself because of him who prospers in his
way,
Because of the man who carries out wicked schemes
(Ps. 37:1-7).

The psalmist challenged us to rest our case with God. He admonished us not to worry to the point of distraction. But just how is this done?

• "Trust in the Lord"—We are reminded of that great promise in the Proverbs which tells us to "Trust in the Lord with all your heart,/And do not lean on your own understanding. In all your ways acknowledge Him,/And He will make your paths straight" (Prov. 3:5-6).

• "Delight yourself in the Lord"—We must find our joy in our relationship to God. There are some who find joy only in their relationship to things and other people. But only the Christian can really "delight in the Lord."

• "Commit thy way unto the Lord"—A part of trust is commitment. When we totally commit our lives to God in Christ, our difficulties are easier to bear.

• "Rest in the Lord"—Only after we have trusted, delighted, and committed are we able to rest in the Lord and wait patiently for Him.

But how can the Christian rest? How can we find rest as we face death? The Christian finds rest in death because death is not the loss of a battle: it is the winning of the war!

The Christian lives his short life in Christ who said, "I came that they might have life, and might have it abundantly" (John 10:10). The Christian enjoys this short life because his Saviour is "the way, and the truth, and the life" (John 14:6).

The psalmist spoke of death as a flood that comes sweeping down over the countryside, taking everything in its path. "Thou hast swept them away like a flood, they fall asleep" (Ps. 90:5). When one stands with Christ, the flood waters of death subside as we hear him say, "I am the resurrection and the life; he who believes in Me shall live even if he dies" (John 11:25).

At the open grave we can stand with the apostle Paul and ask, "O death, where is your victory? O death, where is your sting? . . . but thanks be to God, who gives us the victory through our Lord Jesus Christ" (1 Cor. 15:55-57). The ultimate "put-down" joke in all of life is found in these verses. Think of it! That which more people fear the most is openly mocked! When you can thumb your nose at death, you can laugh your way through any of the circumstances of life.

Speculations or Certainties?

Michael Faraday was asked just before his death, "What are your speculations about the future?"

Faraday replied, "Speculations? I have none. I'm resting on certainties!" What brings such hope in the face of death and the hereafter? Many of us believe that only faith in the living Christ brings such hope. We believe that there is an empty tomb in Jerusalem which proves that our Lord lives and that we serve a risen Christ!

But what are the implications of the resurrection of Christ, and what does it have to do with humor? An ancient custom of the Greek Orthodox Church sets aside the day after Easter as a day of laughter and hilarity. Conrad Hyers claimed that joking and jesting are considered proper even at church because of the big joke God pulled on Satan in the resurrection. He concluded, "Cosmos has been victorious over chaos, faith over doubt, trust over anxiety; and humanity is now truly free to laugh with the laughter of higher innocence."[23]

The resurrection of Christ has far-reaching implications for the believer.

• The risen Lord assures us of the validity of the Christian faith. "If Christ has not been raised, then our preaching is vain, your faith also is vain" (1 Cor. 15:14). One of the best documented facts of history is the resurrection of Jesus Christ! Some have rejected the resurrection because it does not fit into their philosophy, but it happened anyway.

Christ's resurrection remains the final evidence and the ultimate proof that every word and every act of Jesus Christ is true! Jesus Christ was "declared the Son of God with power by the resurrection" (Rom. 1:4). Skepticism and unbelief are silenced by the empty tomb. Easter settles it all!

• In the resurrection, the Christian finds assurance of forgiven sin. Paul concluded, "If Christ has not been raised, you are still in your sins" (1 Cor. 15:17).

• The resurrection assures the Christian of immortality. Without the resurrection, "Those also who have fallen asleep in Christ have perished" (1 Cor. 15:18). The resurrected Christ is the "first fruits of those who are asleep" (1 Cor. 15:20). Just as Adam led in sin and death, Christ leads in forgiveness and life.

A new pastor was making the rounds of the shut-ins on his church field. He made his way up a narrow path to a plateau overlooking a harbor where he found a small cottage. He was ushered into the sparsely furnished house to a dark room in the back. He almost wept at the sight of a one-armed, blind man who was almost deaf.

He shouted into his ear through a speaking trumpet and announced that he was the new pastor. The elderly man indicated that he would like to sing for his pastor.

"Sing? In this prison of silence and darkness? What will he sing about?" thought the pastor.

With a loud, cracking voice the old man sang:

> Blessed Assurance, Jesus is mine!
> Oh, what a foretaste of glory divine!
> Heir of salvation, purchase of God,
> Born of his Spirit, wash'd in his blood.

And why this assurance? Because of the resurrection of Jesus Christ!

The second greatest fear is the fear of circumstances. What's going to happen to me? Will I become ill? Will my job hold out? Will I ever learn to live without my mate? Will I ever raise these teenagers? Will my parents ever understand? Why do bad things happen to me? Why cancer? Why a heart attack? Many of these circumstances never occur. However, the fear of them certainly affects one's self-esteem.

A believer in Christ accepts the promise that "God hath not given us the spirit of fear; but of power, and of love, and of a sound mind" (2 Tim. 1:7, KJV).

Knowing Who Holds Your Future

Many Christians have faced the uncertainties of life and the fear of circumstances with the confident assurance, "We may not know what the future holds, but we know Who holds the future!"

I read recently about the dream an unknown author experienced:

> I dreamed I was walking along the shore with the Lord, and across the sky flashed scenes from my life. For each scene, I noticed two sets of footprints in the sand; one belonged to me, the other to the Lord. When the last scene of my life flashed before me, I looked back at the footprints in the sand. I noticed that many times along the path of my life there was only one set of footprints. I also noticed that it happened at the very lowest and saddest moments.
>
> I questioned the Lord about it. "Lord, you said that once I decided to follow you, you would walk with me all the way. But I have noticed that during the most troublesome times in my life, there is only one set of footprints. I don't understand why in times when I needed you most, you would leave." The Lord replied, "My precious child, I would never leave you during your times of trial and suffering. When you see only one set of footprints, it was then that I carried you.

Carried by God? Yes! But even more than that for the

Christian. In Christ, Christians have a sevenfold promise of God's presence and provision:

(1) He is above us to guard us: "Know therefore today, and take it to your heart, that the Lord, He is God in heaven above and on the earth below; there is no other" (Deut. 4:39).

(2) He is underneath us to support us: "The eternal God is a dwelling place,/And underneath are the everlasting arms" (Deut. 33:27).

(3) He is behind us to keep us from straying: "Surely goodness and lovingkindness will follow me all the days of my life" (Ps. 23:6).

(4) He is at our right hand to protect us: "I have set the Lord continually before me;/Because He is at my right hand, I will not be shaken" (Ps. 16:8).

(5) He is out in front of us to lead us: "I will go before you and make the rough places smooth" (Isa. 45:2).

(6) He is surrounding us to shield us from the storms of life: "As the mountains surround Jerusalem,/So the Lord surrounds His people/From this time forth and forever" (Ps. 125:2).

(7) He is within us as a Companion and Comforter: "I have been crucified with Christ; and it is no longer I who live, but Christ lives in me; and the life which I now live in the flesh I live by faith in the Son of God, who loved me, and delivered Himself up for me" (Gal. 2:20).

If the fear of death and circumstances is erased, genuine humor is possible. One may laugh and cause others to laugh, but secretly live in fear of death and life's problems, and be the most unhappy person in the crowd.

Country humorist Jerry Clower, using his own style of expression, affirms that hell is "hot," heaven is "wonderful," and asserts that only those who know Jesus will "miss hell and hit heaven." "And man," he exclaims, "that's wonderful news and I'm giggling and grinning about it as I go through life."[24]

Clower calls for Christians to be happy and concludes, "I'm convinced there is just one place where there's not any laughter, and that's in hell. And I've made arrangements to miss hell. So, ha, ha, ha. I ain't never going to have to be nowhere where some folks ain't laughing."[25]

3. *Problems of Interpersonal Relationships*—All of us want to love, be loved, and feel a sense of worth to ourselves and to others. We have a need for people to accept us unconditionally and be able to confront us when we are acting irresponsibly. But, even our closest friends have clay feet and may let us down.

Good interpersonal relationships can contribute to our mental stability. But the "ultimate therapy is involvement with our Creator."[26] Then and then only do we really understand the meaning of loving and being loved.

Living the Love Life

A great philosopher who makes no claim to being a follower of Christ said, "The root of the matter is a very simple and old-fashioned thing . . . the thing we need is love—Christian love."

What is "Christian love"? The Greeks had four words for love. One word (*storge*) described the love between children and parents. Another (*eros*) described the love between husband and wife. A third word (*philia*) described the warm, tender affection that one friend has for another.

The Greek word used in the New Testament to describe Christian love is difficult to translate. The word *agape* (pronounced ah-GAH'-pay) is probably best translated "self-giving devotion and dedication to God and mankind."

The first three words describe a love that comes naturally. Parents and children automatically love each other. A man and a woman are said to "fall in love" as if they have no control over this natural impulse. Someone described that "first love" of teenagers as "like falling into a well." Close friends are naturally affectionate toward each other.

But Christian love is a love at which we have to work. It is a love that turns the other cheek and goes the second mile. It is a love that forgets about one's own feelings and rights. It is a love that concentrates so much on giving that it forgets about getting.

It becomes a way of life for the Christian who takes seriously the words of our Lord when He said, "By this all men will know that you are My disciples, if you have love for one another" (John 13:35).

One cannot live the love life without knowing Christ. In the new birth, the believer dies to self. As we grow in Christ, we die more to self each day as did Paul when he said, "I die daily" (1 Cor. 15:31).

Living the love life involves forgetting.

> Brethren, I do not regard myself as having laid hold of it yet; but one thing I do: forgetting what lies behind and reaching forward to what lies ahead, I press on toward the goal for the prize of the upward call of God in Christ Jesus (Phil. 3:13-14).

It involves loving our enemies. "I say to you, love your enemies, and pray for those who persecute you" (Matt. 5:44). This might mean that we reply to bitter words with kind words and to cruel deeds with thoughtful deeds.

Living the love life prompts us to pray for those who "persecute" us. Many doctors claim that the verbal expression of animosity toward others causes a certain bio-

logical reaction within the human body which can unti-
mately cause disease. Some doctors now believe that
many diseases develop when we fatten grudges by re-
hearsing them in the presence of others.

The *agape* kind of love even loves the unlovely. It never
loves to be loved back. A Christian's love for others never
depends on what they are. It never depends on what
others do *to* the Christians, nor what they do *for* them.
Such love can solve interpersonal problems in the home,
at work, and at school. Such love can transform sadness
into laughter.

4. Lack of Meaning—In his book: *Abnormal Psychology and Modern Life,* James C. Coleman stated that modern persons are confronted with a new perspective of
time and space. We now face the problem of finding the
meaning of our existence in a universe in which the earth
and even the whole solar system may be no larger when
compared to the whole than an atom is to the earth. He
further expressed our dilemma:

> At the same time, materialistic values—based on the belief
> that scientific progress would automatically lead to man's
> happiness and fulfillment—have proved sadly disillusion-
> ing. As a result, many people are groping about, bewil-
> dered and bitter, unable to find any enduring faith or to
> develop a satisfying philosophy of life. Despite their fine
> automobiles, well-stocked refrigerators, and other mate-
> rial possessions and comforts, the meaning of life seems to
> be evading them. In essence, they are suffering from exis-
> tential anxiety—deep concern about finding values which
> will enable them to live satisfying, fulfilling, and meaning-
> ful lives.[27]

Have you looked around lately and noticed how few
people seem to have a clear purpose in life and really

believe that they count for something? No wonder so many people are looking on the darker side of life and have found no purpose for being.

A plea for a little good news came from a recent popular song which recounted much of the bad news these days on television, radio, and in the newspapers—from the upheaval in Lebanon to the shooting across town at a local bar. The singer kept punctuating her dismal commentary with the plea for a little good news.

Where is that good news to be found? Those of us who know Christ possess the good news that is needed in a world which is coming apart at the seams. The meaning of *gospel* is "good news." Our Lord greeted His disciples with the words, "Be of good cheer." Vance Havner claimed that our Lord gave every believer "three cheers":

• *The Cheer of Forgiveness:* "Be of good cheer; thy sins be forgiven thee" (Matt. 9:2, KJV).

• *The Cheer of Companionship:* "Be of good cheer: it is I; be not afraid" (Mark 6:50, KJV).

• *The Cheer of Victory:* "Be of good cheer; I have overcome the world" (John 16:33, KJV).

Havner concluded,

Although the New Testament centers in a cross and is bathed in the blood of martyrs and blackened by the fires of persecution, its note from beginning to end is one of triumphant joy. It begins with an angel chorus and ends with rejoicing around the throne of God.[28]

One major key to a good sense of humor is a healthy self-concept. I have, without apology, shared with you in these pages a Christian view of a healthy self-concept. Many humorists use their jokes to enhance their self-worth or mask their emptiness. It is my firm conviction that in Christ we find genuine self-esteem.

Conclusion

We have visited together about an unusual subject in this chapter—laughter and the hereafter. If we have made adequate preparation for the hereafter, we can enjoy laughing and making others laugh here on earth. If we are ready to die, we are ready to laugh. When we are rightly related to the Creator of laughter through Jesus Christ, we possess a healthy self-concept. Guilt and fear are alleviated. Interpersonal conflicts are diffused. Our quest for meaning in life is satisfied.

Paul Burleson, my close friend and fellow minister, recently faced the trauma of learning that one artery in his heart was 99 percent blocked while another was 70 percent blocked. He recently had Angioplasty surgery (balloon dilation) on the 99 percent-blocked artery.

"As usual," he wrote, "it was in this time of physical distress that I learned more about the Lord Jesus than in all the good times combined." He continued, "I'm happy to say that as I lay on that operating table, I was thrilled with the prospect that I could go home to heaven at any moment and got so literally excited about the thought that I laughed out loud."[29]

Paul Burleson survived his surgery. But, you know, if he had died, I think he would have laughed out loud in heaven. I think he might have even heard Claude Chandler say, "Come on in and sit a spell," and I know he and Claude would have found much about which to laugh.

Laughter and the hereafter? Do you see the connection?

Now, let us come back down to earth as we discuss in the following chapters the need for wholesome humor, how to develop a good sense of humor, how to use humor as a communication tool, and how humor often shows up in the most unlikely places. A healthy self-concept plays a major role in developing a sense of humor and using humor as a communication tool.

7

Who Says Humor Must Be Offensive?

"Good morning!" I said as I walked from my car to the front steps of the church that morning.

I had been invited to speak at the twenty-fifth anniversary celebration of a suburban church in Dayton, Ohio. I had parked my car and was walking to the front steps of the church building.

Strange! The two men to whom I had spoken were walking toward their car to leave something or get something before the service started. When I spoke to them they merely looked straight ahead and walked on toward their car.

As they passed me, I turned and said a little louder, "Good morning, friends!" My second salutation received no return.

"Have I come to the wrong church?" I asked myself. "I'm going to try it one more time," I thought as I reached the steps of the church and turned around.

I cupped my hands to my mouth and yelled, "It's a beautiful day, isn't it?" By this time, they had reached their car. However, they made no effort to turn around and return my greeting.

How happy I was as I walked into the vestibule to see the pastor and realize that I *was* at the right church. The pastor handed me a Sunday morning bulletin as we sat down to discuss the service.

The bulletin read, "Welcome to the 25th Anniversary of our Church and the 24th Anniversary of our Deaf Ministry." Then it occurred to me that the two men to whom I had spoken in the parking lot were deaf. And there they were in the deaf section during the worship service!

After the service, I visited with the deaf worshipers for some time. One of the interpreters relayed my words to my "parking lot" friends.

"I was coming through the parking lot this morning and spoke to you two gentlemen and, not knowing you were deaf, I expected you to speak back. In fact, I thought I was in the wrong place when you didn't return my greeting."

When the interpreter had translated my words in sign language, they smiled. Then one of them signed, "You know, deaf people have no way of marking their handicap, like blind people, for instance, who have red-and-white canes."

We laughed together. Then one of my deaf friends suggested, "Maybe all deaf people should paint one ear blue." We laughed again.

Soon I was driving back to Columbus thinking about this interesting encounter. We had experienced tasteful humor in the making. But there is a very thin line between tasteful humor and offensive humor. For instance, if I had told a put-down joke about deaf people, it would have been offensive. But because we were laughing at my ignorance, we could laugh together at their handicap and our humor was still considered wholesome.

When Humor Is Hostile

That leads me to a difficult task: how to define offensive humor. Cal Samra observed, "A sense of humor is a gift from God, but like any gift, it can be abused."[1]

When is humor abused? Thackeray said, "Good humor may be said to be one of the very best articles of dress one can wear in society."[2] Types of "good humor" change from generation to generation. A real knee slapper of another century might not even generate a smile in today's society.

For instance, Josh Billings shared this interesting witticism over one-hundred years ago: "The rite length tu cut oph a dog's tail has never yet bin discovered, but it iz somewhere bak of his ears provided yu git the dog's consent."[3] In those days of long nights, no radio, no television, and fewer magazines to read, American wit and humor depended on the twin tricks of crude phonetic spelling and the use of wrong words.

While types of good humor change from generation to generation, offensive humor remains the same. Offensive humor is hostile humor loaded and aimed to wound a fellow human being.

Michael O'Donahue, former editor of *National Lampoon,* claimed that humor is a release of tension as we react to what is happening in the world around us. His morbid, often tasteless humor is based on his conclusion that "the world is ready to nuke itself out; ... life is a joke and death is the punch line."[4]

Offensive humor is intended to ridicule persons and mock groups. We are indebted to Esther Blumenfeld and Lynne Alpern for their definition of "stress-producing humor."

P okes fun at other people's individual shortcomings.

R eflects anger.

O ffends with inappropriate use of sexual references or profanity.

D ivides a group by put-downs.

U ses stereotypes to denigrate a person or group.

C ruel, abusive, and offensive.

I nsensitive to what causes others real pain.

N egates self-confidence.

G ives license to hurt someone.[5]

Offensive humor is dirty humor which demeans and degrades human sexuality and undermines values. Tom Mullen believes that modern humor has been used in the movies, on television, in books, and in plays in a gradual "devaluation process" of moral values.[6] For instance, even those of us who are opposed to adultery for religious, moral, psychological, and sociological reasons might find ourselves laughing at entertainment which pokes fun at monogamy and the stable family. "If we laugh hard enough and long enough at jokes that deny our beliefs," Mullen contended, "we discover the beliefs themselves have lost their power."[7]

There is such a thing as a clean sexual joke that does not call for a change in accepted norms. However, "clean" is often in the eye and mind of the listener. "Contrary to Mrs. Grundy, sex is not sin," claims Frederick Buechner, and "contrary to Hugh Hefner, it's not salvation either."[8] There is plenty of good sexual humor within the context of marriage to keep us all laughing without forcing us to make fun of our values. Quintilian was right when he said, "Laughter costs too much when purchased by the sacrifice of decency."

Racist Humor

I have a collection of joke books that dates back over a hundred years. It is evident that racial and ethnic jokes have been popular through the years. Unflattering stereotypes of different races have been the order of the day for decades. In recent years, thankfully, we have become more sensitive to racist jokes.

Laughter at the expense of another race is acceptable only when one chooses to tell a joke on one's own race. I am sure our Polish friends are getting a little weary of all the "Polack jokes." However, I saw the tables turned recently at a church where I was speaking.

At the afternoon "dinner on the grounds"—which I always enjoy more than the sermon I preach in the morning service—the pastor asked, "Have you heard the latest Polack joke?"

Knowing that I was preaching that day in an area in which many Polish people resided, I acted as though I didn't hear him and said, "Pass the chicken."

But he persisted! "We want you to know the latest Polack joke," he insisted.

He went down to the end of the table, whispered to one of his members, and the two of them came back to where I was sitting. The pastor proudly announced, "Here is the latest Polack joke! This man is Polish."

I blushed.

My Polish friend leaned over to me with a bright smile on his face and asked, "Do you speak Polish?"

"No," I said, "I don't speak Polish."

"Do you understand Polish?" he queried further.

"No, I don't understand Polish."

"Do you know how to cook Polish food?" he added.

"No, I don't know how to cook Polish food."

He stepped back with a broad smile and a bright chuckle and exclaimed, "How does it feel to be dumber than a Polack?"

Religious Humor

Religious humor can be offensive—depending on who is telling it and about whom it is being told. Catholics can joke about Catholics. In one of Philip Barry's plays, Ethel Barrymore, as a nun visiting her family, asks, "Is everyone here Catholic?" Being assured that they were, she says, "Good! Now we can talk about the pope."[9]

Jews can poke fun at overprotective Jewish mothers and fund-raising, upwardly mobile rabbis. Catholics can joke about golf-playing monsignors, bingo games, and overprotective housekeepers. But Jews don't joke about the Torah nor Catholics about the Eucharist.

Some Catholics may not be offended at describing a football pass thrown in desperation in the waning moments of a football game as "a Hail-Mary pass." But Catholics and Protestants alike were offended when a forward pass thrown in a crucial National Football League game bounced off the hands of a defensive back into the hands of the original receiver and became known as "the Immaculate Reception." Many of us were just as offended when the term *the Immaculate Deception* was given to a controversial play in which one team deliberately fumbled the ball into the end zone.[10]

We Baptists are known for our mode of baptism by immersion. Don't kid us about that, but allow us to share funny incidents related to this sacred ordinance of our church, and it is acceptable—at least to some of us. I have shared this one for many years:

The country church was located so far out in the woods

that there was no "indoor plumbing." However, since baptism was such an important part of the church's life, they improvised by building a baptistry under the pulpit. When it came time to baptize, they would move the pulpit to the side, open the trap door, fill the baptistry with water hauled in by a large tank truck, drop some wooden stairs down into it, and string up some curtains.

The thick curtains were carefully hung on wires. One curtain served as a backdrop to the baptistry as it was pulled around in a circular position. The curtains were also arranged in such a way as to provide a men's dressing room on one side of the baptistry and a women's dressing room on the other side of the baptistry.

The young pastor of this country church was to baptize his first two candidates—an elderly man and a very heavy-set lady.

"Shouldn't we offer to help our young pastor?" asked one of the deacons.

It was decided that the deacons would give special attention to the elderly man lest he fall on the slick wooden steps.

On the evening of the baptismal service, one deacon waited in the baptistry with the pastor and another deacon very carefully helped the elderly gentleman down the stairs. After he was baptized, the deacon in the baptistry helped him up the stairs and followed him back behind the curtains to the dressing room.

But no one thought to help the young pastor with the baptism of the heavy-set lady. Excitedly, she stepped into the baptistry on the first step. The wooden steps, slick from standing under water so long, proved to be her downfall. Her feet slipped, and she promptly sat down on the top step. Then, one by one, she bounced down into the baptistry in the sitting position.

They claim you could hear her scream a mile away. Screaming and bouncing down the stairs, she reached up to grab the only object available—the curtains! So, down into the baptistry with the screaming lady came the men's dressing room and the women's dressing room!

There, visible to the eyes of the whole congregation on one side of the baptistry was the elderly gentleman in the process of getting dressed. He had already donned his longhandled underwear and was in the process of pulling up his trousers. He dropped his trousers to the floor and stood paralyzed, staring at the surprised congregation. Then, he picked up a nearby chair and held it in front of him.

"Do something quick!" one of the deacons shouted. So, a thoughtful deacon ran to the back and turned off all the lights, thinking that the man would take the hint to get dressed in the darkness.

Five minutes later when the lights were turned back on, the man was still standing there in his longhandled underwear, protecting himself with the chair. The lady, still gurgling and bubbling in the water was fighting the curtains. The young pastor, in shock, was standing in the corner of the baptistry with his arms folded and his eyes staring straight ahead![11]

Sexist Humor

Sexist humor, which usually stereotypes women as inferior and incapable, is a form of offensive humor. Some female comediennes have "overcorrected" for this one-sided sexist humor and have added to the polarization between men and women.

Many women are confronted almost daily with "blue humor" in the office. Blumenfeld and Alpern suggest that a woman can make her feelings known related to this type of humor in a humorous, nonthreatening way which will build office morale. They suggest she can:

(1) Reply, "That joke is so good I'm going to submit it for the company newsletter in your name."

(2) Keep a large bar of soap on her desk. Each time he tells a joke, hand him the soap to wash his mouth out. Soon the soap itself will become a joke, and as soon as he begins telling a joke, colleagues may also reach for the soap.

(3) Reply, "Do you have any funny jokes that don't make people feel bad?"

(4) Place a bell on her desk. Each time he tells an offensive joke, ring those chimes. Everyone will come to associate the sound with his jokes, and she will make her point without saying a word.

(5) Place a large, lidded, empty jar in a conspicuous place on her desk labeled "Dirty Joke Jar." It should be accompanied with these typed instructions: "Whisper your dirty jokes in here. Then please put a lid on them."[12]

Have you noticed how much "sick humor" becomes evident as an aftermath to tragedy? Where were you on January 28, 1986? America shall never forget the catastrophic explosion that blew apart the space shuttle Challenger only 75 seconds after lift-off, sending a school teacher and six NASA astronauts to a fiery death in the sky eight miles from Kennedy Space Center.

One late-night host dropped the opening monologue and another opened his show with an acknowledgment of the day's tragedy before pointing out that the show, nonetheless, must go on. It seems that it would have been in unspeakably bad taste to try to joke about such a disaster. But, within days, Challenger jokes were circulating far and wide.

Mel Helitzer, an Ohio University professor who teaches a humor-writing course, claims that this type of humor "is the kind of humor you would say to a friend but wouldn't say publicly." He calls it "entrenous humor."[13]

Sick Humor

Some psychiatrists have dubbed sick humor "a coping mechanism." Bruce Jones, an associate professor of clinical psychiatry at Ohio State University, has pointed out, "One way of handling death is to laugh in the face of it. It is a reminder to people that they are still alive. It's something like children playing hide-and-seek in the graveyard and pretending that they weren't afraid."[14]

There was the same kind of sick humor soon after the assassination of President John F. Kennedy. There were jokes about the Union Carbide disaster in Bhopal, India, and about the Ethiopians in the midst of the famine. Jeffrey Goldstein said, "It comes out of a sort of psychic pain. The death of people suddenly is just a horrendous thing to deal with."[15]

A teenager confided in me recently that one of her dear friends had committed suicide. "This hurts," she said. "But the thing that hurts even as much as his suicide is that, within a few days after he committed suicide, there were jokes going around the school about him."

Some of us can recall the sick jokes about human deformities that were prevalent in the fifties and sixties when America was fighting medical battles against polio and other deformities. More recently, there has been a lot of sick humor related to Acquired Immune Deficiency Syndrome.

Is sick humor offensive? To many people jokes about dead babies, Helen Keller's handicaps, starving Ethiopians, and victims of AIDS are highly offensive. Some believe that sick jokes lead to sick attitudes. However, some believe that cruel laughter and jokes in bad taste may be two different matters.

Tom Mullen conceded that it is naive to believe that all humor is going to remain innocent, warmhearted, playful, and affectionate. "Laughter based only on childhood reminiscences and puppy dogs," he concluded, "would be too safe, too tame, and eventually not very funny." Therefore, he contended, "our young people—and older folks, too—will risk an occasional 'sick' joke."[16]

Slash-and-Burn Humor

"Slash-and-burn humor" is now prevalent among older teenagers and college students. It is satire at its worst. Garry Trudeau claims that the best satire through the years "has always made a distinction between indignation and malice, and even at its blackest, has insisted on the moral premise that something of value remains standing."[17]

Slash-and-burn satire reminds the downtrodden that they are right about themselves—they *are* nobodies. They are "so unhip as to be disadvantaged, to be ignorant, to be physically infirm, or to be black or even female."[18]

Much of our offensive humor reflects the tensions of our time. The stress involved in the nuclear age and McCarthyism led to a marked fall in the quality of humor in the fifties. Watergate cast its satirical shadow across the humor of America as well as the resignation of President Nixon, post-Vietnam problems, and the onset of severe economic problems.

Offensive humor may reflect the conditions of our time. However, good humor ought to lift us above adverse circumstances and serve as a healer instead of a mocker of adversity.

What can be done about offensive humor? There are

several indications that many people are becoming weary of offensive humor and are ready to do some laundering.

A few years ago while recuperating from a heart attack, I took a daily walk with my wife through a mall near our home in Columbus, Ohio. We were appalled as we visited the book store in the mall everyday during the Christmas season to see gross, tasteless, sick, and otherwise-offensive joke books repeatedly appearing on the "best-seller" racks. It was during that time that we determined to do everything possible to offer an alternative to such humor through a series of clean joke books.

A recent survey in *Glamour* magazine indicates that 85 percent of Americans perceive good humor as uplifting, not degrading.[19] Of the 86 percent who have been told a tasteless joke recently, 58 percent spoke up about feeling offended while 22 percent laughed—but felt secretly ashamed.

The survey asked some probing questions:

(1) Is the ability to laugh at things we once ignored a sign of a new social maturity? "No," said 61 percent. A typical comment relating to this subject: "Tasteless jokes stem from an unhealthy need to boost one's own ego by belittling fellow human beings."

(2) Must a joke be at least somewhat offensive to be really funny? Again, 85 percent said no. A typical comment was: "The best humor isn't hurtful or offensive to anyone, and is funny to all."

Laundering Our Humor

A college student claimed that he requested a professor to stop telling rude jokes. "If I want to hear them I'll see a comedian, but otherwise I think tasteless jokes should be told in private," he pointed out. Those who laughed at a tasteless joke but were secretly ashamed had such comments as, "It's not something I'm proud of, but in our society, tasteless jokes are the 'in' thing, and it's not always easy to refuse to go along with the crowd."

Isn't it about time someone refused to "go along with the crowd" as far as offensive humor is concerned? Blumenfeld and Alpern suggest four reactions to an offensive joke:

1. Don't laugh.
2. Reply, "I don't think that's funny."
3. If you're feeling brave and feel the insult was intentional, ask the offender, "Why would you say something that obviously pokes fun at people's shortcomings?" (Fill in the gap with the appropriate phrase from the stress-producing list.)
4. If you want to allow room for the offender to save face, try saying something like, "I'm sure you're not aware of how cruel that joke makes you sound, but many people find that type of humor offensive, and I would appreciate your not repeating it."[20]

They share another very interesting acrostic on using stress-reducing humor to counter stress-producing humor:

R educes tension by joking about universal human frustrations and faults.

E ncourages people to relax and laugh.

D elights in poking fun at oneself.

U nites people by building rapport.

C reates a supportive atmosphere of fun and caring.

I ncludes everyone in the good time.

N otes the positive aspects of human relationships.

G ives everyone a chance to participate.[21]

One of our brighter days for laundering our humor in America was during the presidency of Ronald Reagan.[22] Nearly every one of his speeches offered a joke or two. His repertoire included one liners, put-downs, and feature-length jokes with punch lines that delighted his audiences.

During the 1984 Reagan-Mondale presidential campaign, Mondale often called attention to the age of Mr. Reagan. When the seventy-three-year-old president was asked if age had become an issue, he said, "I will not exploit for political purposes my opponent's youth and inexperience."

President Reagan used humor as a device to help diffuse doubts about his capabilities to serve as President at the age of seventy-five. He told a group of New Jersey high school students: "Your principal showed me your American history book, and I was startled to see that it took almost 400 pages to tell the story of our nation. When I was your age, it only took two stone tablets."

In his opening remarks to a large group of midwesterners, President Reagan observed how it was a "great pleasure" for him to get out of the nation's capital.

"Whoever said 'the worst place to get a perspective on America is Washington, DC,' was absolutely right. You don't have to spend much time in Washington to appreciate the prophetic vision of the man who designed all the streets; they go in circles!"

For a high-school commencement in New Jersey, the president said, "There are advantages to being president. The day after I was elected, I had my high-school grades classified 'topsecret.'"

To the Asia-Pacific Council in Tokyo, he shared an interesting story about a businessman who ordered flowers to be sent to the opening of his friend's new branch office. When the man arrived, he was shocked to see the flowers with the inscription: "Rest in Peace." He was so outraged that on the way home he stopped at the florist to complain.

The florist said, "Don't get so upset. Just think of it this way: today someone in this city was buried beneath a flower arrangement with the inscription, 'Good Luck in Your New Location!' "

To the ministerial meeting of the Association of Southeast Asian Nations in Bali, Indonesia, the president told of two men out in the woods on a hike.

They saw a large bear coming over the hill directly toward them. One of them sat down, took off his knapsack, reached in, got out a pair of tennis shoes, and started to put them on.

The other man looked on and exclaimed, "You don't think that by putting on those tennis shoes you're going to be able to outrun that bear?"

He replied, "I don't have to outrun the bear; I only have to outrun you."

When he met with Soviet leader Mikhail Gorbachev, President Reagan told Mr. Gorbachev the story about a Russian and a American who were discussing how their nations differ.

"I can walk into the Oval Office, slam my fist down on Reagan's desk, and tell him I don't like the way he's running the country," the American said.

The Russian thought for a moment and replied, "But I can do the same in the Soviet Union. I can walk into the Politburo, slam my fist down on Gorbachev's desk, and say, 'I don't like the way Reagan is running the United States.' "

Conclusion

An after-dinner speaker fed his audience a sordid diet of obscene stories punctuated with profanity. Midway in his presentation, he noticed that one of the guests at the head table wasn't laughing. He stopped, looked at him, and noticed a chaplain's insignia in the lapel of his suit.

Embarrassed, the speaker blurted out, "For Christ's sake, are you a chaplain?"

"Yes, for Christ's sake I am a chaplain. For whose sake are you telling these filthy stories?" asked the chaplain.

There was an outburst of laughter, applause, and then silence. The chaplain was then asked to speak, at which time he stood and gave a clean, cheerful speech.[23]

It looks like some people are getting tired of dirty, sexist, racist, and otherwise offensive humor. May their tribe increase!

It is one thing to complain about offensive humor. But what suggestions can be made for developing a wholesome sense of humor? Hopefully, the next chapter will answer that question.

8

Developing a Wholesome Sense of Humor

Our four children ranged from three to twelve years of age when we moved to "the farm"—a ten-acre plot on the edge of Oklahoma City. We had taken for granted many of the conveniences of living in the city. One of those unexpected joys was disposing of our own garbage.

We would "store" the garbage in the barn until it became unbearable. Then we would borrow a pickup truck to make the trek to one of the most interesting places on earth—the city dump!

After dumping our garbage, we would roam the premises to see what other people had thrown away. You know the old saying: "One man's trash is another man's treasure?"

One of those interesting treasures was an artificial leg. We brought it back to the house, disinfected it, and began what would become two years of shear enjoyment and exasperation.

As we rolled out of bed in the morning, we might stumble over this foot protruding from under our bed. On several occasions, the leg appeared *in* someone's bed. It might fall out on us as we opened a closet door. We might even find it in the shower.

It was community property. Any one of our four children could do anything they pleased with it to frighten anyone who might jump. The kids wanted to take it to school, but we explained that it was our own private "leg of joy" to be shared, until now, with no one.

"Get that thing out of this house and take it back to the dump!" Faye ordered one day after she and the leg had an unexpected encounter in the bath tub.

Reluctantly, we piled the leg on the garbage and took it back to the city dump. As I was throwing the leg off of the truck, an elderly man watched me with a great deal of interest.

"Is that your leg?" he asked.

"Yes," I said.

"You don't need it any longer?" he asked.

"No," I yelled, "I've been asked to throw it away."

I jumped down off of the pickup and helped the boys shovel out the remainder of the garbage.

The man looked at the leg and mused, "Your legs look all right to me!"

"Yes, both of my legs feel just like human flesh," I replied.

He came over to where I was and began to feel my legs.

"Holy, moly!" he said. "They really do feel like real flesh! Let me see you walk."

I walked around the truck and he was amazed! Then I explained to him that it was not my leg, but we were returning it to the scene of origin after two years at our home.

We jumped into the truck to drive away. Through the rearview mirror, I saw the old man reach into the trash and retrieve the leg. Leg on shoulder, he lifted his hand to wave as we drove out of sight. And I wondered, *Will it bring as much joy to his household as it did to ours?*

One of the lessons which I learned from our "leg of joy" is that we need to work at developing our own sense of humor. Is humor a natural gift, or is it a developed technique? Why do some people have such a tremendous sense of humor while others seem to lack any trace of a funny bone?

Laughing with Yourself

It is my contention that God gives each of us the seeds of a good sense of humor. But we must plant, water, and cultivate the crop. Perhaps that is what Eivind Berggray meant when he said that the soil in which humor grows must be cultivated.[1] David Seabury pointed out that good humor is not a trait of character but "an art which requires practice."[2]

Developing a wholesome sense of humor involves three phases of laughter: laughing *with* yourself, laughing *at* yourself, and laughing with others.

Laughing with yourself? Yes, before we can enjoy laughter with others, we must be "in fun" with ourselves. Emily Hardy gave us some helpful suggestions for laughing with ourselves.[3]

(1) Accentuate the positive in your inner-personal relationships. Be aware daily of humorous situations, anecdotes, or comical events which will trigger joyous laughter—one wave of chuckles after another that serve as an emotional relief valve.

(2) Build a collection of "moments to remember." These can range from humorous incidents at home to triumphs and compliments on the job. They can include any experience that made you feel good—from something beautiful to look at, like the flaming yellow of the maple tree outside your dining room window, to the spontaneous hug of a child you love.

(3) Once you have started a "happy journal," look for funny happenings to add to your collection that you will

want to share with family, friends, and co-workers. Be sure the collection contains only constructive and creative humor and excludes offensive and ethnic jokes.

(4) Share your humor with yourself. When the daily hassle has drained you of energy, take a few minutes out to sit back and savor one or two of these happy times or funny situations.

Laughing at Yourself

It is said that there are three levels of laughter. The lowest is the laughter of one who laughs only at his or her own jokes. The next is the laughter of one who laughs at the jokes of others. But the highest and best of all is the laughter of people who laugh at themselves. Let's be honest: we have good reason for laughing at ourselves.

Brown Barr said, "A person who can look at his or her own feet without laughing is spiritually deficient."[4] One psychologist suggested, "Stand in front of a mirror and give yourself a big smile. Now try to take yourself seriously."[5]

Lorenz Nieting pointed out that "The power of humor to unseat authority reaches its climax in our society when it is aimed at oneself."[6] Ethel Barrymore claimed, "You grow up the day you have the first real laugh—at yourself."[7]

"Laugh at yourself first, before anyone else can" was the advice of Elsa Maxwell.[8] Theologian Reinhold Niebuhr echoed these same sentiments when he said, "The less we are able to laugh at ourselves, the more it becomes necessary and inevitable that others laugh at us."[9]

When we take ourselves too seriously, we cannot expect to develop a good sense of humor in our homes, on the job, or at school. Each of us must be openly willing to laugh at our own foibles, conceits, and pretensions. In fact, Tom

Mullen claimed that "laughing at ourselves is possible when we are able to see humanity as it is—a little lower than the angels and at times only slightly higher than the apes."[10]

Laughing at ourselves even has spiritual overtones. Theologians have claimed that the ability to laugh at ourselves helps to develop a healthy perspective of our sins and failings.[11] Those who never see anything funny about themselves will probably never see anything sinful about themselves.

"Humor reminds us," said Bernard Ramm, "that we are not gods nor goddesses."[12] From this assertion, he observed that dictators and fanatics always lack a sense of humor because they have classified themselves among the gods and goddesses and refuse to tolerate reminders of their humanity.

Laughing at ourselves in a healthy sort of way may deliver us from pride and give us a "head start on humility."[13] But what does laughing at ourselves do to our self-esteem? If, as indicated in a previous chapter, developing one's self-esteem is essential to developing a sense of humor, where does humility enter the picture?

Ruth McRoberts Ward defined true humility as the "recognition that without God we are nothing."[14] This realization comes only to those who recognize their own limitations and feel free to laugh at some of them. Such an attitude often serves as a prelude to repentance of our sins to God.

While extolling the value of being able to laugh at ourselves, I must register some words of caution, however. For some people, self-laughter can become a masochistic tool of self-abasement. When the "funny" become "unfunny" and cruel to themselves, it ceases to be legitimate humor.

Another pitfall to avoid in laughing at ourselves is the problem of using laughter as a "cover-up." Some use it to avoid doing anything about some of their weaknesses over which they *do* have some control. Some use humor to excuse themselves for unacceptable behavior.

As has been pointed out, laughing at ourselves has spiritual overtones, but the "self-laugher" must be very careful not to use laughter to evade the necessity for repentance. Some spend a lifetime laughing at their sins and moving away from, rather than toward, humility. If laughing at ourselves causes us to delay seeking God's forgiveness for our sins or gaining restitution with others, it is unhealthy in every sense of the word.

The theological, emotional, and physical benefits of laughing at ourselves are often quite complex. However, I have observed on many occasions that those who have the uncanny ability of laughing at themselves seem to make life more enjoyable for the rest of us. In his book: *Preacher You're the Best Pasture We've Ever Had,* Joe Johnson told a hilarious story about himself:

> In a small-town pastorate, I did my share to assist the custodian and "board." It was on a spring afternoon when the ladies of the church were preparing the "fellowship hall" for a bridal shower that night. And we experienced more than a bridal shower. The rain kept falling on our roof.
>
> Like a ministerial Boy Scout, I climbed into the attic to check for the drip-drip-drip we were hearing. I was walking on 2×6's but forgot there were no cross pieces. Precisely as I found the leak, I fell through the ceiling.
>
> Because of my corpulence, I failed to finish the trip. There I was "in suspension" hanging from the ceiling. I couldn't get up and I couldn't get down, and nails were piercing me in the stomach, as my legs flailed in mid-air.

About that time a gracious lady stepped in the side door. A retired school teacher, she had a high level of tolerance, but what she beheld was more than she could stand. She moaned to herself, as she later testified, "Why, oh why, did the preacher have to come to the church to commit suicide? Now, where can I find a knife to cut him down?"

That church strongly considered leaving the hole there and installing a plaque in memory of the occasion.[15]

Laughing with Your Spouse

Humor, like charity, begins at home. There's an old story about a man whose wife smeared a brand of offensive-smelling cheese on his mustache while he was still asleep. She forgot to tell him that morning when he went to work. He came home after work and announced to his wife, "The whole world stinks!" One's attitude during the day is often based on the atmosphere of his or her home.

Husbands and wives need to laugh together. William Thackeray said, "A good laugh is sunshine in a house."[16] Over four-hundred years ago Erasmus exclaimed, "How many divorces [or things worse than divorces] would be happening everywhere if it were not that the everyday life of married couples is supported and sustained by flattery, laughing things off, taking it easy, being deceived, pretending things are not as they are?"[17] In more recent years, Julius Gordon pointed out that "The failure of modern marriage is, in large measure, accounted for by our failure to employ humor in the process of marital adjustment."[18]

Francine Klagsbrun in *Married People: Staying Together In The Age of Divorce,* outlined the secret of lengthy marriages.[19] As a result of interviews with several couples who have been married over fifteen years, the following "abilities and outlooks" that have contributed to lengthy marriages were isolated:

(1) Enjoyment of each other: Wives and husbands in lasting marriages enjoy being together and talking to each other. Even though these couples find each other interesting, they do not necessarily have the same interests.

(2) An ability to change: There is a flexibility among couples that stay together in spite of changes. In short, they continue to make the constant decision "to be married to each other." They willingly choose to change when necessary to keep their marriage alive and vital.

(3) The ability to live with the unchangeable: Couples who live together for a long time have accepted the fact that their personalities, insights, and solutions to problems are quite different. However, they have chosen to overlook their differences in order to stay together.

(4) An assumption of permanence: Couples that stay married intended to stay together before they were married. Divorce is not a viable option. They have a commitment to each other that transcends every problem, adjustment, and heartache related to the home.

(5) Trusting each other: To know that you are the most important person in the life of your mate makes for a happy marriage. Trust presupposes "exclusivity."

(6) A balance of dependencies: Happy marriages are built on one partner sharing his or her strengths with the other. When they talk about "needing each other," they are talking about strengths, not weaknesses, which are mutually shared.

(7) A shared and cherished history: Because so many marriages end in divorce and do not have a history to share with their children, couples that stay together do so on the assumption that they are building together a history.

Klagsbrun claimed that "Humor is the universal salve, easing tensions and marriage fatigue." But how does humor ease tension and marriage fatigue? Like nothing else, humor can surface delicate problems and solutions between husbands and wives. While some teasing and kidding within a marriage is often done to deliver messages, it is almost a proven axiom that "husbands and wives who laugh together stay together."

Martin Grotjahn said, "I can assure young women that they'll never be battered wives if they choose a mate who's witty."[20] George Jean Nathan claimed, "Nothing lives on so fresh and evergreen as the love with a funny bone."[21]

Tom Mullen encourages husbands and wives to cultivate their relationship with private jokes and the discovery that they both laugh at the same things. In fact, he concluded, "Courtship often focuses on laughing together as a primary form of attraction."[22] Grady Nutt was being about as serious as he was funny when he said, "Sometimes the best joke you know, you're sharing your twenty-seventh anniversary with, or you are aging with."[23]

Laughing with Your Children

Our children need to learn laughter at home. Phylis Campbell Dryden was right when she exclaimed, "Life, love, and laughter—what priceless gifts to give our children."[24] It is important to instill values, impart spiritual truth, build self-esteem, and develop abilities in our children. However, it is also important to have fun with our children. We have a little motto at our house:

Be Fair . . . Be Firm . . . Be Fun

I like Julius Gordon's appraisal of children: "By being

frequently in the company of children, we may learn to
recapture the will to laugh and the art of laughing at
will."[25] The older we get, the more prone we are to suppress laughter, but children are spontaneous laughers.

Using humor in the home can help a child to develop
a personal positive image and a more positive image of
the world outside the home. Blumenfeld and Alpern
claim that a close observation of children who seem naturally cooperative will reveal mutual respect, a sense of
fairness, affection, and good-natured humor "enhancing
the sense of family cohesiveness and we're-all-in-this-
together attitudes."[26]

Many helpful suggestions have been given for developing humor in the home with younger children by psychologists and specialists in childhood education. But
what can be said of what Tom Mullen calls "one of God's
most complex creations"—the teenager?[27]

Many teenagers never hear laughter in their homes.
Many families have substituted the laughter gained
through television and the movies for the laughter they
could be sharing with their teenagers.

While speaking in a church recently, I met a woman
with a sparkling personality and an amazing sense of humor. In her earlier years, she had lived the life of a juvenile delinquent. Over twenty years ago, she became a
Christian and has dedicated her life to encouraging troubled teenagers and teenagers in trouble. With the help of
her church and the encouragement of her husband, she
has been able to minister to hundreds of teenagers
through the years.

She shared an unusual letter with me from a teenaged
boy whom she had visited in a youth detention center.
There was about a page and a half filled with information

about him, his family, and the usual stuff a teenage boy would share with an adult.

Then, the letter said, "Here are some jokes."

(1) What's yellow, sings, and weighs 1,000 pounds?
Answer: Two 500-pound canaries.

(2) What did the big beach ball say to the child?
Answer: "I get a kick out of you."

(3) What do you get when you cross a mink and a kangaroo?
Answer: A mink coat with pockets.

(4) What kind of room has no windows, no doors, and no walls?
Answer: A mushroom.

(5) Why doesn't a motorcycle stand up?
Answer: Because it is two tired.

(6) In what way is a teacher different from a train?
Answer: A teacher says, "Take out the gum," and a train says, "choo-choo."

This fine Christian lady said, "I have always used humor to bridge the gap between me and teenagers. If I can laugh with them, I can help them."

Youth counselor and chaplain Byron W. Arledge claims that the most frequent question he asks delinquent teenagers is: "What do you do for fun?" His most popular answer is: "Nothing!"[28]

Teenagers come in assorted sizes, weights, and colors, but, according to Tom Mullen, they share a common creed—"to keep all adults in a state of anxiety, fluctuating between high hopes for the future of the world and complete despair for all living things."[29]

I write these words from experience. During the writing of this book, my two teenage sons and I had several

"interesting conversations" about the usual warfare between parental authority and teenage takeover. A few
days after one of these episodes, my wife purchased a
couple of small posters and suggested that I might want
to ease the tension by passing them on to our sons. I liked
the idea, and I liked the message on the posters:

<blockquote>
Attention Teenagers!
If You Are Tired of Being Hassled by
Unreasonable Parents,
Now Is the Time for Action!

Leave Home and Pay Your Own Way
While You Still Know Everything
</blockquote>

I slipped a poster under each door that night and was
pleased to see that both of them had taped them to their
mirrors the next day. They got the message, and we all
had a good laugh!

At an annual Christmas staff dinner a few years ago, a
friend shared a touching essay on "When the Kids Finally
Leave Home." Upon my request, he shared it with me
indicating that he was not sure of its source. I have since
updated it, added some "personal embellishments," and
shared it in many places. It speaks of fun at home and the
urgency of laughing with your kids *now:*

SOMEDAY WHEN THE KIDS FINALLY LEAVE
HOME, things are going to be a lot different around our
house. The garage won't be cluttered with bicycles and
garbage bags on their way to trash cans. I'll be able to park
both cars in just the right places and never again stumble
over skateboards, a bag of rabbit food, and eggshells from
the garbage bags that someone forgot to tie.

SOMEDAY WHEN THE KIDS FINALLY LEAVE
HOME, the kitchen will be incredibly neat. The sink will

stay free of dirty dishes. The garbage disposal won't get clogged up with rubber bands, paper cups, or a stray spoon. The refrigerator won't be crowded with four cartons of milk—all opened and half used. We won't lose the tops of jelly jars or catsup bottles anymore. The honey will stay inside the container, and no one will wonder again what's going to explode next in the microwave oven.

SOMEDAY WHEN THE KIDS FINALLY LEAVE HOME, Mom will actually have time to get dressed leisurely. She can take long, hot baths without interruptions. She will even have a chance to have her hair done without trying to squeeze it between the orthodontist, soccer practice, and piano lessons.

SOMEDAY WHEN THE KIDS FINALLY LEAVE HOME, the instrument called the "telephone" will actually be available. It won't look like it's growing out of a kid's ear. It will simply hang there . . . silently and amazingly available! It will be free of peanut butter, mayonnaise, and pimple medicine. And, miracle of miracles, the cord won't look like a spider web; and I will never again have to say, "Can you hang up and let me call you right back after I get out from under my son's bed and get this telephone cord straightened out?"

SOMEDAY WHEN THE KIDS FINALLY LEAVE HOME, old Dad will gasp in unbelief when he finds the hammer where he left it last, and he doesn't have to call in an FBI agent to find his special "one-size-fits-all" wrench. He will be utterly amazed that, for the first time, there *is* a place for everything, and everything *is* in its place.

SOMEDAY WHEN THE KIDS FINALLY LEAVE HOME, we will return to normal conversation around our house—you know, just plain English. "Yuk" will never be heard again. Nothing will ever be described as "totally awesome" or "gross" or "neat" or "nasty." "It's my turn!"

will not require a referee or a karate expert to restore harmony to our otherwise happy home.

SOMEDAY WHEN THE KIDS FINALLY LEAVE HOME, we'll be able to see through the car windows again. Fingerprints, tongue licks, footprints, and dog tracks will be conspicuous by their absence. The back seat won't be a disaster area, and the trunk will no longer be mistaken for a garage sale.

SOMEDAY WHEN THE KIDS FINALLY LEAVE HOME, we won't run out of toilet paper. The refrigerator door will stay shut. The microwave will always be clean, and the vacuum cleaner will work. The screens will return to our windows. Knives, notes from teachers, rocks, and grass will no longer be found in the washing machine.

YES, SOMEDAY WHEN THE KIDS FINALLY LEAVE HOME, things are going to be a lot different around our house. When a kid's voice is no longer heard at our house, it will be quiet and calm. The crackling of the fireplace will echo in the hallway. From the dining room you will hear the clink of china and silver on special occasions. When the telephone rings, you will know it is for you.

Yes, it will be quiet and calm and clean and organized around our house, but it will also be empty and lonely.

SOMEDAY WHEN THE KIDS FINALLY LEAVE HOME, we will sit and think and talk about how wonderful it was when the kids were home. And one of us will suggest, "Maybe we could baby-sit for someone tonight and get some life back into this old house for a change!"

Laughing on the Job

But what about humor in the marketplace? Strangely enough, many are singing the praises of "yukking it up the corporate ladder."[30]

It was recently reported by the National Council on Compensation Insurance that 15 percent of the 100,000 occupational-disease claims filed during the year were stress related—a more than 30 percent jump over the previous year.[31] With the increase of stress on the job has come the necessity for relieving tension with humor.

A good manager is usually socially adept and very witty, according to Robert Billings who teaches industrial psychology at Ohio State University. "He's not a stand-up comic, but he is certainly humorous and can respond to other people's humor."[32]

One bank dealt with more than its share of "extra nasty customers." A consultant convinced the employees that they should make a game of their problems, competing with each other over who had endured the worst customer that week. The results? A happier, more cheerful workplace.

Blumenfeld and Alpern have found that "the positive force of humor can help you reduce the stress involved in both your personal and business relationships with other people."[33] The wise executive these days realizes that constructive humor can help create a positive office atmosphere and he or she often uses humor to spice up memos, illustrate points, and add spice to otherwise boring meetings.

In his book: *What They Don't Teach You at Harvard Business School,* Mark McCormack claimed that the most important personal asset in business is common sense, followed closely by a sense of humor, which he defined as "the ability to laugh at yourself or the situation." McCormack saw four values of humor in the business world.[34]

(1) It diffuses business tension: When one can find the humorous and absurd about a situation or confrontation, tension can be relieved because laughter allows two people to share the same feeling.

(2) It creates long-term impressions: A single humorous

incident in which one fails to take himself or herself too seriously will never be forgotten by business associates.

(3) It is the best way to start a meeting: "You don't need to have them rolling in the aisles, but a mildly pleasant remark at the outset will create the right atmosphere for everything that follows."[35]

(4) It brings back perspective: next to profits, perspective is the easiest thing to lose in business.

McCormack shared an interesting story about the Ford Motor Company in the days when Robert McNamara was the president, and several plants were being closed to cut costs. After the closing of plants in Massachusetts and Texas, top executives sat down to discuss a recommendation for the closing of another plant.

No one was in favor of closing the plant, but the accountants made the situation look rather grim. Finally, a veteran of many years spoke up and said, "Why don't we close down all the plants, and then we'll really start to save money?" This really brought the meeting back into perspective.

John D. Yeck is the founder of a revolutionary organization called, "The Let's Have Better Mottoes Association, Inc."[36] He collects and shares humorous mottoes that are designed to be used in the workplace.

Sometimes Yeck shares definitions. A committee is "a device to share the blame with," and a friend is "one who takes you to lunch even when you are not deductible." Some of his mottoes shared in his monthly newsletter which tickled my funny bone are as follows:

Fools Rush in Where Fools Have Been Before.

I'm so Completely Open-Minded on the Issue that I'll Even Listen to Your Fantastically Stupid, Idiotic Opinion.

To Avoid Duplication, Make Three Copies.

Don't Ridicule Your Employees. If They Were Perfect, You'd Be Working for Them!

Do Not Disturb—Genius at Werk.

To Stop Gossiping in the Office, Turn the Clock to 5:01.

It's Called "Take Home" Pay Because You Can't Afford to Go Anywhere Else with It.

Success Comes Before Work, But Only in the Dictionary.

Success Is Relative; the Greater the Success, the More Relatives.

My Work Is so Secret Even I Don't Know What I'm Doing.

Anyone Can Be a Winner—Unless, of Course, There's a Second Entry.

It's Better to Have Loafed and Lost Than Never to Have Loafed at All.

The Slower You Work, the Fewer Mistakes You Make.

For Every Vision There Is an Equal and Opposite Revision.

If Murphy's Law Can Go Wrong, It Will.

You Can Say Anything You Please Around Here But Some Things Only Once.

If at First You Succeed, Try to Hide Your Astonishment.

You Must Have Learned from Others' Mistakes. You Haven't Had Time to Think All Those Up Yourself.

Your Visit Is the Highlight of My Day; so You Know What Kind of Day I've Had.

If You Look Like Your Passport Picture, You Probably Need the Trip.

Never Do Your Best, It Leaves No Room for Improvement.

Never Be Redundant—Never, Never, Never, Never.

I Like Criticism. Just Keep It Positive and Flattering.

We Learn More from Failure than We Do from Success —Because We Fail More.

Pur Spellrs of the World Unyte.

Indecision May or May Not Be the Problem Here.

It's OK to Let Your Mind Go Blank. But Please Turn Off the Sound.

I Tolerate All Opinions—Even Stupid Ones Like Yours.

People Claim I'm Indecisive, But I'm Not so Sure.

Truth Is Precious—Don't Waste It.

Experience Is What Tells You You've Made a Mistake . . . Again.

I Am *Not* Arbitrary, and I Won't Discuss It Further.

I'm Going to Become More Assertive if It's 100 Percent OK with You.

Please Don't Argue. I've Changed My Mind Already.

Self-Praise May Be Sickening But at Least It's Sincere.

Worry Kills More People than Work Because More People Worry than Work.

I Never Make a Mistake, But I'm Getting Tired of Doing Nothing.

I Respect Your Opinion, But I'd Respect It Even More if You'd Keep It to Yourself.

If at First You Don't Succeed . . . Look in the Wastebasket for the Directions.

Procrastination Avoids Boredom—There's Always Something Left to Do.

Laughing at School

I began to notice something about my children and their school several years ago. They came home from school talking about their favorite subjects and, almost invariably, the teacher of those classes had a good sense of humor. In fact, more than one teacher had developed the habit of reading a few clean, discreet jokes at some time during the class period.

Humor can be overdone in any setting. I am not recommending that parents and children, employers and employees, and students and teachers become stand-up comedians. However, many teachers are now realizing that humor can be a very effective teaching aid.

Blumenfeld and Alpern give good advice to the teacher: "If you accept the idea that humor is a positive attitudinal approach to life, valuable and not merely frivolous, then as a teacher, you can use it (with reasonable limitations) as a positive approach to your class."[37]

No less an authority on humor than Allen Funt has concluded, "When people are smiling they are most receptive to almost anything you want to teach them." He believes that this can be applied "industrially, academically, technically and in almost every other way."[38]

Blumenfeld and Alpern consider humor an oasis in the classroom. They discuss ten accomplishments of this humor oasis, using the words as an acrostic:[39]

    H umanizing effect on self-image . . .

    U nderstanding . . .

    M otivating . . .

    O pening communication . . .

    R especting individual differences, divergent thinking . . .

O pportunity to be creative . . .

A ttitude . . .

S timulating learning . . .

I nspiring and illustrating . . .

S afety valve for tension and aggressive behavior
. . .

Conclusion

Developing a wholesome sense of humor involves laughing *with* yourself, *at* yourself, and with others. Let's laugh in our homes, on the job, and at school. We desperately need wholesome laughter. A good sense of humor may, indeed, be the best sense of all!

9

When It's Laughter You're After

"Share with us some humorous church happenings" came the request at a meeting of ministers in Kentucky. For almost an hour, we laughed, roared, slapped our knees, and even cried.

It was a hilarious time. One minister seemed to enjoy laughter more than anyone else. On several occasions, he almost fell out into the aisle. I later learned that this was partially due to the fact that he had only one leg.

Later that evening at dinner, he walked over to my table on his crutches to visit.

"I guess you think you've heard it all when it comes to humor in the ministry," he said. "But I'll bet you've never heard of a wrestling match between a roto-tiller and a preacher!"

"No," I admitted, "I don't think I've ever heard such a story."

He explained to me that he had lost his leg several years ago while serving in the United States Navy. Because his had been a radical amputation of his left leg and almost all of his left hip, he wore an artificial limb only occasionally. However, he has managed an effective ministry through the years.

He and his wife live on a small farm in Kentucky where they have a large vegetable garden each year. He explained how he hopped behind the rototiller on one leg plowing his garden.

"One of the biggest problems I have is this extra trouser leg," he said. "When I'm hopping behind the rototiller, I usually stick it in my back pocket."

"The other day as I was hopping along behind my rototiller, the trouser leg kept falling down. I stopped several times to stuff it back into my hip pocket. Then it happened! The trouser leg came out of my pocket and was strangely drawn to the blades of the rototiller. Before I knew what had happened, the rototiller had literally stripped me of my clothing. I had already shed my shirt to get a good suntan. But I didn't expect to shed everything except my shorts in the twinkling of an eye."

"What did you do?" I asked.

"I shut off the rototiller," he continued, "and began the long, arduous task of winding my trousers back out of the rototiller. There I was, sitting in the dirt with nothing on but my shorts and praying that no one would drive by. Luckily, no one did drive by and I was able to don my slightly damaged trousers, start the rototiller, and go on my merry way of making a garden."

Laughing to Become Serious

All of those at my table could hardly stop laughing after my friend had told this story. As he walked back to his table, I realized that he was a living illustration of what humor can do as a tool of communication.

(1) He relieved tension: I was somewhat tense about his handicap, and he may have been as well. However, as he shared his humorous story, all tension was relieved.

(2) He retained my attention: I couldn't wait to hear what he was going to say next.

(3) He removed barriers: we were total strangers but,

within a few minutes, I felt as though we were friends who had known each other for years.

(4) He communicated several ideas to me: He not only told me a humorous story, he also demonstrated his ability to laugh at himself and to overcome adversity.

(5) The telling of his story enhanced my memory: I shall not soon forget the picture he painted of his wrestling match with the rototiller.

Mark Twain once said that he was sorry that he had a reputation for being humorous because nobody took him seriously. Of course, if you happen to be a humorist, your job is to entertain and not to be taken seriously.

On the other hand, most of us just want to know how to use humor as an effective tool for communication while being taken seriously by those who hear. This chapter does not deal with humorous talks but how to use humor in informational, inspirational, and persuasive speeches or sermons as an illustration of the ideas which we are attempting to communicate.

Why should we use humor? Where do we find humorous material? How can we make the best use of humor in communicating ideas to others from the speaker's platform? Hopefully, this chapter will answer these important questions.

George Q. Lewis said, "The business of making people laugh is the toughest in the world."[1] If making people laugh is so difficult, why then should we use humor as a tool of communication? Remember my friend's wrestling match with the rototiller?

The use of humor relieves tension. The relief of tension is a two-way street when humor is used in communication: it causes both the speaker and the audience to relax. If, as indicated in previous chapters, laughter is both physically and emotionally helpful, it goes without saying that the use of humor will serve well to relieve the tension of the speaker.

Relieving Tension to Get Attention

A congressman from Texas came back to his district to give a speech in which he would attempt to answer the charges related to his support of what many of his people considered questionable legislation. Most of the information that his constituents had received was false.[2]

The congressman began his speech with a story of a man who rushed up to a friend and said, "Hello, Bill, congratulations!"

Bill said, "What for?"

"For making fifty thousand dollars in oil."

"It wasn't I; it was my brother."

"Oh, it was your brother?"

"Yes, and it wasn't oil; it was coal."

"Oh, it was coal?"

"Yes, but he didn't make fifty thousand; he lost it."

"Oh, he lost it? Well, I was approximately correct," said the friend.

By this time, the congressman's audience had relaxed and they were ready to hear him say, "The charges which you have heard concerning me are not even 'approximately correct.'"

Roger C. Palms surmised that a joke or a funny story is a "hook, a means of pulling along the minds of the hearers." Palms concluded, "It even gives a little mental vacation in the midst of concentration."[3] Such "mental vacations" will allow your audience to relax. And, as they relax, laughter may also pave the way for other emotional expressions and for seriousness. William K. Zinsser said, "What I want to do is to make people laugh so that they'll see things seriously."[4]

Many ministers are aware that the Scriptures say, "There is . . . A time to weep, and a time to laugh" (Eccl. 3:1-4). While weeping is never banned from their pulpit, many of them feel that laughter should be left in the vestibule of the church. Many speakers, including ministers, are missing a golden opportunity for communicating serious truth by their failure to use humor.

The use of humor gets and keeps the attention of the audience. "Get a laugh and you've got an audience," claimed Stewart Harral.[5] If humor is used effectively by a speaker, it will serve as a window to the thoughts being shared and will help retain the attention of the audience. Some specialists in communication have even recommended that a humorous story or a humorous sentence appear every seven minutes in a speech.

A friend of mine felt the call to the ministry at the height of a very successful career as a television announcer. He first pastored a small, struggling church. Then, he moved on to a small county-seat town to a medium-sized, but influential church. He shared with me on one occasion that he was using a television camera in his worship services.

"Are you recording your sermons and playing them back later to see how you can improve on your preaching?" I asked.

"No," he said, "I'm not just recording my sermons. I'm recording the reactions of my congregation to my sermons."

He explained to me that he had trained the camera on his congregation each Sunday and studied these films to measure the effectiveness of his communication skills as a speaker.

"I noticed that when I injected humor into the sermon, the people took this occasion to shift in the pew, cross their legs, and generally become more comfortable," he noted. He continued, "It seemed that they listened much more intently after a humorous illustration than they were listening before humor was injected into the sermon."

This minister has developed a style of preaching that draws often on humor to illustrate the deep and abiding truths of the gospel message. He now pastors one of the great churches of America and has, for many years, made effective use of television in his ministry. If more ministers could learn to use humor effectively, perhaps Tom Mullen's prayer for sermons might be answered:

> O Lord, be present in the churches,
> so that preaching and listening to
> sermons will begin and end at the same
> time.[6]

Removing Barriers to Share Ideas

The use of humor removes barriers caused by gaps in age, education, background, experience, and other factors. Motivationalist Jim Savage has claimed that "Getting an audience to laugh is a good way to warm them up to you as a speaker."[7]

As a minister, I have found that the use of humor often removes barriers caused by preconceived ideas. One lady, with a sad tone in her voice and a miserable countenance, asked a friend, "Do you want to become a Christian?"

The other lady answered, "No, I'm already miserable enough as it is!" Admittedly, many people associate piety with sadness. When a minister uses humor, it often removes the barrier caused by false impressions of ministers in particular and religion in general.

Another barrier often faced by a speaker is resistance

to conflicting ideas held by those in the audience. Henry Ward Beecher considered the use of humor as "the most civilizing of all the influences in the soul of man." His reason? He claimed that when he used humor to communicate truth he was able to "bring in the truth which men do not like."[8]

Billy Graham has overcome resistance on many occasions with an effective use of humor. He once addressed the student body of the prestigious London School of Economics. When he stood to speak to a packed auditorium, some booed. Shortly after he began to speak, one young man jumped out in front of the audience and began to heckle Graham, acting like an ape, using gestures, scratching, and making noises like a monkey. As the student body roared with laughter, it seemed that Graham had lost his audience.

After a good hearty laugh of his own, Graham turned to his audience and said, "He reminds me of my ancestors." The hall was filled with laughter again. Then, he said, "Of course, all of my ancestors came from Britain." After this, all barriers were broken, and Graham was able to communicate effectively with his audience.[9]

Humor is a great communicator. It helps drive home a point and communicate truth and knowledge. As Samuel Butler said, "A little levity will save many a good heavy thing from sinking."[10] Sam Jones was fond of saying, "Some men open their mouths to laugh, and you can drop a great brickbat of truth right in."[11]

Actually, however, people do not even need to laugh in order for communication to take place. They may do no more than smile or "laugh with their eyes," but, according to Charles R. Brown, "They will be all the more ready to recognize and to accept the full value of the solid truth which is thus proclaimed."[12]

There is a woeful lack of knowledge concerning the Bible in many of our churches. I have often told the humorous story of a man, about to be ordained, who was asked if he were knowledgeable of the Scriptures.

"Yes," he said. "I'm a good Bible scholar. I know my Bible well."

"Well," requested one of the older ministers, "Share with us your favorite parable."

The young man leaned back, took a deep breath, and shared the following collage of information:

Once there was this man traveling from Jerusalem to Jericho, and he fell among thorns, and the thorns sprang up and choked him. And as he went on, he didn't have no money, and he met the Queen of Sheba and she gave him 1,000 talents of gold and 100 changes of raiment. And he got into a chariot and drove furiously, and, when he was driving under a big juniper tree, his hair caught on the limb of that tree, and he hung there many days, and the ravens brought him food to eat and water to drink, and he ate 5,000 loaves of bread and two fishes.

One night when he was hanging there asleep, his wife Delilah come along and cut off his hair, and he fell on stony ground. But he got up and went on, and it began to rain, and it rained forty days and forty nights, and he hid in a cave, and he lived on locusts and wild honey.

Then he went on till he met a servant who said, "Come, take supper at my house!" And he made excuse and said, "No, I won't, I have married a wife, and I can't go!" And the servant went out in the highways and in the hedges and compelled him to come in. After supper, he came on down to Jericho. And when he got there, he looked up and saw that old Queen Jezebel sitting down away up high in a window. And she laughed at him, and he said, "Throw her down out of there!" And they threw her down out of there seventy-times-seven, and, of the fragments that remained, they picked up twelve baskets full besides women and children, and they said, "Blessed are the peacemakers." Now, whose wife do you think she will be in the Judgement Day?

Those who are serious students of the Bible, and those who are not so serious can see the humor. I often use this story to illustrate the following truths:

(1) Being aware of the context of Bible verses helps to understand the meaning of those verses.

(2) Those who insert "Bible talk" into their conversation do not necessarily know the Bible.

(3) One of our greatest needs is effective Bible teaching and Bible preaching.

Sharing Ideas to Be Remembered

The use of humor enhances our memory. When evangelist Vance Havner died in 1986, Billy Graham was called upon to preach his funeral. Havner, often called the "Will Rogers of the pulpit," was ordained at the age of fifteen and delivered his first sermon when he was only twelve years of age. His ministry spanned over seventy-two years, and he was the author of thirty-eight books. He had the uncanny ability of driving home his point with easily remembered stories and humorous statements.

Havner often told of a little girl and her mother who were regular worshipers at a small country church that had a picture of Jesus behind the pulpit. One Sunday morning when the preacher was slow coming to the pulpit the little girl asked, "Where is the man who stands so you can't see Jesus?"

Here's a sample of some of Havner's short humorous statements about preachers:

- "Some preachers have more degrees than temperature."
- "If the Lord can defeat the devil with only three verses from Deuteronomy, we ought to be able to do it with the whole Bible."
- "Have you learned the fine art of almost saying something when you preach?"
- "Some church services start at eleven o'clock sharp and end at twelve o'clock dull."

Havner had a way of communicating truth to the churches:

> I'm amused and amazed at some of the stunts the churches are playing these days. You take the Ichabod Memorial Church for instance. They pack 'em in for folk music. Ephesus brings in a television personality. Pergamos has somebody who can play a fiddle, tap dance, play drums, and blow a harmonica all at the same time. And the church at Sardis, not to be outdone, says that they're going to have Aunt Dinah's quilting party—come dressed like you did 100 years ago and we'll all sing "Aunt Nellie's Bonnet." Laodicea puts in a talking horse. . . . They asked him how many Commandments there are, and he stomped ten times. They asked him how many disciples there were, and he stomped twelve times. Someone in the back asked him how many hypocrites there are in the church and he danced all over the front of the church.[13]

Finding Humor Everywhere

The two major keys to successful speaking, as well as the use of humor as a tool of communication, are good materials and good delivery. Where do you find good humorous material? Just about anywhere you want to look. Emily Hardy said, "You are missing something vital if you're not finding situations or anecdotes or comical events daily that will trigger joyous laughter."[14]

Have you noticed the humor in radio and television advertisements these days? A Texas supermarket chain features a funny man selling frozen turkeys. "With the right dressing, the turkey can become an attractive addition to anyone's table," he tells TV viewers. Then he holds up one of the birds and flips it over to reveal a red necktie and pocket handkerchief.

In another TV spot, a man talks about eggs which he describes as "the hobby of chickens." Chickens, he claims, "can't drive recreational vehicles or water ski, so in their spare time they lay eggs. Please buy them; otherwise we're going to have chickens hanging out in pool halls."[15]

Will Rogers, one of the funniest men who ever lived, is famous for several meaningful statements. His most famous seems to be, "I never met a man I didn't like." A close second was, "There's no trick to being a humorist when you have the whole government working for you." He also said, "All I know is what I read in the newspapers."

If Will Rogers were alive today, he would find more humor in magazines and newspapers than he ever dreamed possible. From time to time, almost every major magazine will include humorous stories, quips, and one liners which can be used to develop ideas in a speech or sermon.

An Associated Press release sometime ago told about a writing exercise given to first graders at Alexander Elementary School in Duncanville, Texas. The first half of some of our favorite clichés were given to the first graders, and they were asked to complete the sentences.

- "Don't count your chickens—before you cook them."
- "Don't put all your eggs—in the microwave."
- "All's fair in—hockey."
- "People who live in glass houses—better not take off their clothes."
- "If at first you don't succeed—go play."
- "All work and no play—is disgusting."
- "Eat, drink, and—go to the bathroom."
- "He who laughs last—did not understand the joke."

Some newspapers have employed columnists who are well trained in the art of writing humor. Columnist Mike Harden of the *Columbus Dispatch* writes a humor-filled column usually related to events in or around Columbus, Ohio.

One of Harden's Sunday features, for some reason or another, dealt with the subject of ugliness.[16] He began his article by wondering, "Why is it, tell me, that we seem to have so many more graphic and creative descriptions for ugliness than for beauty?" Here are some of those descriptions shared throughout the body of his article:

- One woman was so ugly that when she looked up the word "ugly" in the dictionary, her picture was next to it.
- One fellow was so ugly that, when he was a kid, they had to tie a pork chop around his neck just to get the dog to play with him.
- He was so ugly that when he was born, the doctor spanked his father.
- He was so ugly that his mother sat him in a corner and fed him with a slingshot.
- He looks like someone set his face on fire and then put it out with a track shoe.
- He is so ugly that when he passes you, your clothes wrinkle.

- He is so ugly that if he moves in next door, your lawn will die.
- His face would not only stop a clock, it would stop a sundial.

Harden concluded, "beauty is only skin deep; ugly goes to the bone."

Reading the Signs of Our Time

Another good source of humorous material is to be found in the many joke books that have been published through the years. Admittedly, you may have to wade through some of the offensive material often included in these books. In fact, there is a whole series of dirty, gross, and tasteless joke books that I cannot recommend for anyone's bookshelf.

Another risk you run in the use of published joke books is that you might be sharing old jokes. However, I wouldn't worry too much about that if I were you. Bennett Cerf once said, "If Adam came to earth again, I daresay the only thing he would recognize would be the current jokes."[17]

Milton Berle was often accused of borrowing other people's jokes. Fred Allen said, "Milton Berle for years has been bragging to audiences that he has stolen jokes from other comedians. There has been no reason to doubt his word."[18] Berle claimed however, "If it sounds like a new joke, it's been taken from someplace."[19] In his defense of using other people's materials, Berle came to some interesting conclusions:

> Comedy never changes. There are only eight to nine formats of jokes. . . . Funny is funny. There is nothing new that's old. There's nothing old that's new. Everything has been done before with switches.[20]

Bennett Cerf seemed to agree when he said that there's really no such thing as a new story, and experts insist that there are only about fifty basic humorous stories in the world, "and most of them date back to Homer and Aristophanes."[21]

One of the best sources of humorous material is the newsletters of current jokes and one liners written specifically for public speakers by professional speech writers. Robert Orben, who has written over forty books on humor, shares some of the best up-to-date material in *Orbin's Current Comedy*.

Esther Blumenfeld and Lynne Alpern in *The Smile Connection* and Lawrence J. Peter and Bill Dana in *The Laughter Prescription* have shared some of the most exhaustive lists of resources for humorous material in recent years.

Sometimes the best humor to be found is when we merely open our eyes and look around. Have you noticed those ubiquitous "Baby on Board" signs hanging in the back windows of cars? A young entrepreneur named Michael Lerner began to manufacture these popular signs in the interest of child safety.[22] Almost overnight, humorous parodies of his very serious sign began to appear:

- "Baby Driving"
- "Nobody on Board"
- "Mother-in-law in Trunk"
- "Workaholic on Board"
- "No Radio on Board"

In a message recently on the need for improving husband and wife relationships, I called a congregation's attention to one of these signs I had recently seen in the back of a car: "Former Husband in Trunk." As the woman driver passed me, I noticed a necktie flapping in the wind from the trunk door.

Just open your eyes and look around. You will often find some very humorous signs.[23] For instance, a sign in the office of a Denver psychoanalyst said, "Be a better psychiatrist, and the world will beat a psychopath to your door." Here are some other interesting signs:

- Sign in a doctor's office: "Doctor is very busy. Please have your symptoms ready."
- Sign in a coffee shop: "Do not insult our waitresses by tipping them."
- Sign on each table in the same coffee shop, on a cardboard box with a slit across the top: "Insults."
- Sign on a truck carrying explosives: "Give me room—or we both go boom!"
- Sign in the window of a Washington, DC, laundry: "We do not tear your clothes with machinery. We do it carefully by hand."
- Sign on the rear of a school bus in Erie, Pennsylvania: "Approach with care. Driver under the influence of children."
- Sign on a tow truck in Merced, California: "Puff the Magic Drag-in."
- Sign in a Denver motel: "Do not smoke in bed without umbrella. Extrasensitive sprinkling system."
- Sign on a plumbing truck in Elko, Nevada: "Sewers drained, pipes unplugged, and if there's anything your husband has fixed lately, I can repair that, too."
- Sign in a beauty shoppe in Tampa, Florida: "We can give you the new look if you still have the old parts."
- Sign in a hot dog stand near the bus garage in West Hollywood, California: "Bus drivers must have exact change."

- Sign on a university bulletin board: "Shoes are required to eat in the cafeteria."
- Sign attached to the same sign: "Socks can eat wherever they want to."
- Sign in a dinner theatre in New Jersey: "Do not photograph the performers while they are on stage. You may come backstage and shoot them after the show."
- Sign on a country road in Arkansas: "When this sign is under water, road is impassable."

Delivering Your Message with a Smile

The second major key in the use of humor is delivery. Rusty and Linda Wright claim that three important factors are at work in all sorts of communication—between individuals and between a speaker and the audience.[24] The ancient Greeks called these three factors *ethos, logos,* and *pathos.* Successful delivery of any sort of message, be it humorous or serious, will involve understanding and developing these three.

(1) *Ethos* involves ethical appeal. Does the speaker come across as reliable? Can he or she be trusted? Does his or her background and experience substantiate what is being said?

(2) *Logos* deals with the speaker's logical appeal. Does he or she make sense? Is anything really being said? Is the point being logically and persuasively made in this presentation?

(3) *Pathos* involves the speaker's emotional appeal. Your audience is asking such questions as "Do you really care about me?" "Do you really understand me?" and, "How am I going to feel if I listen to you?"

Depending on the nature of the audience and the purpose of the speaker, it is generally agreed that humor can be effectively used in the introduction, body, and conclusion of any sort of communication with an audience.

Blumenfeld and Alpern contend that every speaker should be prepared for the unexpected at the beginning of his or her presentation. Here are some of their suggestions:[25]

- When something is being repaired: "When you are finished here, my car could use an oil change."
- When you have to raise the mike: "I prayed my talk would be well received, but I wasn't planning on kneeling throughout the whole thing."
- When you have to lower the mike: "I guess when it was suggested that I give an elevating speech, you meant that I give it on stilts."
- When someone drops a folding chair: "Why can't you carry a briefcase like everyone else?"

One pastor, finding it difficult to get into the introduction of his sermon, noticed that his minister of music was talking on a platform telephone to the sound booth giving instructions regarding the sound. He also noticed that all eyes were fixed on the music director sitting on the platform with the telephone to his ear.

He turned to the music director and asked, "Randy, what are you doing? Ordering pizza?" Even ministers ought to be prepared to deal humorously with the unexpected as they begin their sermons.

Lawrence Peter and Bill Dana suggest that the purpose of an introduction to a speech is to "win the audience's favorable attention to you and, in particular, to your subject matter."[26] They also contend that a joke, just off the top of one's head, is not necessarily a good way of beginning a presentation. They suggest that humor be used in the introduction only if it is relevant to the topic and if the speaker can provide a transition from the joke or story into the subject at hand.

The use of humor can be delightful or dangerous in an introduction. Nothing can warm up an audience faster than laughter. However, nothing can turn them off quite as fast as an unsuccessful attempt to be funny. They will not forget their first impression, and they will remember very little you say thereafter.

Within the body of a presentation, humor can often be used to strengthen the theme and the main idea you are attempting to communicate. Humor may also call your audience back to the subject of your presentation. Jim Sites, while serving as special assistant to the secretary of the treasury, was addressing a rather sophisticated audience on what many considered a very dry subject. Reportedly, in the middle of his presentation, he added this humorous item:

> The more learned economists might tell you that a slowing up of the slowdown is not as good as an upturn in the down-curve. But even this is a good deal better than either a speed-up of the slowdown or a deepening of the down-curve. And it does suggest that the climate is just about right for an adjustment to the readjustment. All of which indicates that there may be a letting up of the letdown. Of course, if the slowdown should speed up, the decrease in the rate of increase should turn an increase in the rate of decrease. In other words, the rate of deceleration would be accelerated.[27]

Humor can also be effectively used at the conclusion of a presentation. The audience's last impression of you is often the longest remembered. If you have ruffled any feathers, now is the time to end on a positive note. Peter and Dana have shared some interesting concluding remarks that can "leave them laughing or smiling":28

- "As you leave this hall tonight, I'd like you to remember one thing—where you parked your car."
- "I leave you with the words of Luther Burbank—'Never look down on a lily—tomorrow it may be looking down on you.' "
- "Before I go, I leave you with this thought: Keep your words soft and sweet—you never know when you might have to eat them some day."
- "Be good to each other and may you live among people who care."
- "Let me leave you with the words of Elbert Hubbard: 'Don't take life too seriously; you will never get out of it alive.' "

I cannot emphasize enough that the purpose of one's presentation always dictates his or her use of humor. While the minister may want to use humor to communicate the truth of the message, the congregation might be highly offended at a humorous quip just before the invitation or closing prayer.

Timely Tips for Effective Speakers

When it's laughter you're after, there is no end to the suggestions you might receive. My list is not exhaustive, however, here are six suggestions that I have found most helpful for using humor as an effective tool in communication.

1. Know your audience. Some occasions do not lend themselves to laughter. Sometimes comic humor is both inappropriate and insensitive and should be avoided. A knowledge of who is in the audience will help you know when to use humor and whether to use humor.

A university professor who was a humor behavior scientist was speaking to a group of insurance salespersons on motivation.[29] All of his stories and illustrations were about factory workers in the metal trades. For instance, he shared how one company had motivated its milling machine operators. However, most of those in his audience had never even seen a milling machine. It was an excellent talk for factory foremen and supervisors, but most of the insurance salespersons yawned through the whole presentation.

2. *Realize that some people are humor insulated.* As Samuel Johnson put it, "That frolic which shakes one man with laughter will convulse another with indignation."[30] In other words, some people are just not going to get the joke, nor the point of what you are trying to illustrate with your humor.

Martin Grotjahn said, "I seriously doubt that humorless people can be taught to be witty or to appreciate those who are."[31] Humorist Jerry Clower, speaking on the use of humor in the pulpit said, "The same people who don't want to hear humor in the pulpit would probably say they don't want you to be emotional."[32]

Every speaker who wants to use humor effectively must realize the truth of the old saying: "The success of humor lies in the ear of him who hears it—never in the tongue of him who makes it."

3. *Be natural.* If you can't be funny, don't force yourself to be funny. Humorous stories, jokes, and witty remarks are used by a large number of effective speakers. But there are also many dynamic and successful speakers who never tell a funny story or use a witty remark. The best kind of humor is that which naturally flows through one's personality.

Josh Lee contended, "The style of joke-telling best

fitted to you is that which comes most natural and which gives the easiest outlet to your sense of humor."[33]

But don't let this suggestion be a cop-out. Anyone can improve on timing, diction, facial expressions, animation, and self-confidence in order to be a better speaker. Blumenfeld and Alpern suggest that "Any person can learn to be funny if they are willing to become a different kind of person." They make three pertinent suggestions: change the way you view people and events, improve your style while building on what's already there, and take a few risks.[34]

While it is always advisable to be natural, it is also wise to at least attempt to develop that which we know will be a tremendous aid to communication.

4. Let humor aid communication without calling attention to itself. Cicero said it well when he said, "Joke with good reason, not to appear jesters, but to obtain some advantage."[35] Joke telling should never be a substitute for poor research. Jacob Braude describes the shallow storyteller as "all frosting and no cake." He concludes that "this is no more desirable than his opposite counterpart who never lightens his speech or conversation with wit."[36]

Halford Luccock has an appropriate word for ministers at this point:

> The only kind of humor which, in sermons, is more than, at its best, an interruption and, at its worst, an impertinence is that which is struck off incidentally while the preacher is moving directly on his way, just as sparks are struck off by the wheels of a railroad engine while it is going to a destination. There is no stopping the train for the purpose of showing off some sparks!"[37]

5. Don't be offensive. If you offend your audience with the kind of offensive humor described in the seventh chapter, your audience will become hostile. Hostile audiences are never receptive to any ideas which you might attempt to share.

Some wonder if a minister should use humor at all in the pulpit. To be sure, in every congregation there are those present who are spiritually depressed or are dealing with some sort of emotional problem. There may be some in the congregation who, even though humor might be good for them, they are just not ready for it at that particular time. The laughter of those around such a person often reinforces his or her loneliness and pain. While others are laughing, that person may be made to feel worse by the laughter of others.

Most ministers will be sensitive to those with special needs in the congregation and will want to be very careful in how humor is used from the pulpit. However, a minister can be cautious and, at the same time, quite effective in the use of humor in communicating spiritual ideas.

6. *Don't overdo it.* Don't use long, involved stories that tend to lose your audience before you get to the punch line of your presentation. Josh Lee's suggestions for a short speech can also be applied to the need for short bits of humor.[38] He contended that some speeches are like a dog's tail—it is bound to a cur (occur). Some speeches are like a cat's tail—fur (far) to the end. But, he contended, most people like a speech that's like a rabbit's tail—a mere suggestion![39] Every speaker needs to remember that wit is the salt of the speech—not the food.

Josh Lee advised, "Never dull the keen edge of humor by covering it with verbiage."[40] Jacob Braude directed, "Use humor tastefully, knowingly, and effectively—but not indiscriminately or overwhelmingly."[41]

Of all people, the minister must be on guard for the overuse of humor. People come to church not to hear a clerical jester, but to hear a word from the Lord. Only when God's Word can be clarified and better communicated though humor should humor be used in the pulpit.

Conclusion

It would seem appropriate to conclude this chapter with an admonition from the apostle Paul in which he said, "Let your speech always be with grace, seasoned, as it were, with salt, so that you may know how you should respond to each person" (Col. 4:6). This scriptural admonition encourages us to speak from the standpoint of an inner understanding and compassion for others. When humor is used to communicate truth in the spirit of this admonition, the highest and loftiest of ideas can be better communicated.

Move now with me to our last chapter where we shall simply share some unexpected situations which produce laughter. By the way, these too are good sources for material when it's laughter you're after.

10

Laughter Where It's Least Expected

"Mr. Bonham, do you have two sons whose names are Randy and Tal David?" the lady asked rather coldly on the phone.

"Yes, I do. What's the problem?" I asked.

"Your two sons have been involved in an accident; they are on their way in an ambulance to a hospital in Florence, Kentucky," she replied.

"How badly are they hurt?" I asked.

"I don't know anything about their injuries. I'm just the dispatcher who was asked by a police officer to call and let you know about the accident," she reported. "You need to call the hospital and authorize them to treat your sons when they arrive."

Tal David, a freshman in high school, had spent his spring break with Randy, a senior at Cumberland College in Williamsburg, Kentucky. They were to meet us at a youth conference in Dayton later that evening.

It was 3:00 in the afternoon, and I hadn't even shaved or taken a shower. Faye was downstairs ironing. I decided to call the hospital before informing her of the accident. *Were they unconscious? Were there any broken bones? Would they survive?* These questions were churning through my mind as I dialed the hospital emergency room.

"Please give me the birth dates of your two sons," the nurse asked. My mind went blank!

I yelled downstairs to Faye, "What year was Randy born? What year was Tal David born?" She knew that something was wrong, and, as I hung up the phone, she was standing beside me.

"Our two sons have been in a car wreck. They are on their way in an ambulance from the scene of the accident to the hospital," I explained. We embraced and fell to our knees for prayer. Then, we began to prepare for the drive to the hospital about 100 miles away.

The nurse in the emergency room informed us by phone that they had arrived at the hospital. "Both of them were unconscious at the scene of the accident," she explained.

It was the longest two-hour drive of our lives. We stopped twice to call for an update on their condition, but no additional information was available.

I drove the car around the back of the hospital to the emergency room entrance. We jumped out and ran in to see our sons.

"You have a couple of funny kids," the nurse said at the desk. "They're cracking jokes with the doctors and nurses!" I knew now that they would be all right.

Tal David was behind a curtain over in one corner of the emergency room. Randy was lying on a bed in front of the nurse's station.

Randy was a little disoriented, but he managed a smile and the reassuring words, "I'm doing fine." He talked about the knot on his head and the scrapes and cuts all over his body caused by being thrown through a window to a dirt median. "There's enough dirt in my ear to raise a garden," he joked.

"What happened?" I asked.

"Dad," he replied, "it's like the guy who spilled a cup of water in his lap."

"What?" I asked. "And what in the world does a cup of water in your lap have to do with this accident?"

"Well," he explained, "when you spill a cup of water in your lap, people believe whatever they want to believe regardless of what you tell them."

We laughed. In the emergency room of a hospital? Yes, in a place where laughter was least expected.

Tal David didn't look quite as bad as Randy. He claimed that his back was hurting, and he proudly held up his left hand to show us four stitches in his little finger.

Faye and I rented a motel room nearby and spent the next three days as close to our sons as possible. Their recovery was speedy, and they left the hospital with no serious aftereffects.

As they were taken from the emergency room to a hospital room, there was a mix-up in room numbers. They had canceled a previous room assignment for Tal David so that he and Randy could be together in the same room.

I followed Tal David's stretcher into the elevator with a nurse's aide who was transporting him to his room. I had just learned that the hospital, less than five years old, was named "Booth Hospital" after William Booth, the founder of the Salvation Army.

"There has been a change in room assignments for Tal David," explained a nurse at the desk near the room where we were planning to take him. "He is on the next floor down," she explained.

The nurse's aide rolled him into the elevator. It was plain to see that she was quite upset about the whole situation. She indicated her displeasure by uttering some expletives under her breath. I could hardly believe my ears!

"Lady, if William Booth knew you were talking like that he would turn over in his grave," I said. "What would you think if I told you that I am a captain in the Salvation Army?"

As we moved from one floor to the other, she literally tried to blend into the back side of the elevator. Her face turned white, and she didn't say another word. As she rolled Tal David out of the elevator, I smiled and said, "I'm really not a captain in the Salvation Army. I was just kidding."

"Thank God!" she said.

After getting Tal David situated in his bed, she stayed awhile to visit. She apologized for her language, and we laughed together about the incident.

She was the best friend we had in the hospital during those days. Every time I saw her in the hallway, we laughed about our experience in the elevator, and she addressed me as "Captain." The humorous incident relieved our tension and made our hospital ordeal a little more bearable.

Defying Defeat with Laughter

The best kind of laughter is often found where it is least expected. In fact, such laughter is probably our most effective coping mechanism and the funniest of all humor.

Humor is often expressed as a certain heroic defiance in the face of life's most crushing defeats. It is often the last weapon is our arsenal with which we battle some of our greatest problems. Grady Nutt properly related seriousness and humor when he surmised in his own unique, free style:

> Humor understands ecstasy
> joy

hurrah!
bliss
giggles
because it knows pain
death
hurt
loneliness
reality.[1]

In 1983, two window washers in Philadelphia dangled thirty stories off the ground for ten minutes after their scaffold collapsed. When the ordeal was over and they were on the ground, they agreed that joking helped them cling to their safety belts until they were rescued. "You know, my mother, she's going to kill me when she finds out," said twenty-six-year-old Donald Miller.[2]

Concentration camp humor has been pointed to by many as their escape hatch from the reality of such unbelievable suffering. As Victor Frankl told of the incredible circumstances in a Nazi concentration camp, he claimed, "Humor was another of the soul's weapons in the fight for self-preservation."

Frankl contended that developing a sense of humor is a trick learned while mastering the art of living, and declared, "It is possible to practice the art of living even in a concentration camp although suffering is omnipresent."[3]

Soon after James Thurber learned that he was going blind, he overheard a young woman say, "We're not going to hide our heads in the sand like the kangaroos!"

Depressed from his recent bad news, Thurber recalled that this was "Just what my harassed understanding and tortured spirits needed! Whenever I think I hear the men coming with the stretcher or the subpoena," he fondly recalled, "I remember those kangaroos with their heads in the sand, and I am ready to face anything again."[4]

Joking About Disappointments

Abraham Lincoln and Mary Todd possessed two diametrically opposed personalities. Physically, they presented an amusing contrast. Lincoln was tall and thin while Mary was short and obese. When Lincoln looked at a full-length picture, taken of himself and his wife after their wedding, he remarked, "Well, this is the long and short of it!"

Mary Todd was the aristocrat while Abe Lincoln was the great commoner. Mary Todd was given to fits of anger, bordering on hysteria, while, on the other hand, Lincoln was endowed with the patience of Job. Mary was extremely ambitious and impatient. Even though Abe was not unambitious, he enjoyed brooding and meditating on ideas before sharing them with others.

Lincoln was aware, according to those who knew him best, of the marked difference between him and his wife. According to Carl Sandburg, Lincoln was fond of quoting a statement passed down by his father which actually summarized his philosophy of marriage: "If you make a bad bargain, hug it all the tighter."[5]

Will Rogers said more than once that the main source of his humor was the government. While we Americans enjoy the freedom of joking about our leaders, some people in other parts of the world do not enjoy that luxury.

It is said that there are certain government restrictions in East Germany regarding organized religion and encouraging the support of that country's atheistic stance.[6] Prior to the death of Russian Communist party chief Leonid Brezhnev, an East German border guard and a West

German border guard were at their checkpoints only a few feet apart.

The West German said, "It's almost time to go off duty. Thank God!"

The East German said, "It's almost time to go off duty. Thank Brezhnev!"

The West German asked, "But what will you say when Brezhnev is dead?"

The East German answered, "Thank God!"

Many have learned to poke fun at their handicaps. Jimmy Durante was known far and wide for his big nose. Through laughter, he not only capitalized on his nose, but he shared his philosophy for dealing with life's problems.

Durante asserted that as long as you can laugh, you are safe from the world and safe from yourself. "All of us have schnozzles—are ridiculous in one way or another," he claimed, "if not in our faces, then in our characters, minds, or habits. When we admit our schnozzles," he continued, "instead of defending them, we begin to laugh, and the world laughs with us."[7]

Barbra Streisand, also noted for her schnozzle, once said to an audience, "If I'd known you were planning to seat people on both sides of me, I'd have had my nose fixed."[8]

Giggling at Our Adversities

Are we really ready to laugh in the midst of our most adverse circumstances? Ed Hower claimed, "If you don't learn to laugh at trouble, you won't have anything to laugh at when you're old."[9]

Bob Hope asserted that laughter has a constructive power. "I have seen what a laugh can do," he claims. "It can transform almost unbearable tears into something bearable, even hopeful."[10]

Thomas Higginson pointed out that, "There is no defense against adverse fortune which is so effectual as an habitual sense of humor."[11] Some have even claimed that the next best thing to solving a problem is finding some humor in it.

While going through our adversity, nothing ever seems funny. But, as Steve Allen says, "Tragedy plus time equals comedy."[12]

Bryon Arledge, chaplain of a juvenile court in Akron, Ohio, has shared in his book *Laugh with Your Teenager* how he has used humor in counseling many youths and families in crisis. He called for parents to "make 'em smile!" "We do not have to go to clown school or imitate Bob Hope," he contended. "We must, however try to bring a relaxed atmosphere into our homes."[13]

Arledge has been so bold as to use humor in dealing with young suicide victims. He shared the following interesting story:

> I had been counseling for the Protestant Youth Counseling Service only a few months when a young woman client came to say, "Good-bye, and thanks for the four sessions." She was carrying an empty bottle as proof she would be dead in a few minutes.
>
> I urged her to voluntarily have her stomach pumped. She said she would run if I called an ambulance. She only wanted to talk.
>
> I quickly began telling her of the unsearchable riches of Christ, and that God loved her. But she would not listen to either a religious or a psychological approach.
>
> Since she was an obese girl and I knew she enjoyed humor, I said, "I feel sorry for your pallbearers. They will all get hernias."
>
> I got her attention!
>
> "Besides," I continued, "all your chins are going to look

funny while you lie in the casket." I suggested she reduce before suicide.

She began to think.

I asked her about her family.

"I hate 'em all," she snapped.

I told her I did not think it was fair not to express this to them.

I asked about her little boy.

She said she loved him very much.

I did not think it was fair for her to leave him, but she was sure he would be better off without her. I advised that she knit him a beautiful afghan to express her love.

It worked! She went to the hospital and had her stomach pumped.

There we made a simple plan. She was to complete the following: (1) lose two pounds, (2) tell her mother she hated her, (3) recite her husband's faults to him, (4) knit the afghan for her son, and (5) read the Gospel of John.

I told her I would pray that something would happen to change her life.

Releasing her bottled-up feelings to her husband brought so much satisfaction that she started to go see her mother to do the same. However, as she was running to her car, she slipped and fell on a patch of ice, breaking her arm.

After she had finished screaming, my response was, "Maybe all things do work together for good."

Eventually she completed the first plan and several others as well, and suicidal symptoms receded after her success.[14]

The matter of suicide has also been treated with a sense of humor by poet Dorothy Parker:

> Razors pain you;
> Rivers are damp;
> Acids stain you;
> And drugs cause cramp.

Guns aren't lawful;
Nooses give;
Gas smells awful—
You might as well live.[15]

Taking Laughter to Church

In religious circles, humor has historically received a bad rap. In the early centuries, Christian leaders faced the "eat, drink-and-be-merry" philosophy of the Greco-Roman world. It is understandable that their warfare with hedonism may have affected their theological attitude toward humor.[16] Our running battle with secular humanism may also affect our sense of humor in the twentieth century.

Ambrose cautioned the ministers under his charge to avoid joking "even in small talk, so that some more serious topic is not made light of." He maintained that "not only loose jokes, but jokes of any kind must be avoided."

Augustine concluded that "The pleasures of the table, of playing and joking, break down manly dignity and seriousness."

The archives of homiletics reveal that the Puritans not only failed to joke when they preached, but they preached against jokes. Some even accused them of altering the lines of the one hundredth Psalm in the Geneva Psalter from "Him serve with mirth, His praise forthtell," to "Him serve with fear, His praise forthtell."[17]

For many people, the church is the last place on earth to experience joy. One of my favorite theologians writes a daily column for many of our newspapers. Her name is Erma Bombeck. A few years ago, she told the following story:

In church the other Sunday I was intent on a small child

who was turning around smiling at everyone. He wasn't gurgling, spitting, humming, kicking, tearing the hymnals, or rummaging through his mother's handbag. He was just smiling. Finally, his mother jerked him about and in a stage whisper that could be heard in a little theater off Broadway said, "Stop that grinning! You're in church!" With that, she gave him a belt and as the tears rolled down his cheeks, added, "That's better," and returned to her prayers.

Erma Bombeck continued with some piercing observations:

> We sing, "Make a joyful noise unto the Lord" while our faces reflect the sadness of one who has just buried a rich aunt who left everything to her pregnant hamster. We chant, "If I [sic] have not charity, I am become as sounding brass, or a tinkling cymbal." Translated in the parking lot it comes out, "And the same to you, fella!"
>
> Suddenly, I was angry. It occurred to me the entire world is in tears, and if you're not, then you'd better get with it. I wanted to grab this child with the tear-stained face close to me and tell him about my God. The happy God. The smiling God. The God who had to have a sense of humor to have created the likes of us. I wanted to tell him He is an understanding God. One who understands little children who pick their noses in church because they are bored. He understands the man in the parking lot who reads the comics while his wife is attending church. He even understands my shallow prayers that implore, "If You can't make me thin, then make my friends look fat."

It was interesting to see how Erma Bombeck concluded her column with a few words about laughter at church:

I wanted to tell him I've taken a few lumps in my time for daring to smile at religion. By tradition, one wears faith with the solemnity of a mourner, the gravity of a mask of tragedy, and the dedication of a Rotary badge.

What a fool, I thought. Here was a woman sitting next to the only light left in our civilization—the only hope, our only miracle—our only promise of infinity. If he couldn't smile in church, where was there left to go?[18]

If you think there is no humor at church, just pick up the church bulletin sometime and read the announcements. These funny errors were found in orders of worship:

"O, Rest in the Lard"

"Blest Be the Tie that Blinds"

Anthem—"Jesus, Grant Me This I Pray"
Sermon—"Money! Money! Money!"

Sermon—"Gossip"
Invitation Hymn—"I Love to Tell the Story"

The following announcements have been made on lighted churchyard bulletin boards:

No Healing Service Sunday Due to Our Pastor's Illness

Sermon—"How Much Should a Christian Drink?"
Music By a Full Choir

Sermon—"Do You Want to Know What Hell Is Like?"
Come in and Hear Our Choir!

The following announcements have appeared in church bulletins:

Not everyone who enters this church has been converted, so please watch your handbags and wallets.

Ladies, don't forget the rummage sale. It is a good chance to get rid of those things not worth keeping around the house. Bring your husbands.

Next Sunday, Mrs. G. C. is the soloist in the morning service. The pastor will speak on "It's a Terrible Experience."

This afternoon there will be a meeting in the north and south ends of the church. Children will be baptized at both ends.

The Ministry of Mirth

If you think the ministry is dull, you haven't been going to church where I've been the last thirty-five years. One young preacher in Texas preached on Samson and called him Tarzan throughout the entire sermon!

Another pastor came to the time during prayer meeting when he asked all who had special prayer requests to raise their hands. His mind must have been on the previous business meeting when he said, "All those opposed by the same sign."

A pastor in California was preaching in a revival where there were few visible results. Finally, after several verses of an invitation hymn, a young man started forward.

"And a little child shall lead them!" exclaimed the excited evangelist. The boy walked toward the pastor, turned to the left, and walked into the hall on his way to the bathroom!

A Baptist congregation in Florida loaned its baptistry to a neighboring Methodist congregation for the purpose of baptizing a new convert who requested immersion.

The host pastor arrived at the afternoon baptismal service just in time to see the young Methodist pastor standing outside the baptistry on the arms of choir chairs reaching over the baptistry to lower the candidate into the water. The candidate for baptism was wearing the baptismal boots and robe usually worn by the pastor.

Two women were sitting together in the church services one Sunday morning. One, recently widowed, became upset during the service and left. Her friend, obviously wanting to minister to her, got up to leave, stepped in the aisle, and fell down. She got up, started again, and fell again! She got up, started a third time, and fell again!

That afternoon as soon as the pastor arrived home, he called the husband of the staggering parishioner to inquire of her problem.

Her husband announced, "Her foot went to sleep!"

The pastor asserted, "I accept no responsibility for putting anyone to sleep below the waist!"

One minister of education prayed, "Oh Lord, make us more offensive . . . er—what I mean, Lord, is put us on the offensive!"

One pastor introduced his new music director to the congregation on Sunday with the words, "We are delighted he is coming to lead us in our sinning!"

A large denominational gathering in the Midwest a few years ago heard a keynote speaker begin his message, "Puke and weany men that we are . . . I mean, weak and puny men . . ."

At a testimony meeting on the campus of a Christian college, a tearful freshman concluded his personal testimony with a memorable request: "Please pray I'll not be found sleeping with the five foolish virgins when Jesus comes," he sobbed. They say that at every homecoming since, several recall that choice moment of laughter.

Several thousand people were present at a Seventh-day Adventist conference in Oregon several years ago where

Elder Belleau (pronounced "Bellow") was slated to offer the morning prayer.

A nervous ministerial intern, whose only responsibility for the occasion was to introduce this church leader, got up before the crowd and solemnly announced, "Elder Pray will now bellow!"[19]

Even Billy Graham has not escaped an occasional slip of the tongue. No one will ever let Graham forget that in Atlanta, Georgia, while preaching to a Youth for Christ rally back in 1944, he roared, "David slew Goliath, and then he turned around and killed him!"

One of Graham's most embarrassing moments occurred before thirty thousand people in Memphis, Tennessee. The police chief had asked him to help promote a traffic safety campaign.

Graham pointed to a neon sign behind the platform which said, "150 days." He dramatically singled out the sign and announced, "You see this sign back here? That 150 days?"

When all eyes were focused on the sign, Graham explained, "That means that there has been 150 days without a *fertility*."

Grady Wilson reported, "There was soon a swelling tide of laughter. Dr. Robert G. Lee, world-renowned clergyman, almost fell off the platform in hysterics."[20]

Cliff Barrows, the music director for the Billy Graham Evangelistic Association, cupped his hands and in a stage whisper said to Graham, "Fatality!"

Beware of Frowning Theologians

And who can forget some of the embarrassing circumstances in which pastors often find themselves? My favorite stories are usually related to young pastors and those first pastorates. Some of these are passed from generation to generation, and the characters remain nameless. Here is one of the funniest I have heard:

The young pastor was on two "honeymoons." He had just married, and he and his new bride had moved to their first pastorate. Their first home was the parsonage located next door to the church building.

The deacons announced, "Pastor, on your first Sunday night as our pastor we have planned to have the Lord's Supper." It was his responsibility to prepare the elements for the Lord's Supper service. So on Sunday afternoon, he and his wife poured the grape juice into the little cups and prepared the unleavened bread for what would be his first experience of administering the Lord's Supper.

It was an unusually large crowd that night. As the deacons served the juice, the young pastor stood reverently at the front of the church observing the congregation. Suddenly, it occurred to him that the crowd was larger than the number of juice containers.

He leaned over the front row and whispered to his wife, "We are going to run out of grape juice!"

"What do you want me to do?" asked his anxious bride.

"Run next door to the parsonage and get that bottle of grape juice out of the refrigerator. If you run fast enough, you can be back here by the time the deacons get back down the aisle."

The pastor's wife bolted out the side door of the church into the kitchen of the parsonage next door. She didn't bother to switch on the lights. She rushed to the refrigerator, reached in, and got what she thought was a bottle of grape juice. But it was not a bottle of grape juice. It was a bottle of green persimmon juice!

In the midst of the emergency, neither she nor her husband bothered to read the label. Frantically, she handed the bottle to her young husband/pastor. He uncapped it and poured its contents into the small juice containers for himself and the deacons.

It was like clockwork! Just as he had finished filling the cups for himself and the deacons, the deacons were reverently marching down the aisle with empty trays after having served the congregation.

The pastor picked up the tray of juice glasses and slowly served his deacons. Then, he led the whole congregation in drinking the juice.

Suddenly strange things began to happen. The young pastor's lips began to pucker. He knew he was in trouble.

"Deacon Jones," he wheezed, "will you please lead us in the closing prayer?"

Deacon Jones was having his own problems with the persimmon juice. He smacked his lips and barely managed to say, "Pastor, please excuse me!"

The pastor surveyed the situation and called on Deacon Smith to lead in the closing prayer. Deacon Smith made some funny noises through his puckered lips and begged to be excused from leading the closing prayer.

The young pastor turned to the bewildered congregation, motioned for them to stand, and said, "Well, friends, let's all stand, whistle the Doxology, and go home!"[21]

And why shouldn't we laugh in church? Laughter and praise are closely related. With the command to be filled with the Spirit is the command for joyful praise (Eph. 5:18-20). Contemplation of God's salvation, His goodness to us in the past, and His prospects for us in the future, may even lead us to burst out with joyful laughter.

The psalmist encourages us to "shout for joy," "Be glad," "Sing," "Bless the Lord," "Rejoice," "Oh give thanks to the Lord," "O clap your hands," "Sing praises," and "Make a joyful noise unto God" (KJV).

Even though laughter is often least expected at church, it should be considered a gift to the church to be encouraged instead of suppressed. Martin Clark even suggested, "Every parish should have a humor committee."[22]

Conrad Hyers claimed, "Humor apart from holiness may be irresponsible; but holiness apart from humor is inhuman."[23] I agree with Bernard Ramm when he cautioned us to "Beware of theologians without a sense of humor!"[24]

Laughing at Death

Death is probably the least humorous situation known to us. We try to put it off as long as possible. I heard Red Skelton describe a woman who had so many face lifts that there was no skin on the bottom of her feet. "Her skin was so tight that her mouth came open when she sat down," he claimed. She is probably typical of most of us as we try to slow down or cover up the aging process.

When death finally comes, we often camouflage it. When we view a dead friend at a funeral we often say, "Doesn't he look natural?" Why don't we just say, "Doesn't he look dead?"

I like the way Catholic priest James G. O'Malley faced the possibility of death when he was informed that cancer would allow him to live only about six more weeks. He decided to arrange his own funeral service and to share it with his friends and family.

O'Malley, who had already undergone five operations for cancer, sent letters and telegrams to his friends and family saying, "You are cordially invited to the wake of Rev. James G. O'Malley at Philadelphia Naval Hospital."[25]

The "corpse" had a marvelous time at his wake. He shook hands with his friends, hugged and kissed their wives, shared humorous stories, and insisted that his friends follow the tradition of making speeches praising him. Among those present was his surprised doctor.

O'Malley laughed throughout the entire wake and said good-bye to each of his friends with a big smile on his face.

That was back in 1972 when O'Malley was an air force chaplain. Now, over sixty years of age, he is still laughing and claims that the eleventh commandment is, "Thou shalt laugh."

The healing process was long and painful, but O'Malley claimed, "I feel very sure that it was a sense of humor, as well as praying, which helped me beat this rap."

Others have tried to lighten the blow of death with humorous comments.[26] Pancho Villa's last words were, "Don't let it end like this. Tell them I said something."

When "Professor Backwards," a comic whose speciality was pronouncing words and sentences in reverse, died as a result of a mugging, comedian Chevy Chase reported of the incident, "Passersby ignored Professor Backwards' cries of 'Pleh! Pleh!' "

"I'm not afraid to die," Woody Allen once quipped. "I just don't want to be there when it happens."

Epitaphs on tombstones have caused many to laugh at death in the cemetery. Here are three choice epitaphs from some old New England tombstones:[27]

> In memory of
> Beza Wood
> Departed this life
> Nov. 2, 1837
> Aged 45 yrs.
> Here lies one Wood
> Enclosed in wood
> One wood
> Within another.
> the outer wood
> Is very good:
> We cannot praise
> The other.

Sacred to the Memory of Mr. Jared Bates
who Died Aug. the 6th 1800.
His Widow Aged 24 who mourns as one
who can be comforted lives at 7 Elm Street
this village and possesses every qualification
for a Good Wife.

Here lies as silent clay
Miss Arabella Young
Who on the 21st of May 1771
Began to hold her tongue.

In Montgomery, Alabama, the following words appear
on a tombstone:

Under the clover and under the trees;
Here lies the body of Jonathan Pease.
Pease ain't here, only the pod,
Pease shelled out and went home to God.

From the old West come these memorable lines:

Here lies Les Moore.
Six shots from a forty-four
No Les. No More.

On a more serious level, Benjamin Franklin's epitaph is
often quoted even to this day at many funerals.

The body of Benjamin Franklin, Printer,
Like the covering of an old book, its contents
    torn out and stripped of its lettering and
    gilding, lies here, food for worms;
But the work shall not be lost, it will
    (as he believed) appear once more, in a new
    and more elegant edition, revised and
    corrected by the Author.

But what fun when one can have such an epitaph, though not written on a tombstone, as the apostle Paul when he said, "I have fought the good fight, I have finished the course, I have kept the faith" (2 Tim. 4:7).

Why the Reaper Is Grim

The Bible certainly makes no effort to camouflage death. The apostle Paul said,

> For this perishable must put on the imperishable, and this mortal must put on immortality. But when this perishable will have put on the imperishable, and this mortal will have put on immortality, then will come about the saying that is written, 'Death is swallowed up in victory?' " (1 Cor. 15:53-54).

An understanding of the biblical view of death will allow anyone to laugh at our most feared enemy. According to the Bible, death is the cessation of life as we know it and a change from one kind of existence to another.

According to the biblical account of creation, life itself is a gift from God: "Then the Lord God formed man of dust from the ground, and breathed into his nostrils the breath of life; and man became a living being" (Gen. 2:7). The psalmist added, "For with Thee is the fountain of life;/In Thy light we see light" (Ps. 36:9).

The living of our lives is dependent on God's earthly provisions. Then this life that has been given by God returns to God at death: "Then the dust will return to the earth as it was, and the spirit will return to God who gave it" (Eccl. 12:7).

Death is intimately related to sin: "Therefore, just as through one man sin entered into the world, and death through sin, and so death spread to all men, because all sinned" (Rom. 5:12). In fact, the eternal existence of those who die without making peace with God is called "the second death" (Rev. 20:14-15).

With the coming of Christ, even the concept of death is made new. When Jesus arrived at the home of Jairus whose daughter had died, He said, "Why make a commotion and weep? The child has not died, but is asleep" (Mark 5:39).

When He learned of the death of His good friend Lazarus, Jesus said, "Our friend Lazarus has fallen asleep" (John 11:11). In Christ, therefore, death brings peace and rest rather than fear.

Jesus also said, "Everyone who lives and believes in Me shall never die" (John 11:26). Paul asserted that Jesus Christ "abolished death, and brought life and immortality to light through the gospel" (2 Tim. 1:10). This is why Christians can claim the promise, "Blessed are the dead who die in the Lord" (Rev. 14:13).

Nelvin Vos concluded that laughter in the face of death is possible because God always has and always will have the last laugh.

> Once in Eden and later on Golgotha, the demons thought they had made the whole plight of man one of never-ending seriousness. The monster death was allowed to close its jaws, and then, suddenly, it burst asunder, teeth, jaws, and all, with a party-balloon bang.
>
> To witness that man can be free from sin, the devil, and the world, what could be more appropriate than to laugh —to laugh, for God's sake?[28]

Conrad Hyers echoed some of the same sentiments when he said, "The first and last word belong to God and therefore not to death but life, not to sorrow but joy, not to weeping but laughter. For surely it is God who has the last laugh."[29]

Tom Mullen said, "The reaper is grim because the joke is on him."[30] Why shouldn't we be able to laugh at death? In spite of the grief related to it, death itself is not final for those who have placed their trust in Christ. Tom Mullen concluded, "Fortunately, the Christian faith says the graveyard is not the last stop. Thus, we are free to enjoy funny things that happen along the way."[31]

Conclusion

It has been my contention throughout this book that a mirthless spirit is a distortion of our basic humanity. We were created in the image of God. Even as children, we did not have to learn to laugh, but when not to laugh.

A mirthless spirit is a contradiction of Christian theology often based on a misunderstanding or denial of the Scriptures. We have been created in the image of God. Therefore, we have the capacity for laughter. As Christians we have been recreated in the image of God through Jesus Christ—the Christ who laughed, enjoyed laughter, and taught us the secret of real happiness.

Wholesome laughter relates to the hereafter. If you have acquired peace with God and are ready to die, you have every reason to laugh.

Let the theological killjoys and the philosophical sadsacks who discourage humor and laughter once and for all bow down at the feet of Jehovah God, who not only loves but also laughs!

There is a tablet in an English cathedral which contains an unusual prayer with which I would like to end our journey together:

Give me a good digestion, Lord,
    And also something to digest.
Give me a healthy body, Lord,

And the sense to keep it at its best.

Give me a healthy mind, Lord,
  To keep the good and pure in sight.
Which seeing sin, is not appalled,
  But finds a way to set it right:

Give me a mind that is not bored,
  That does not whimper, whine, or sigh.
Don't let me worry over much
  About that fussy thing called "I."

Give me a sense of humor, Lord,
  Give me the grace to see a joke,
To get some happiness from life
  And pass it on to other folk.

For everything there is a season,
  So spoke the ancient author.
He has made everything beautiful in its time
  And put eternity in our hearts.[32]

Quotable Quotations

Subject Index

Adversity and Defeat: Humor's Targets

"Humor is the sense of the absurd which is despair refusing to take itself seriously."—Arland Ussher[1]

"It is a sort of survival quality that came down with us through the ages that we must take adversity with a smile or a joke."—Stephen Leacock[2]

"There are two insults which no human will endure: the assertion that he hasn't a sense of humor; and the doubly impertinent assertion that he has never known trouble."
—Sinclair Lewis[3]

"If you can use humor to distance yourself momentarily from your problems, it can sometimes be enormously healing."
—Esther Blumenfeld and Lynne Alpern[4]

"Comedy is an escape, not from truth but from despair: a narrow escape into faith."—Christopher Fry[5]

"Nothing, no experience good or bad, no belief, no cause is in itself momentous enough to monopolize the whole of life to the exclusion of laughter."—Alfred North Whitehead[6]

"Laughter and the awareness of humor become doubly important when individuals are in abnormal, non-humorous situations."
—Herman Ryber[7]

"Being able to laugh at the frustrations and painful things in life means we are on our way to overcoming them."
—Esther Blumenfeld and Lynne Alpern[8]

"The saving grace of humor, then, is not only an ability to laugh, but (most savingly, most gracefully) an ability to laugh at ourselves. It involves a willingness to be cut down to size and emerge liberated rather than devastated by the experience."—Robert McAfee Brown[9]

"Laughter is more contagious than tears."—Anonymous[10]

"Laugh and the world laughs with you; cry and you simply get wet!"—Anonymous[11]

"The human race has only one really effective weapon, and that is laughter."—Mark Twain[12]

"Laugh, and the world laughs with you;
    Weep, and you weep alone,
For the sad old earth must borrow its mirth,
    But has trouble enough of its own."
—Ella Wheeler Wilcox[13]

"I think the next best thing to solving a problem is finding some humor in it."—Frank A. Clark[14]

"It is well known that humor, more than anything in the human makeup, can afford an aloofness and an ability to rise above any situation, even if only for a few seconds."
—Victor Frankl[15]

"Humortality is overcoming enough pain, embarrassment, stupidity to begin to say 'I did that dumb thing before and lived!' "—Grady Nutt[16]

"Down through the ages, what have most jokes been about? Unpaid bills, bad taste, pomposity, drunks, taxes, going to the bathroom, sexual inadequacy, stinginess and stupidity. Not to mention mothers-in-law, corpses, politicians, and tramps. These matters have to do with unpleas-

antness, yet they are the stuff of which jokes are made."
—Tom Mullen[17]

"Humor is blended with pathos until the two are one and represent, as they have in every age, the mingling heritage of tears and laughter that is our lot on earth."—Carlo Bos[18]

"Against the assault of humor, nothing can stand."—Mark Twain[19]

"Tragedy plus time can lead to humor. Tragedy without enough time or distance can produce refined cruelty."
—Tom Mullen[20]

Anxiety and Stress— Humor's Power to Relieve Tension

"One of the most remarkable characteristics of humor is the capacity to enjoy the messiness of existence, and to laugh relative to the very things that otherwise frustrate and dismay us."—Conrad Hyers[21]

"Humor, unlike most techniques for relaxing, can be applied at the moment of discomfort, wherever problems arise."—Esther Blumenfeld and Lynne Alpern[22]

"A sense of humor will help the minister and missionary more than any psychiatric therapy, for it palliates disappointments and alleviates tensions."—Paul King Jewett[23]

"Joking in the middle of suffering indicates neither masochism on the part of the sufferer nor sadism on the part of others."
—Tom Mullen[24]

"If you can once make a funny connection with a particularly stressful situation, then the next time you encounter a similar situation, you will be able to recall the humorous reaction and become an instrument to ease the stress not only for yourself but for those around you."—Esther Blumenfeld and Lynne Alpern[25]

"At a time in which anxiety forms the subject of so many publications . . . it is a good thing when the gospel of good humor, founded on detachment, is also preached."—Jean Leclercq[26]

"Humor can liven up your conversations, allow you to communicate more freely, help illustrate points you want to make. It can help release tension in yourself and others —tension that, if not dissipated, could seriously damage relationships."—Rusty and Linda Wright[27]

"There are alternative ways to deal positively with stress. Some people meditate, others exercise. The immediacy of humor, however, gives it a decided advantage as a stress reliever."—Esther Blumenfeld and Lynne Alpern[28]

"It is very hard to sustain humor, or the desire for humor, in a period when we seem to be trying, on the one hand, to invent a pill or a miracle drug that will cure us of everything, and on the other hand to invent machines for instant annihilation!"—James Thurber[29]

"Like anger, humor can release some of your frustration and give you momentary relief. But unlike anger, humor will relax you, ease the tension, and consequently help open new doors to creative solutions."—Esther Blumenfeld and Lynne Alpern[30]

"When the daily hassle has drained you of energy, take a few minutes out to sit back and savor one or two of these happy times or funny situations again."—Emily Hardy[31]

"Because hostility is at the root of humorous put-downs, getting caught in a cycle of one-downmanship is stress-producing and creates a tense atmosphere."—Esther Blumenfeld and Lynne Alpern[32]

"We should not be surprised that the hectic, stressful pace of life today makes it difficult for people to pay attention to the preacher. People aren't relaxed enough to give their full attention."—John W. Drakeford[33]

Bible—Its Humorous Content

"Our use of Scripture, whether in catechesis or for our own pleasure, should be a time of joy and laughter."
—Eugene J. Fisher[34]

"Humor is of the essence of life, and some of the supposed irrelevance of the Christian message may be charged up to failure to appreciate the biblical perspective of humor and laughter."—Frederick W. Danker[35]

"We have tended to separate out seriousness as sacred and laughter as profane, and in that way to flatten out the uses of language and the meaning of words in biblical literature. But it is easy to miss some punchlines that way, particularly if you don't believe there are any to begin with."—Conrad Hyers[36]

"Without the capacity to laugh, the Bible is cut off from the human condition. Without humor there is no irony, without irony no tragedy. Without tragedy, there is no Good News."
—Eugene J. Fisher[37]

"The gospel is about the unexpected and the unforeseeable which reverse the patterns of things known to be true, and therefore the gospel evokes hilarity and Sarah laughs."
—Frederick Buechner[38]

"There are also those who, on hearing the words *humor*

and *comedy* associated with the Bible, suppose that the intent is to make fun of the Bible. If anything, it is the other way around. The Bible pokes fun at human pride and pretension, selfishness and greed, and the myriad other sins to which flesh and spirit are heir."—Conrad Hyers[39]

Christ, the Humorist—The Smiling Messiah

"Because Jesus has overcome the world, because he will carry us through death, because he can heal grief, we are free to be his children and laugh at princes, kings and ourselves."—Herb Barks[40]

"Everyone who draws near to Jesus seems to acquire something of his humor."—Henri Cormier[41]

"If so many health professionals from so many different disciplines are using humor in their practices, surely Jesus Christ, the Great Physician, the greatest psychiatrist of all time, the healer of healers, must have used humor in his healing ministry."—Cal Samra[42]

"Would it be treading on too holy ground to say that perhaps the reason there is so little space for a clown in the world, or in the church, is the same reason there is so little space for a Christ?"—Larry M. Taylor[43]

"He [Jesus] makes the most sense to me, the most profound impact on me, when I envision him as Will Rogers in sandals . . . or as Andy Griffith being patient with the first-century Barney Fife, . . . Simon Peter."—Grady Nutt[44]

"Jesus never told anyone to lie down on the analyst's couch. . . . When Jesus finds a person lying on his bed or stretcher, he usually tells him to get up."—Henri Cormier[45]

"Christ came to us bringing peace, love, joy, laughter and healing. And when he returns again, he will lead his disciples in a chorus of laughter, because, as the old saying goes, the Devil can't stand the sound of laughter."—Cal Samra[46]

"How could Jesus have managed to attract children, women, simple people, if he was always aloof and serious?"—Jean Leclercq[49]

"Jesus had little to leave his disciples. Even his clothes would soon be divided among those who crucified him. Peace was one thing that could not be taken from him."
—T.B. Maston[48]

"Humor is as divine as pathos, and I cannot study the life of Jesus without finding humor there."—G. Campbell Morgan[49]

"The Pharisees were dignified. They would have put any ecumenical convocation to shame. Contradict me if I'm wrong, but I simply cannot read ministerial dignity into the Lord Jesus."—Joe Johnson[50]

"Believe me, Jesus Christ was a joy-filled person. He had problems, but He knew how to handle them creatively and constructively."—Robert Schuller[51]

"The main reason we miss Jesus' humor is the fact that we worship him, and that is usually serious business."
—Larry M. Taylor[52]

"To recognize and interpret laugh-provoking factors in Jesus' message, it is necessary both to adopt first-century viewpoints and deliberately look for elements that enter into humor."
—Gary Webster[53]

"We must take seriously the fact that Jesus did make jokes."
—Humphrey Palmer[54]

"What Christian cannot but 'shout with joy' concerning the Christ?"—Joseph K. Neumann[55]

"The Christian life begins with our union with Christ, it continues and develops in the consciousness of fellowship with and in him, it ends with the anticipation of life with him in the ages to come. How glorious to be in Christ and for him to be in us!"—T.B. Maston[56]

"Better it were that we should be clowns for Christ than to be the devil's fools."—Delos Miles[57]

"Be of good cheer; laugh! Beyond the clinging doubt and beyond the unruly deed—God. Has He not 'found' us in Jesus Christ? So that door is always open—into laughter."
—George A. Buttrick[58]

"Since religion was so much a part of my life as a child, and since my childhood was so happy and so full of laughter and joy, I associate the two. Even my concept of Jesus goes along with this association of happiness and religion."
—Minnie Pearl[59]

"As much as we may enjoy our humor, we will all ultimately come to the place where laughter will be temporarily laid aside, and we will take the shoes off our feet with the realization that the ground upon which we stand is holy. Then we will move on to join with the heavenly hosts in the heavenly laughter that comes when a prodigal returns home to the Father: 'It was meet that we should make merry and be glad, for this thy brother was dead, and is alive again, was lost and is found.' "
—John W. Drakeford[60]

Clowns: Humor in Uniform

"Humor, as such, overcomes the world only so long as the clown and the fool use their insight into the tragi-comedy of life to assert their humanity-in-weakness, kicking and being kicked, falling and rising to fall again, continuing in the narrow space that allows laughter not to dissolve into tears too bitter for laughter."—Robert Thomas Haverluck[61]

"A clown is a poet in action. . . . It's the same story over and over again—adoration, devotion, crucifixion." —Henry Miller[62]

"The clown reminds . . . a person that in all life, including theological life, he or she is fallible and errant, and at times tragically stupid and at other times comically stupid."— Bernard Ramm[63]

"Our recognition and acceptance of the fool or clown that we really are puts us in touch with the truth about ourselves, stripping from ourselves the many masks we wear, the false pride and pretensions; at the same time it places a high value on the dignity of personhood."—Marie-Celeste[64]

"In every epoch of history those who have had something to say but could not say it without peril have eagerly assumed a fool's cap. The audience at whom their forbidden speech was aimed tolerated it more easily if they could at the same time laugh and flatter themselves with the reflection that the unwelcome words were clearly nonsensical." —Sigmund Freud[65]

"If, as Jesus and Paul said, joy is a gift of the Spirit, the daughters of joy—humor, clowning and laughter—also must be gifts of the Spirit."—Cal Samra[66]

"I would thus argue that humor, like childhood and play, can be seen as an ultimately religious vindication of joy .... The gestures of the clown have a sacramental dignity."—Peter Berger[67]

Death and Aging: How Humor Helps

"We all came into the world crying while everyone else was laughing. By Joe I mean to go out laughing, let others do the crying."—Count Felix von Luckner[68]

"Laughter in, around, or in spite of grief is an affirmation that death itself is not final."—Tom Mullen[69]

"If people are too grouchy too long, they don't get old. They die."—Anonymous[70]

"One way of handling death is to laugh in the face of it. It is a reminder to (people) that they are still alive. It's something like children playing hide-and-seek in the graveyard pretending that they weren't afraid."—Bruce Jones[71]

"I'm not afraid to die. I just don't want to be there when it happens."—Woody Allen[72]

"Life does not cease to be funny when people die, any more than it ceases to be serious when people laugh." —George Bernard Shaw[73]

"Serenely greet the journey's end, as an olive falls when it is ripe, blessing the branch that bare it and giving thanks to the tree which gave it life."—Marcus Aurelius[74]

"If you live right, death is a joke to you, so far as fear is concerned."—Will Rogers[75]

"I am ready to meet my Maker. Whether my Maker is prepared for the ordeal of meeting me is another matter." —Winston Churchill[76]

"If we can laugh in the face of death, then we certainly can enjoy funny things on the way to the cemetary."—Tom Mullen[77]

"Those who know God is with them even in death also know that death itself is not to be taken too seriously."
—George Bernard Shaw[78]

"It is not too far-fetched . . . laughter is related in several ways to longevity—mainly through the reduction of stress and hypertension."—Jeffrey Goldstein[79]

"A doctor acquaintance of mine whose specialty is geriatric medicine has concluded that one thing which almost all his very healthy elderly patients seemed to have in common is a good sense of humor."—Raymond A. Moody[80]

Easter: the Ultimate Put-down

"The life of the Christian is not lived in the time of Good Friday and Crucifixion, but in the time of Easter and Pentecost."—Conrad Hyers[81]

"Christian faith, just because it strives for clear perception, cannot look at Don Quixote through the eyes of Sancho Panza. The windmills of the Quixote attack are the battlements of the New Jerusalem, as yet dimly seen on the horizon. But it is toward this horizon that the human caravan is moving. Don Quixote rides toward the dawn of Easter morning."—Peter L. Berger[82]

"He was for us both a Victor and a Victim—a Victor because a Victim."—Augustine[83]

"The crucifiers meant to put an end to the visible activities of a rabble-rousing rabbi, and succeeded in inaugurating a new age in which all certainties are transvalued to the background music of divine laughter."—Chad Walsh[84]

"In the midst of the awful is the absurd; in the process of frenzy there is boisterous laughter. Man causes Good Friday; then, God responds with Easter."—Grady Nutt[85]

"The traditional association of comedy with spring rites, and of resurrection hope with Easter, confirms the connection between humor and hope."—Conrad Hyers[86]

Emotional Health: Humor's Coping Power

"Jesus comforted the afflicted and afflicted the comfortable. Some preachers and mental health professionals these days have been comforting the comfortable and afflicting the afflicted."
—Cal Samra[87]

"A hearty laugh gives one a dry cleaning, while a good cry is a wet wash."—Puzant Kevork Thomajan[88]

"There are reports, both in the professional literature and in the context of anecdote and folk belief, of persons who have been cured, or at least eased, in numerous medical and/or psychological conditions, by the use of laughter and humor."
—Raymond A. Moody[89]

"This world is a comedy to those who think, a tragedy to those who feel."—Horace Walpole[90]

"Humor has always stood out as a unique and puzzling psychological phenomenon, and the scant attention it has received from psychologists does them little credit."
—Paul McGhee and Jeffrey Goldstein[91]

"What we laugh at is a window to our minds."—Paul King Jewett[92]

"Sometimes youth seek to use emotional symptoms as a way of running from pain. The ultimate end of running away is, of course, suicide. Even in these extreme cases, the theology of God's presence on earth and the theology of hope can bring healing."—Byron W. Arledge[93]

"Laughter is such a marvelous tool to help us hang loose."—Ken Olson[94]

"A sense of humor often seems to be the best sense of all."—Anonymous[95]

"The effect of laughter upon the mind not only brings relaxation with it, so far as mental tension is concerned, but makes it also less prone to dreads and less solicitous about the future. This favorable effect on the mind influences various functions of the body and makes them healthier than would otherwise be the case."—James J. Walsh[96]

"Humor can unmask human pretension, and it can also mask it more effectively. It is able to reach out in friendly embrace, and lash out in animosity and distain."—Conrad Hyers[97]

"Laughter thus is not a mask which hides us from ourselves and others and even from God, but a means toward self-discovery."—Nelvin Vos[98]

"In my opinion, deviations in laughter and the sense of humor play a very profound role in mental illnesses, and the understanding of humor and laughter play a correspondingly significant role in understanding patients with mental illnesses."—Raymond A. Moody[99]

"The ability to laugh is a measure of man's adjustment to his environment."—Jacob Levine[100]

"Something special happens when people laugh together over something genuinely funny, and not hurtful to anyone. It's like a magic rain that showers down feelings of

comfort, safety and belonging to a group."—Mary Jane
Belfie[101]

"While disease is not all psychosomatic, I feel that whose
that are can be influenced by our emotions. I find that
humor can be useful to boost the spirits of patients."
—William S. Rutti[102]

"In the area of emotions, the muscles are one of the most
obvious ways of observing emotion in people and the face
is one of the most glorious ways of doing that."—Gary
Schwartz[103]

"Although it is difficult to state with any great precision,
there does seem to be some sense in which humor, laughter, and mirth are, in effect, the opposite of certain negative emotional states, such as anger, or a vengeful or
punishing attitude."
—Raymond A. Moody[104]

"People who enjoy the humor columns of magazines and
newspapers, or who find relaxation in cartoons and comic
strips generally are found to be in sound mental health."
—Jacob Levine[105]

"The humorous attitude is a kind of mental equipment
with which one meets any and every possible experience,
rather than a quality of single experiences no matter how
numerous or varied they be."—Dudley Zuver[106]

Employers and Employees: Laughing on the Job

"An architect without a sense of humor is called an engineer."
—Tim Jones[107]

"A manager who initiates humor should feel flattered
when employees are comfortable enough to use humor
back—as long as neither the boss nor the employee ridi-

cule the other."—Esther Blumenfeld and Lynne Alpern[108]

"Well-rounded people are happy people and better workers."—Mel Dodgo[109]

"One of the greatest contributions a boss can make is a liberal donation of humor. It can grease the wheels of progress, lift the spirits and make dreary work seem to fly by."—Rusty and Linda Wright[110]

"Health and humor are important to professional success."
—Elsa Maxwell[111]

"Good morale is indicated, not by a total lack of complaints, but by how employees express them and temper them with a hint of humor."—Esther Blumenfeld and Lynne Alpern[112]

"When you laugh at your boss' joke, it may not prove you have a sense of humor, but it proves you have sense."
—Anonymous[113]

"The good news is . . . the bad news can be turned into good news . . . when you change your attitude."—Robert Schuller[114]

"Humor puts others in an agreeable mood and breaks down social and business barriers between people."
—Esther Blumenfeld and Lynn Alpern[115]

"Humor can be used to achieve social acceptance, to gain status, and to reinforce group cohesiveness. It can oil the wheels of face-to-face relations, but it can also pour sand in them."
—Avner Ziv[116]

"We live in a world that is ravenously hungry for humor."
—Canon Alfred Price[117]

"Men show their characters in nothing more clearly than in what they think laughable."—Johann Wolfgang von Goethe[118]

"A new joke acts like an event of universal interest. It passes from person to person like news of the latest conquest."—Sigmund Freud[119]

"Successful executives realize that constructive humor can help create a positive office atmosphere, and often use humor to spice up memos, illustrate points, and add color to their meetings."—Esther Blumenfeld and Lynne Alpern[120]

"I must be free to laugh at you. You must be free to laugh at me. And we both must be free to laugh at people in authority."
—Martin Grotjahn[121]

"I have never met leadership without a sense of humor; this ability to stand outside oneself and one's circumstances, to see things in perspective and laugh. It is a great safety valve!"
—A. E. Norrish

"Laughing with unites, binds, and overcomes. It doesn't necessarily solve problems nor resolve conflicts, but it helps build trust out of which kinship can develop."—Tom Mullen[122]

God: His Gifts of Humor and Laughter

"If we are committed to humor as a part of our inheritance from the Creator, then we must one day give account of our stewardship."—Paul King Jewett[123]

"God is a humorist. If you have any doubts about it, look in the mirror."—Ken Olson[124]

"The whole point of history is peace, laughter, and satisfaction. The grief-striken may rise up in hope to say 'laughter, not crying, is the deepest purpose that God wills for man.' "—Edward Schillebeechx[125]

"Grace is the hilarious unexpectedness that God has done something about our sin. In the comedy of grace we all receive more than we deserve."—Larry M. Taylor[126]

"Our Heavenly Father, we thank Thee for a saving sense of humor. May we learn to smile through tears and to laugh in spite of sorrow and know that real humor is rooted in an unconquerable faith in the ultimate goodness of God. Help us to laugh at ourselves and not take ourselves too seriously."—Canon Alfred Price[127]

"A basic contention for me is that a humorist notices fun, he doesn't invent fun . . . God does that."—Grady Nutt[128]

"Keep your humor, keep the faith, and God bless you." —James I. McCord[129]

"It is pleasing to the dear God whenever thou rejoicest or laughest from the bottom of thy heart."—Martin Luther[130]

"Humorous laughter is a gift God has given humanity." —Tom Mullen[131]

"Is not reality itself to be understood and experienced as much on the analogy of play as of work—the 'play of God' as much as the 'work of God'?"—Conrad Hyers[132]

"That we should be loved by One greater than we are is the ultimate incongruity. To believe it is to be able to indulge in laughter—not the laughter of nervousness or the laughter of being unmasked, but the laughter of pure joy that, despite everything, it should be so."—Robert McAfee Brown[133]

"I don't believe we know much about God if we have never heard Him laugh."—Henlee Barnette[134]

"The Creator possesses a rarefied sense of humor. How else could He survey this earth and observe some of His children standing in chambers of justice, swearing to tell the truth, so help them God, and then playing the child's game of show and tell."—Goodman Ace[135]

"Religion is not a melancholy, the spirit of God is not a damper."—John Donne[136]

"God laughs, it seems, because God knows how it all turns out in the end. God's laughter is not that of one who can safely chortle, from a safe distance, at another's pain. It comes from One who has also felt the hunger pangs, the hurt of betrayal by friends, and the torturer's touch."
—Harvey Cox[137]

"Does God have a sense of humor? Yes, if he doesn't I'm in serious trouble. But because He does I feel real comfortable."
—Grady Nutt[138]

"Be of good cheer: this counsel is of Heaven."—Homer[139]

"If humor and laughter are gifts from God, . . . losing the ability to laugh is poor stewardship."—Tom Mullen[140]

"Humor is, in fact, a prelude to faith; and laughter is the beginning of prayer."—Reinhold Niebuhr[141]

"Laughter can also find its way into prayer. I've heard of more than one saint who broke into a sort of holy hilarity while enjoying a time of communion with God."—G. Roger Schoenhals[142]

Happiness: Our Inalienable Right

"The Constitution only guarantees the American people the right to pursue happiness. You have to catch it yourself."—Benjamin Franklin[143]

"The best way to cheer yourself up is to try to cheer somebody else."—Mark Twain[144]

"In a society which promotes the pursuit of happiness as a constitutional right, to be against fun is as bad as opposing baseball, hot dogs, apple pie, and Chevrolet."—Tom Mullen[145]

> "I'm going to be happy today!
> Though the skies are cloudy and gray,
> No matter what comes my way—
> I'm going to be happy today!
> —Ella Wheeler Wilcox[146]

"Cheerful crusaders are cheerful lovers of humanity—warts and all—and they relate to the human race as if they belonged to it."—Tom Mullen[147]

"Most people are about as happy as they choose to be." Abraham Lincoln[148]

"I just can't conceive of an individual who's got a home in heaven, who knows that he has eternal security and is living in this world, preparing the best retirement plan ever, and not being happy."—Jerry Clower[149]

"The ability to laugh is one of the most characteristic and deep-seated features of man."—Raymond A. Moody[150]

"Genuine laughter is a vent of the soul, the nostrils of the heart, and it is just as necessary for health and happiness as spring water is for a trout."—Josh Billings[151]

"Laughter dwells within most of us, and adults discipline themselves to suppress it. The result is that we deny ourselves the fun of being 'in fun'."—Tom Mullen[152]

Home and Family: Laughing Together and Staying Together

"Today's young people have grown up in a culture almost constantly brainwashed by mass-produced humor." —Steve Allen[153]

"Including plenty of fun and laughter around the dinner table helps develop bonds and can lessen the discouragement from a difficult day at school."—Rusty and Linda Wright[154]

"Humor during sibling fights also shifts attention from the source of conflict, allowing room for making constructive suggestions to resolve the problem."—Esther Blumenfeld and Lynne Alpern[155]

"A family is blessed when some among its members assume the role of Head of Horseplay. Most families depend upon certain ones to provide the life of the party, just as they look to other members for strength or responsibility." —Tom Mullen[156]

"Before we can have a positive relationship with our children, we must have a positive relationship with ourselves."—Byron W. Arledge[157]

"I believe the trait of being able to see what is laughable in oneself is learned from others, and the best teachers are our parents."—Phylis Campbell Dryden[158]

"An authentic response to life demands a chuckle as well as a boohoo. We're dang close, I think, in this era in our nation, to forgetting humor."—Grady Nutt[159]

Hope: a By-product of Humor

"In the world of laughter and in the laughter of the world lies one of the hopes for peace on earth."—Yuri B. Boryev[160]

"Humor is hope. Humor brings strength where there is weakness. Humor puts fun into the drama of sickness. Healing is accelerated."—Barry Brunsman[161]

"You must examine your sense of humor to determine how it has served you. Is it chiefly a repository for jokes and anecdotes? Or does it function—as it should—to help you perceive your own occasionally ludicrous aspects?"
—Meyer Friedman and Ray Rosenman[162]

"We charge our image-makers with assuming a tragic model for society, whereas the comic model contains man's only hope."
—Joseph C. McLelland[163]

"Many times in the history of divine and human affairs, Holy Folly has been the cause of deliverance and salvation."
—Belden C. Lane[164]

"Where there is humor, there is still hope."—Conrad Hyers[165]

Humor: Definitions

"One odd thing about humor is that it is almost impossible to write about it in a humorous way. The magic of the thing disappears under analysis and one is left with a puff of dry dust."—Steve Allen[166]

"Humor is emotional chaos remembered in tranquility."
—James Thurber[167]

"Humor is a mechanism of disengagement and a means of objectifying painful life situations."—Fred D. Layman[168]

"Wit is the sudden marriage of ideas which before their marriage were not perceived to have any relationship."—Mark Twain[169]

"Humor is not a reserved sense to be indulged on special occasions, but a kind of spice for all seasons."—Wilbur Mullen[170]

"Gags die; humor doesn't."—Jack Benny[171]

"Trying to define and analyze humor is a waste of time. Somebody tickling you with a feather will make you laugh, but it's not funny."—Laurence J. Peter[172]

"Humor is a balancing, disarming, and therefore peacemaking force that touches on the divine."—Cal Samra[173]

"Good humor isn't a trait of character, it is an art which requires practice."—David Seabury[174]

Humor is unpredictable because it is personal, and people are unpredictable."—Roger C. Palms[175]

"Humor is nothing other than perfect self-awareness. It is the delighted recognition of one's own absurdity, and a loving cynicism with respect to one's own pretension."—Alan Watts[176]

Joy: Illusive but Available

"The opposite of joy is not sorrow. It is unbelief."—Leslie Weatherhead[177]

"The Christian life that is joyless is a discredit to God and a disgrace to itself."—Maltbie D. Babcock[178]

"There is an old saying that the blood of the martyrs is the seed of the church. But we hardly ever hear of the joy of the martyrs. It was a contagious joy, and the early Christians, especially, had it in abundance, passing it on from generation to generation."—Cal Samra[179]

"Without kindness there can be no true joy."—Thomas Carlyle[180]

"The surgeon must forbid anger, hatred and sadness in the patient, and remind him that the body grows fat from joy and thin from sadness."—Raymond A. Moody[181]

"Joy is not gush; joy is not jolliness. Joy is just perfect acquiescence in God's will because the soul delights itself in God Himself."—Hammer William Webb-Peploe[182]

"When we are in a state of fun, we are probably not in a mood to save the world—nor destroy it. But we may be able to do one Good Thing—enjoy a moment of the time God has given us."—Tom Mullen[183]

"Great joy is only earned by great exertion."—Johann Wolfgang von Goethe[184]

"Science cannot restore the joy of life and help us laugh again."—Gerald Kennedy[185]

"Joy is more divine than sorrow, for joy is bread and sorrow is medicine."—Henry Ward Beecher[186]

"Jesus Christ can put joy into the joyless work of the twentieth century."—Bernard Ramm[187]

"Desire joy and thank God for it. Renounce it, if need be, for other's sake. That's joy beyond joy."—Robert Browning[188]

"Happy are they whose ability to rejoice is great. They will find much to celebrate."—Tom Mullen[189]

"Grief can take care of itself; but to get the full value of joy you must have somebody to divide it with."—Mark Twain[190]

"A man isn't poor if he can still laugh."—Raymond Hitchcock[191]

"Humor takes on a religious dimension when it helps in some measure to free us inwardly to be in the world more creatively, more loving more joyously."—Harvey Potthoff[192]

La ughter: Definitions

"Laughter is a safe and civilized alternative to violence."—Martin Grotjahn [93]

"There is always a laugh in the utterly familiar."—James Thurber[194]

"Laughter is caused by the spectacle of a human being responding mechanically to an unexpected situation."—Henri Bergso [195]

"In the nuclear age, laughter is the only weapon that may be praised without violating humanitarian principles, for laughter is a creative, not a destructive weapon, in other words, an an -weapon."—Yuri B. Boryev[196]

"Laughter occurs when aggressive energy is freed from repression; the more energy that is suddenly expressed, the louder and deeper the laughter will sound."—Martin Grotjahn[197]

"Laughter is the bark of delight of a gregarious animal at the proximity of his kind."—Wyndham Lewis[198]

"Man is distinguished from all other creatures by the faculty of laughter."—Joseph Addison[199]

"Laughter is fundamentally an act of celebrating existence. Laughter is an expression both of enjoyment and of thanksgiving."—Conrad Hyers[200]

Life: More than a Bad Joke

"The very fact that living does not dim the luster of our humor is in itself the finest tribute to the worthwhileness of life."
—Julius Gordon[201]

"Humortality is a bandage for the open-sored self-consciousness of life—when what you do is how you think people discover what you are."—Grady Nutt[202]

"We can laugh at the incongruities of life so long as we believe life is not just a joke, a bad joke."
—Harvey Potthoff[203]

"The more thoroughly and substantially a human being exists, the more he will discover the comical."
—Kierkegaard[204]

"We cannot control all of the things that happen to us in our life, but we do have a certain degree of control over our reactions to them.
—Esther Blumenfeld & Lynne Alpern[205]

"When we take away the ability to laugh with chemicals, we destroy an important aspect of humankind. The first symptom of the emotionally ill person is his lack of laughter. I believe we have to celebrate life with laughter."
—John McBride[206]

"Life is a jest,
    All things show it.
I thought so once,
    But now I know it."
—Anonymous[207]

"To the portent of laughter Christian faith gives the

Christ-event, the historical drama of uncoercive love. So we may now choose how to laugh. We can laugh because life, despite its darkness, is good."—George A. Buttrick[208]

"I believe the good Lord created humor in us to help us make it through life. Laughter is a relaxant. The opposite of laughter is criticism. Criticism destroys relationships; laughter builds them."—Edward E. Ford[209]

Offensive Humor—Bad Use of a Good Gift

"It hurts to be the target of laughter. Some humor is intended to wound others, and we can use it to as a deliberate act of hostility. We can use hurtful humor as a prophetic instrument—exposing wickedness and hypocrisy."—Tom Mullen[210]

"Thou canst not joke an enemy into a friend, but thou may'st a friend into an enemy."—Benjamin Franklin[211]

"Sticks and stones may break our bones, but spoofing our beliefs is as funny as water to a drowning man."
—Tom Mullen[212]

"A person reveals his character by nothing so clearly as the joke he resents."—G. C. Lichtenberg[213]

"If not all food is good for the stomach, not all humor is necessarily good for the soul."—Cal Samra[214]

" 'Laughing at' is humor at the expense of someone else, but 'laughing with' builds sympathy with another. We become kindred spirits. 'Laughing with' does not alienate us from others; it does not identify enemies. It identifies our friends and how funny they are."—Tom Mullen[215]

"We all like to see our sense of decency threatened, but no one likes to see it outraged."—Dudley Zuver[216]

"Put-downs not only hurt others but also can backfire,

leaving the user unsatisfied and even more hostile."—Esther Blumenfeld and Lynne Alpern[217]

"Humor won't backfire if you tell it properly and it's not putting anybody down."—Jerry Clower[218]

"He that will lose his friend for a jest deserves to die a beggar by the bargain."—Thomas Fuller[219]

"Tellers of racist jokes are sometimes innocent of bad motives but guilty of poor taste, that is, insensitivity."—Tom Mullen[220]

"I don't know what humor is. Anything that's funny—tragedy or anything, it don't make no difference so long as you happen to hit it just right. But there's one thing I'm proud of—I ain't got it in for anybody. I don't like to make jokes that hurt anybody."—Will Rogers[221]

"Such let thy jests be, that they may not grind the credit of thy friend."—Thomas Fuller[222]

"I am of the opinion the amount of anti-feminine hostility in a considerable portion of sexual humor is based on man's biological weakness.—Avner Ziv[223]

"The real wit tells jokes to make others feel superior, while the half-wit tells them to make others feel small."—Elmer Wheeler[224]

Physical Health—Humor's Healing Power

"What better way is there to cope with the absurdity of being roused from bed at 3 AM to treat a patient's sniffles (he has had them, he tells you, for three weeks now!) than to laugh at the incident?"—Raymond A. Moody[225]

"On a healing mission I usually tell several jokes and then tell the congregation that God's healing love is working in them as they are laughing."—K. Womble[226]

"A sure sign that an alcoholic is recovering is the return of a sense of humor."—Joseph Martin[227]

"Pain reduction and prevention of violence toward self and others through humor raise questions about the mutual interplay of endorphins, immunology, and humor."
—Walter E. O'Connel[228]

"The very act of laughing is actually good exercise."
—Anonymous[229]

"Nothing is more essential in the treatment of serious disease than liberating the patient from panic and foreboding."—Norman Cousins[230]

"Blue Cross reports that laughter supplies six times as much oxygen to body tissue as a deep breath."—Claudia M. Dewane[231]

"In the case of jokes, we feel the effect of this slackening in the body the oscillation of the organs, which promotes the restoration of equilibrium and has a favorable influence upon health."—Immanuel Kant[232]

"Humor can keep us healthy. It has kept all the Keane family healthy for three decades."—Bil Keane[233]

"Let the surgeon take care to regulate the whole regimen of the patient's life for joy and happiness."—Henri de Mondeville[234]

"Laughter is not all 'ho, ho, ho' and 'ha, ha, ha.' It's also a quiet inner warmth that spreads good vibes throughout the mind and body. There is no doubt in my mind that laughter of any kind promotes better health."
—Bil Keane[235]

"Laughter is the best medicine for a long and happy life. He who laughs—lasts."—Winfred A. Peterson[236]

"As every dedicated athlete knows, to stay in top physical condition you should do some kind of exercise every day: running, swimming, dancing—or laughing."—Dick Robinson[237]

"Illness is not a laughing matter. Maybe it should be."
—Norman Cousins[238]

"It is amazing how a little bit of humor can get rid of a lot of tension. When you help patients laugh, they let go of anger, frustration, anxiety, and hostility."—Vera Robinson[239]

"If laughter promotes health, it also reflects health. People who are happy and who laugh together are saying something positive about themselves."—Roger Schoenhals[240]

"Clearly, if Christians can agree on little else, there is an almost unanimous ecumenical consensus that humor is healing."
—Cal Samra[241]

"The old man laughed joyously and loud, shook up the details of his anatomy from head to foot, saying that such a laugh was money in a man's pocket because it cut down the doctor's bills like everything."—Mark Twain[242]

"The great majority of people, especially after middle life, do not laugh nearly enough for the good of their hearts."
—James J. Walsh[243]

"It is helpful for the physician to have a stock of good honest stories to make patients laugh."—John Arderne[244]

"Crisis is real and often not immediately compatible with laughter. But with time and perspective, humor can be an important step toward healing."—Esther Blumenfeld and Lynne Alpern[245]

"Laughter is primarily and fundamentally the antidote of sympathetic pain."—William McDouglass[246]

"If a man cannot laugh there is some mistake made in putting him together, and if he will not laugh he warrants as much keeping away from as a beartrap when it is set."
—Josh Billings[247]

"It's an essential management skill to have a sense of humor about yourself."—Matt Weinstein[248]

"If you can't take a joke, then you'll have to take medicine."
—Anonymous[249]

"You don't play when you feel better, you feel better when you play."—Matt Weinstein[250]

Religion, Theology, and Faith: Humor's Place

"No wonder that the surge of laughter and the sense of comic joy in a death-haunted, misery-prone creature could be seen as a natural intrusion of the miraculous into the self, that is, as a religious experience."—Roger Polhemus[251]

"One who professes an interest in religion and the comic sense may properly be supposed to be, at least mildly, religious."
—Dudley Zuver[252]

"When religion gets sick, it becomes humorless and narrow."
—Larry M. Taylor[253]

"Laughter is a vestibule to the temple of confession; but laughter is not able to deal with the problem of the sins of the self in any ultimate way."—Reinhold Niebuhr[254]

"A Christian theologian without a sense of humor seems to be a contradiction in terms."—John E. Benson[255]

"Humor passes over into despair if it has no groundedness in the sacred, if it is not essentially and inwardly related to holy things. But if it has this foundation, it can play its own peculiar role in the inner dialectic of the sacred and the comic."—Conrad Hyers[256]

"It may be politely asked of the Calvinists, if the Arminians are so wicked why did God decree that they exist?" —Bernard Ramm[257]

"A person of good humor actually mediates grace."—Harvey Potthoff[258]

"It is laughter which knows full well that one has been a recipient of outrageous grace, a radical mercy, which is neither anticipated nor deserved."—John Vannorsdall[259]

"The comic is not a wart on the human soul but a part of the soul, and the soul is diminished if the comic is excised by any kind of spiritual X-ray."—Chad Walsh[260]

"A good joke is the one ultimate and sacred thing which cannot be criticized. Our relations with a good joke are direct and even divine relations."—G. K. Chesterton[261]

"Healthy religion is religion of grace. It knows how to laugh."—Larry M. Taylor[262]

"Although tragedy has held the most fascination for literary theorists, there is general agreement that comedy most accurately embodies the Christian message."—Nelvin Vos[263]

"The person of faith knows something others do not know. He or she has something up his sleeve, and so can chuckle

when others are just plain uptight. Faith vindicates laughter.
—Harvey Potthoff[264]

"Should we not see that lines of laughter about the eyes are just as much marks of faith as are the lines of care and seriousness?"—Helmut Thielicke[265]

"Men can laugh only when they believe."—Gerald Kennedy[266]

"Perhaps we are simply too insecure to laugh at ourselves and by ourselves and by laughter gain with the Biblical authors a healthy perspective on our sins and our failings."
—Eugene J. Fisher[267]

"Holy laughter is a gift of grace. It is the human spirit's last defense against banality and despair. Sometimes I think that, along with martyred missionaries, comedians—those of gentle type—can be God's emissaries in a mean-spirited time like ours."—Harvey Cox[268]

"It is amusing to think of a camel's going through the eye of a needle; but it is divine comedy indeed, amazing, laughable, wonderful—to be a redeemed sinner entering Heaven's feast!"—Anonymous[269]

"A great part of the malaise afflicting Christianity today, particularly in its Protestant forms, is that it has forgotten (or never learned) how to laugh."—Chad Walsh[270]

"I've taken a few lumps in my time for daring to smile at religion."—Erma Bombeck[271]

"In my opinion, evangelical theology and practice have been quite uptight about feasts, festivities and fun."—Wilbur Mullen[272]

"Laughter must be heard in the outer courts of religion;

and the echoes of it should resound in the sanctuary; but there is no laughter in the holy of holies. There laughter is swallowed up in prayer and humor in fulfilled by faith."
—Reinhold Niebuhr[273]

"There are Christians who have been killjoys by identifying the Christian spirit with a long face, stern countenance, and grave demeanor, or the Christian life with a square-jaw, bull-dog disposition, judgemental look, and militant temperament."—Conrad Hyers[274]

"The forests of theology become an impenetrable jungle without the constant pruning of holy wit; and life, both theoretical and practical, becomes opaque and intolerable."
—Jackson Lee Ice[275]

"Only in humor can evangelical theology avoid the humorless theological dictator and theological fanatic. If we have no sense of humor in our theology, we then take ourselves with an inhuman seriousness."—Bernard Ramm[276]

"Only if we are secure in our beliefs can we see the comical side of the universe."—Flannery O'Connor[277]

"As far as philosophy and theology studying humor, there has not been a great deal done and most of us think there's something to it."—John P. Newport[278]

"Laughter, of course, can be strained, cruel, artificial and merely habitual. It can mask our true feelings. But where it is real, laughter is the voice of faith."—Harvey Cox[279]

"People who believe in little laugh at little."—Leonard Feeney[280]

"Humor helps us to see how incongruous it is that we finite creatures make infinite claims about ourselves; faith helps us see how incongruous it is that infinite claims should be made on our behalf by another."—Robert McAfee Brown[281]

"But laughter in the holy place is not a guffaw."—Wilbur H. Mullen[282]

"A church is in a bad way when it banishes laughter from the sanctuary and leaves it to the cabaret, the nightclub, and the toastmasters."—Helmut Thielicke

"Laughter knows no denominational barriers, but I have always hastened to add in my quest that I definitely do believe in reverence. It's just that I have a sneaking hunch even the angels sometimes must bend over in laughter over the unexpected."—Jan. S. Doward[283]

"Humor in theology serves the function of reminding every theologian that he or she is a human being performing a very human task."—Bernard Ramm[284]

"Humor without holiness may be vulgarly unaesthetic. Holiness without humor may be a 'clean, well-lighted place,' but trival and boring."—Wilbur Mullen[285]

"It is a great gift to be allowed to get outside ourselves and smile at our worship, our robes, and our dignity."
—Herb Barks[286]

"I wonder why preachers never preach on the fun of being good. Religion is really a form of fun."—Charles Jefferson[287]

"If God created laughter, playfulness, and humor, few theologians, biblical scholars, or doctors of the church have ever heard about it. And if there is such a thing as the humor of God, it has never come through in our creeds, confessions, or catechisms. No wonder, for these are the things about which we endlessly quarrel."—Conrad Hyers[288]

Self-Laughter: Where Humor Starts

"Learning to laugh at ourselves, with our strutting and our pretensions, may be the prelude to repentance. And there are times when laughter can become a form of worship of the living God."—Kenneth Chafin[289]

"To laugh at other people is often a sign of mockery. To laugh with other people can be a sign of humor. But to laugh at oneself, this is certainly a gift of humor."—Henri Cormier[290]

"If we are to have a good, positive humor attitude, it is necessary for us to avoid laughing at people and learn to laugh with them. One of the best ways of doing this is to be willing to laugh at ourselves."—John W. Drakeford[291]

"The one offense which a sense of humor cannot tolerate is that we forget our humanity—the finite quality of our most deeply cherished causes."—Tom Mullen[292]

"The ability to laugh at one's self may be one indication of an integrated personality."—Claudia M. Dewane[293]

"Like individuals, nations that take themselves too seriously become intolerant. And intolerance ultimately makes people and nations intolerable."—Martin Grotjahn[294]

"Men will confess to treason, murder, arson, false teeth, or a wig. How many will own up to a lack of humor?" —Frank Moore Colby[295]

"By being part of a group, mutually sharing a historical, religious, or cultural background, and also the burden of society's prejudices, you can poke fun at your own people because you are also poking fun at yourself. Everyone is included and no slur is intended."—Esther Blumenfeld and Lynne Alpern[296]

"Humor not only recognizes the comic discrepancy in the human condition; it relativizes it, and thereby suggests that the tragic perspective on the discrepancies of the human condition can also be relativized by laughing at the imprisonment of the human spirit."—Peter Berger[297]

"An inability to laugh at human foibles is blasphemy. It treats human beings as if they were godlike, and they aren't."—Tom Mullen[298]

Seriousness: Its Dependence on Humor

"Christians are wary of too much laughter, limiting themselves most of the time to two jokes, one spouse, and no drinks. Humor is—how shall we put it—less responsible than seriousness."—Tom Mullen[299]

"The Christian faith relates to men stripped of their social roles; Christian ethics humanizes the social comedy and frees men from the bondage of deadly earnestness."
—Peter L. Berger[300]

"What is funny about us is precisely that we take ourselves too seriously."—Reinhold Niebuhr[301]

"The hallmark of a psychological society seems to be an unremitting seriousness. The problem for us is that the serious tone of the therapists' office has crept into all the areas of our lives. Any ordinary remark we make seems to require analysis by our friends. Where does this psychological seriousness come from? It comes from the attempt to take the place of God."—William Kirk Kilpatrick[302]

"Laughing because we are unwilling to deal with serious matters is a serious matter. It is a distortion of reality."
—Tom Mullen[303]

"The more serious we become, the more our awareness of humor diminishes and in many cases becomes completely dormant."—Esther Blumenfeld and Lynne Alpern[304]

"Without laughter, life on our planet would be intolerable."
—Steve Allen[305]

"It seems rather to be a fact that only people who can be serious also possess a liberating sense of humor, and that the serious-minded person who never laughs suffers from some kind of flaw in his seriousness."—Eivind Berggrav[306]

"The most utterly lost of all days is that in which you have not once laughed."—Sebastien Bach Nicolas Chamfort[307]

"Unfortunately, theologians and moralists have had much to say about man's responsibility to work, but little about his responsibility to play; many words about seriousness and sobriety, few about nonsense and laughter."—Conrad Hyers[308]

"Because the man of comedy is essentially human, he is aware that only the serious man can really laugh; the rest only mock or giggle."—Nelvin Vos[309]

"Humor is a good way to tamp down the level of nastiness and violence in the world. We really ought to take humor more seriously."—Jeffrey Keefe[310]

"Man is the only animal that weeps and laughs and knows that he weeps and laughs, and wonders why. He is the only creature that weeps over the fact that he weeps, and laughs over the fact that he laughs. He is the most humor-seeking, humor-making, and humor-giving species that has walked the earth."—Jackson Lee Ice[311]

"Sometimes humor is useful in saying serious things which just can't be said flat out."—John Vannorsdall[312]

"Those in the mood of play will laugh for any reason, good or bad. Those in a serious mood will watch a baby smile and assume it is feeling gas pains."—Tom Mullen[313]

"Philosophers have told us through the ages that comedy and tragedy are separated by a very thin line."—Ann Landers[314]

"I think we need to know that we are lovable just as we are. Then we can laugh at ourselves and feel comfortable as others laugh with us."—Paul Alvey[315]

"In trying to emphasize the great issues of life, the church may have too readily turned away from the message of humor, laughter, joy, and play."—John W. Drakeford[316]

Smile: Humor's Silent Language

"If I can make people smile, then I have served my purpose for God."—Red Skelton[317]

"True humor springs not more from the head than from the heart. It is not contempt, its essence is love. It issues not in laughter, but in still smiles, which lie far deper."
—Thomas Carlyle[318]

"The thing that goes the farthest
    toward making life worthwhile
That cost the least, and does the most,
    is just a pleasant smile."—Wilbur D. Nesbit[319]

"Someone once figured out that it takes seventy-two muscles to frown, and only fifteen to smile."—Cal Samra[320]

"There's a town called Don't-You-Worry
    On the banks of the River Smile
Where the Cheer-up and Be-happy
    Blossom sweetly all the while."—I. J. Bartlett[321]

"Often truth spoken with a smile will penetrate the mind

and reach the heart; the lesson strikes home without wounding because of the wit in the saying."—Horace[322]

"Better by far you should forget and smile Than that you should remember and be sad."—Christina Rossetti[323]

Speeches and Sermons: Using Humor in Communication

"If he can remember so many jokes
With all the details that mold them
Why can't he remember with equal skill
How many times he told them?"—Anonymous[324]

"A joke that has to be explained is at its wit's end."
—Anonymous[325]

"One thing is certain about all humor: used tastefully and with discretion, it can do more to spice up a speech, liven up a social gathering, ease an uncomfortable atmosphere, bail out an awkward situation—and, incidentally, gain for its user a reputation of sincere good fellowship—than any other single accomplishment."—Jacob Braude[326]

"The jest loses its point when he who makes it is the first to laugh."—Johann Christoph Friedrich von Schiller[327]

"A preacher who becomes obsessed with being funny loses his ability to communicate the gospel in all its seriousness. It all comes out as nonsense."—John W. Drakeford[328]

"A preacher can occasionally laugh at himself, but he must never be guilty of laughing at others from the pulpit."—Allen F. Harrod[329]

He Has to Prove It
"When a fellow says, 'I'm not a speaker.'
That subject should then be quite shut.
His listeners' spirits rest easy
Until he continues with, 'But . . .' "—Anonymous[330]

"Smile and the congregation will smile with you. Frown and the congregation will cut out and take a short nap."—Allen F. Harrod[331]

"The Bible speaks of 'the foolishness of preaching,' but has no commendation for *foolish* preaching."—John W. Drakeford[332]

"A good twenty-minute speech will always be perceived as being better than a good long one. After twenty minutes, only 20 percent are listening, 30 percent have dozed off, and the other 50 percent are having sexual fantasies."—Robert Orben[333]

"Humor lends pungency, originality and eloquence to sermons."
—J. Oswald Sanders[334]

"It is pretty generally admitted that sermons may wisely be adorned with a fair share of illustrations; but anecdotes used to that end are still regarded by the prudes of the pulpit with a measure of suspicion."—C. H. Spurgeon[335]

"Few sinners are saved after the first twenty minutes of a sermon."—Mark Twain[336]

"It is unlikely that the hearers of sermons will see humor in God's redemptive acts if humor is not regularly present in sermons."—John Vannorsdall[337]

"We can talk about the most important and significant things in life and still find a place for a humor that will make our points even more telling."—John W. Drakeford[338]

"Humor can unmask human pretension, and it can also mask it more effectively. It is able to reach out in friendly embrace, and lash out in animosity and distain."—Conrad Hyers[339]

"Make not jests so long that thou becomest one."—Thomas Fuller[340]

"If you want to tell people the truth, make them laugh, or they will kill you."—George Bernard Shaw[341]

"Far more research has been devoted to the visual system of the frog than to what makes people laugh."—Jim Hassett and Gary Schwartz[342]

"One of the extraordinary qualities of a humorous response is that it is so instantaneous and brief, and yet its effects are so positive and in some cases permanent."—Esther Blumenfeld and Lynne Alpern[043]

"Perhaps the best rule on appropriateness in humor is that love must temper laughter. When you keep that rule, you and your listeners can benefit from your joviality."—Rusty and Linda Wright[344]

"The pleasure which I cause them tells me that for at least a short moment, they love me."—W. C. Fields[345]

"I learned quickly that when I made others laugh, they liked me. This lesson I will never forget."—Art Buchwald[346]

"It is easier to make people laugh when they expect to, and this is why the established comedian has an advantage."—Esther Blumenfeld and Lynne Alpern[332]

"The minister who is given to laughter is not going to be awarded 'Who's Who' in the gallery of the Sanhedrin. But, bless your tickle box, the rank and file will relate to that preacher."—Joe Johnson[348]

"The surprising power of humor is that the laugh is so

short lived, and yet its effects can be so lasting."—Esther Blumenfeld and Lynne Alpern[349]

"Used well, humor may allow the hearer momentarily to respond in an appropriate way, which need not necessarily be audible laughter."—Allen F. Harrod[350]

"But humor, if it is just a veneer slapped on the surface of your personality, will not ring true."—Esther Blumenfeld and Lynne Alpern[351]

"Humor is a gift to the church, but there are people in all churches who would discourage and suppress it."—Cal Samra[352]

"A preacher of the gospel is not primarily a humorist or an entertainer, but if he is wise he learns to use humor in his sermons."—John W. Drakeford[353]

"Humor in one form or another, has always leavened religion."
—Maurice Bozarth[354]

"Humor can be applied effectively to enhance every aspect of life though few have explored its practical benefits."—Elsa Maxwell[355]

"Laughter is contagious. It is social behavior. If you watch a funny movie alone, you might not laugh out loud. But if you watch the same show with friends, you will probably all laugh together."—Esther Blumenfeld and Lynne Alpern[356]

"There is no harm in laughter. The preacher with a good sense of humor ought to use it in the pulpit, though always with restraint. The gospel becomes drab when it is delivered in a drab tone."—Bishop Gerald Kennedy[357]

"If you split a gut at just about every joke you hear, it could

mean that you need help, rather than praise as a great wit."
—Charles R. Gruner[358]

"Blessed are they who get the joke." —Frederick Buechner[359]

"A storyteller is a person who has a good memory and hopes other people haven't."—Irvin S. Cobb[360]

"Some authorities claim there is one serious lapse of attention in any audience about once every seven minutes. A humorous response by the preacher may be necessary to cope with this situation."—John W. Drakeford[361]

"If you would rule the world quietly, you must keep it amused."
—Emerson[362]

"Humor may ultimately turn out to be the royal road to learning."—John W. Drakeford[363]

Study of Humor: a Funny Thing

"Those who have toyed with the idea of studying humor are usually a little funny to start with—or so they like to think. Put two of them together to ponder the essence of wit, and they begin to act like Abbott and Costello."
—Jim Hasseett & Gary Schwartz[364]

"There seems to be no lengths to which humorless people will not go to analyze humor."—Christopher Byron[365]

"Of puns it has been said that they who most dislike them are least able to utter them."—Edgar Allan Poe[366]

"The world like humor, but treats it patronizingly. It decorates its serious artists with laurel, and its wags with Brussels sprouts."—E. B. White[367]

"The problem with most essays on the comic . . . is that they proceed in a solemnity of tone and style more suited to earning a degree in philosophy or being named bishop than inviting us to celebration and laughter."—Chad Walsh[368]

"Everybody is ignorant, only on different subjects."—Will Rogers[369]

"Without claiming too much for it, I would say that the reason for the popularity of a joke is its extraordinary condensation; a character is presented and disposed of, a problem is stated and solved, all in one breath."—Louis Untermeyer[370]

"Men will let you abuse them if only you will make them laugh."
—Henry Ward Beecher[371]

Notes on Chapters

Chapter One

1. Allen James, comp., *Keep Smiling and Have a Happy Day* (New York: Random House, 1972), p. 53.

2. Laurence J. Peter and Bill Dana, *Laughter Prescription* (New York: Ballantino Books, 1982), p. 185.

3. William Barclay, *The Mind of Jesus* (New York: Harper & Brothers, 1960), p. 94.

4. Allen James, *Keep Smiling*, p. 53.

5. Allen James, *Keep Smiling*, p. 375.

6. Grady Nutt, "More on the Humor of Christ," *The Student*, Feb. 1974, p. 22.

7. Grady Nutt, "Humortality," *The Student*, 53, Feb. 1974, p. 6.

8. Allen James, *Keep Smiling*, p. 54.

9. Ibid., p. 33.

10. Peter and Dana, *Laughter*, p. 188.

11. John Morreall, *Taking Laughter Seriously* (Albany, N.Y.: State University of New York, 1983), p. 4.

12. *International Dictionary of Thoughts* (Chicago: J. G. Ferguson Publishing Co., 1969), p. 372.

13. John Morreall, *Taking Laughter Seriously*, pp. 16-17.

14. Tom Mullen, *Laughing Out Loud and Other Religious Experiences* (Waco: Word Books, 1983), p. 17.

15. Allen James, *Keep Smiling*, p. 9.

16. John Bussey, "U.S. Presidents are Very Funny Fellows, Often on Purpose," *The Wall Street Journal* 17 Sept. 1986, pp. 1 & 27.

17. Rusty Wright and Linda R. Wright, *Secrets of Successful Humor* (San Bernardino, Calif.: Here's Life Publishers, 1985), p. 23.

18. Tom Mullen, *Laughing Out Loud*, p. 18.

19. John Morreall, *Taking Laughter Seriously*, p. 126.

20. Tom Mullen, *Laughing Out Loud*, p. 18. (Waco: Word Books, 1983).

21. Martha Wolfenstein, *Children's Humor* (Glencor, Ill.: Free Press, 1954), pp. 105-106.

22. Gary Webster, *Laughter in the Bible* (St. Louis: The Bethany Press, 1960), p. 142.

23. Conrad Hyers, "Christian Humor: Uses and Abuses of Laughter," *Dialog*, 22 (Summer 1983), p. 199.

24. Jackson Lee Ice, "Notes Toward a Theology of Humor," *Religion in Life*, 42 (Autumn 1973), p. 392.

25. *International Dictionary of Thoughts* (Chicago: J. G. Ferguson Publishing Co., 1969), p. 427.

26. Max Eastman, *Sense of Humor* (New York: Charles Scribner's Sons, 1921), p. 226.

27. Allen James, *Keep Smiling*, p. 52.

28. John E. Benson, "Divine Sense of Humor," *Dialog*, 22 (Summer 1983), p. 192.

29. Julius Gordon, *Your Sense of Humor* (New York: Didier, 1950), p. 5.

30. Leslie B. Flynn, *Serve Him with Mirth—The Place of Humor in the Christian Life* (Grand Rapids: Zondervan, 1960), p. 2.

31. Paul King Jewett, "Wit and Humor of Life," *Christianity Today*, 8 June 1959, p. 8.

32. Farrell Cross and Wilbur Cross, "Cheers! A Belly Laugh Can Help You Stay Well," *Science Digest*, 82, Nov. 1977, p. 20.

33. Allen James, *Keep Smiling*, p. 54.

34. Gene Perret, *How to Write and Sell Your Sense of Humor* (Cincinnati: Writer's Digest Books, 1982), p. 15.

35. William J. Tobin, "Your Sense of Humor," *Talent* (Summer 1983), p. 15.

36. Grady Nutt, "More on the Humor of Christ," p. 23.

37. Frank B. Minirth and Paul D. Mier, *Happiness is a Choice* (Grand Rapids: Baker Book House, 1978), p. 73.

38. Willard Scott, "Living on the Sunny Side" *Saturday Evening Post*, Dec. 1983, p. 65.

39. Norman Vincent Peale, *The Positive Power of Jesus Christ* (Wheaton: Tyndale House Publishing, 1980), pp. 33-34.

40. Raymond A. Moody, *Laugh after Laugh* (Jacksonville, Fla.: Headwaters Press, 1978), pp. 87-88. Moody contends that this story, often told as true, may be apocryphal.

41. Ruth McRoberts Ward, *Self-Esteem: Gift from God* (Grand Rapids: Baker Book House, 1984), pp. 219-220.

Chapter Two

1. Grady Wilson, *Count It All Joy* (Nashville: Broadman Press, 1984), p. 248.

2. Reinhold Niebuhr, "Humour and Faith" in *20 Centuries of Great Preaching*, Vol. 10, p. 373.

3. Jackson Lee Ice, "Notes Toward a Theology of Humor," *Religion in Life*, 42 (Autumn 1973), p. 390.

4. Cal Samra, *The Joyful Christ: The Healing Power of Humor* (San Francisco: Harper & Row, 1986), p. 12.

5. Conrad Hyers, "Funny Faith," *One World*, July 1982, p. 10.

6. Ice, "Notes Toward a Theology of Humor," p. 400.

7. Arthur T. Pearson, *Knowing the Scriptures* (New York: Gospel Publishing House, 1910), p. 6.

8. Grady Nutt, "Gift of Laughter" (Louisville: Oakriver Productions), audio cassette.

9. George A. Buttrick, *Sermons Preached in a University Church* (New York: Abingdon Press, 1959), p. 52.

10. Arthur T. Pearson, *Knowing the Scriptures* (New York: Gospel Publishing House, 1910), p. 1.

11. Marcian Strange, "God and Laughter," *Worship*, Jan. 1971, p. 11.

12. Conrad Hyers, "The Day that Jonah Swallowed the Whale," *L.I.G.H.T.*, 1 (Fall 1984), p. 13.

13. For an extensive study of several Greek words related to laughter, humor, happiness, and joy see *The New International Dictionary of New Testament Theology*, pp. 352-361, 429-436.

14. Fred D. Layman, "Theology and Humor," *Asbury Seminarian*, 38 (Winter 1982-83), pp. 11-12.

15. David A. Redding, *Jesus Makes Me Laugh with Him* (Grand Rapids: Zondervan, 1973), p. 69.

16. *International Standard Bible Encyclopedia*, s.v. "Humor in the Bible," by C. D. Linton, p. 779.

17. For an extensive study of these puns and the significance of the original language, see A. T. Pierson, *Knowing the Scriptures* and also Eugene Fisher's article "The Divine Comedy: Humor in the Bible" in the November, 1977, issue of *Religious Education*.

For some striking examples of onomatopoeia (a word which imitates the sound of its referent) see p. 780 of *International Standard Bible Encyclopedia*.

18. *International Standard Bible Encyclopedia*, p. 779.

Chapter Three

1. Elton Trueblood, *The Humor of Christ* (San Francisco: Harper & Row, 1964), p. 15.

2. Gaines S. Dobbins, "Is It Folly to be Jolly?" *Baptist Messenger*, 87, 14 Dec. 1972, p. 2.

3. Cal Samra, *The Joyful Christ: The Healing Power of Humor* (San Francisco: Harper and Row, 1986), p. 36.

4. Leslie B. Flynn, *Serve Him with Mirth—The Place of Humor in the Christian Life* (Grand Rapids: Zondervan, 1960), p. 116

5. Samra, *The Joyful Christ*, p. 16.

6. Leslie B. Flynn, *Serve Him with Mirth—The Place of Humor in the Christian Life* (Grand Rapids: Zondervan, 1960), p. 115.

7. Minnie Pearl and John Dew, *Minnie Pearl: An Autobiography* (New York: Simon and Schuster, 1980), p. 249.

8. Samra, *The Joyful Christ*, pp. 149-170.

9. "Christ: the Essence of Life, Light, Love and Laughter" by Joyce Martin. Prints available from Mrs. Martin at the Franciscan Family Retreat at 21661 Highway 550, Montrose, Col. 81401.

10. "Smiling Christ" by Lawrence Zink, art director, *St. Anthony Messenger* Magazine. Available from Praise and Joy Annex, 4014 Schuster Drive, West Bend, Wis. 53095.

11. "Smiling Christ" by Frances Hook. Copyrighted and distributed by John Brandi Co., Inc., Yonkers, N.Y. Available through Christian book stores throughout the United States.

12. "My Friend," smiling Christ with young girl, by Frances Hook. Available in plaques and cards from Apostleship of Prayer, 661 Greenwood Ave., Toronto, Ont. Canada M4J 4B3.

13. "Jesus Laughing," a color screen-print adaptation by Ralph Kozak of an original drawing by Willis Wheatley. Color screen prints are available in various sizes from Praise and Joy Annex, 4014 Schuster Drive, West Bend, Wis. 53095; or from Praise Screen Prints, 11325 Blue Water Drive, Traverse City, Mich. 49684.

14. *The Joyful Noise* letter is available at the following address: Fellowship of Merry Christians, P. O. Box 668, Kalamazoo, Mich. 49005-0668.

15. James R. Cameron, *God, The Christlike* (Nashville: Broadman Press, 1986), p. 73.

16. Delos Miles, *Master Principles of Evangelism* (Nashville: Broadman Press, 1982), pp. 70-77.

17. Tal D. Bonham, *The Treasury of Clean Church Jokes* (Nashville: Broadman Press, 1986), p. 105-106.

18. Conrad Hyers, ed., *Holy Laughter* (New York: Seabury Press, 1969), pp. 244-245.

19. Robert Schuller, *The Be-Happy Attitudes* (Waco, Texas: Word Books, 1985), p. 20.

20. Willard Scott, "Living on the Sunny Side" *Saturday Evening Post*, Dec. 1983, p. 89.

21. Carl F.H. Henry, *Christian Personal Ethics* (Grand Rapids: Wm. B. Eerdmans Publishing Co., 1957), p. 278.

22. Tal D. Bonham, *The Demands of Discipleship* (Pine Bluff, Ark.: Discipleship Book Company, 1967), p. 14.

23. Joe L. Ingram, "Viewpoint," *Baptist Messenger* 1 June 1980, p. 7.

24. David Augsburger, *Medicine of Laughter* (Harrisonburg, Va.: Mennonite Hour, No. 113), p. 6.

25. Yuri B. Boryev, "The World Will Never Die if It Dies Laughing" *UNESCO Courier*, Apr. 1976, p. 22.

26. Leslie B. Flynn, *Serve Him with Mirth—The Place of Humor in the Christian Life* (Grand Rapids: Zondervan, 1960), p. 125.

27. Gary Webster, *Laughter in the Bible* (St. Louis: The Bethany Press, 1960), p. 100.

28. Trueblood, p. 127.

29. Grady Nutt, "More on the Humor of Christ," *Student*, Feb. 1974, p. 24.

Chapter Four

1. Allen James, comp. *Keep Smiling and Have a Happy Day* (New York: Random House, 1972), p. 19.

2. *International Dictionary of Thoughts* (Chicago: J.G. Ferguson Publishing Co., 1969), p. 428.

3. Ibid., p. 372.

4. James, *Keep Smiling*, p. 19.

5. Ibid., p. 52.

6. Ibid., p. 18.

7. Joe Johnson, *"Preacher You're the Best Pasture We've Ever Had!"* (Nashville: Broadman Press, 1972), p. 1.

8. Claudia M. Dewane, "Humor in Therapy," *Social Work*, 23, Nov. 1978, p. 509.

9. Laurence J. Peter and Bill Dana, *Laughter Prescription* (New York: Ballantine Books, 1982), p. 47.

10. Meyer Friedman, MD, and Ray H. Rosenman, MD, *Type A Behavior and Your Heart* (New York: Fawcett, 1974), p. 298.

11. Friedman, and Roseman, p. 76.

12. Cynthia Gorney, "Everyday Therapy Helps Type A's Calm Down," *Columbus Dispatch*, 19 Sept. 1984, p. G5.

13. Raymond A. Moody, *Laugh after Laugh* (Jacksonville, Fla.: Headwaters Press, 1978), p. 109.

14. Ibid.

15. Ibid., p. 49.

16. Ibid.

17. Ibid.

18. Norman Cousins, *Anatomy of an Illness* (New York: W. W. Norton, 1979).

19. Norman Cousins, *Healing Heart* (New York: W. W. Norton, 1983).

20. Norman Cousins, "Healing Heart," *Ladies' Home Journal*, 100 Oct. 1983, p. 42 *ff.*

21. Norman Cousins, "Anatomy of an Illness," *Reader's Digest*, 110, June 1977.

22. Cousins, *Healing Heart*, p. 50.

23. Ibid., p. 25.

24. Ibid., p. 264.

25. Ibid.

26. Moody, *Laugh after Laugh*, p. 18.

27. Cousins, *Healing Heart*, p. 256.

28. Ibid., pp. 235-236.

29. Moody, *Laugh after Laugh*, p. 120.

30. "Why Laughing Is Good for You," *Science Digest*, 89, June 1981, p. 27.

31. Cousins, *Healing Heart*, p. 154.

32. Ibid., p. 157.

33. Ibid., p. 158.

34. Ibid.

35. Tal D. Bonham, *The Treasury of Clean Church Jokes* (Nashville: Broadman Press, 1986), pp. 68-69.

36. Moody, *Laugh After Laugh*, p. 21.

37. Robbie W. King, "Humor Holds Untapped Healing," *SBC Today*, Apr. 1985, p. 6.

38. Ibid.

39. Ibid.

40. Ibid.

Chapter Five

1. Cal Samra, *The Joyful Christ: The Healing Power of Humor* (San Francisco: Harper & Row, 1986), p. xi

2. "Use of Humor Lauded," *Columbus Dispatch*, 27 Nov. 1980), p. F1.

3. Samra, *The Joyful Christ*, p. 24.

4. Allen James, comp., *Keep Smiling and Have a Happy Day* (New York: Random House, 1972), p. 39.

5. Anthony J. Chapman and Hugh C. Foot, eds., *Humour and Laughter, International Conference on Research Into: "It's a Funny Thing, Humour"* (Oxford: Pergamon Press, 1976), p. xiv.

6. "Laughter Instead of Violence," *USA Today*, Apr. 1982, pp. 2-3.

7. Steve Allen, *Funny People* (Briarcliffe Manor, N.Y.: Stein and Day Publishers, 1982), p. 2.

8. Esther Blumenfeld and Lynne Alpern, *The Smile Connection* (Englewood Cliffs, N.J.: Prentice-Hall, 1986), p. 3.

9. Conrad Hyers, ed., *Holy Laughter* (New York: Seabury Press, 1969), p. 245.

10. Samra, *The Joyful Christ*, p. 36.

11. Steve Allen, *Funny People*, p. 1.

12. Blumenfeld and Alpern, *The Smile Connection*, p. 37.

13. Farrell Cross and Wilbur Cross, "Cheers! A Belly Laugh Can Help You Stay Well," *Science Digest*, Nov. 1977, p. 15.

14. Samra, *The Joyful Christ*, p. 23.

15. Claudia M. Dewane, "Humor in Therapy," *Social Work*, 23, Nov. 1978, p. 510.

16. Frank B. Minirth and Paul D. Mier, *Happiness is a Choice* (Grand Rapids: Baker Book House, 1978), p. 195.

17. Samra, *The Joyful Christ*, p. 21.

18. Ibid., p. 23.

19. James, comp., *Keep Smiling,* p 14.

20. A. Russell Lee, MD, Contra Costa, and Charlotte P. Ross, "Suicide in Youth and What You Can Do About It." Pamphlet. (San Mateo County, Calif.: Suicide Prevention and Crisis Center), p. 2.

21. Nancy Allen, M.P.H., and Michael L. Peck, Ph.D., "Suicide in Young People." Pamphlet (West Point, Pa.: Merek, Sharp & Dohme, n.d.), p. 2.

22. "Baby Boom Suicide Wave," *Columbus Dispatch*, 8 Sept. 1986, p. 1.

23. Allen and Peck, "Suicide in Young People," p. 6.

24. A. Russell Lee, MD, Contra Costa, and Charlotte P. Ross, "Suicide in Youth and What You Can Do About It." Pamphlet. (San Mateo County, Calif.: Suicide Prevention and Crisis Center), p. i.

25. Norman Cousins, *Healing Heart* (New York: W.W. Norton, 1983), p. 154.

26. Samra, *The Joyful Christ*, p. 194.

27. Ibid., p. 104.

28. Michael Korda, "The New Pessimism," *Newsweek*, 14 June 1982, p. 20.

29. James Lee Young, "Psychologist Cites Ways to Be Positive Thinker," *Rocky Mountain Baptist*, 30 Aug. 1979, p. 2.

30. Tom Mullen, *Laughing Out Loud and Other Religious Experiences* (Waco, Texas: Word Books, 1983), p. 95.

31. Blumenfeld and Alpern, *The Smile Connection*, p. 48.

32. "Face It: Smiles, Frowns Reveal Emotional Health," *Dallas Times Herald*, 24 Apr. 1982, p. 22.

33. Tal D. Bonham, "Suggestions for Stress," *Ohio Baptist Messenger*, 26 July 1984, p. 8.

Chapter Six

1. Allen James, comp., *Keep Smiling and Have a Happy Day* (New York: Random House, 1972), p. 36.

2. Harvey Potthoff, "Humor and Religious Faith," in *Summary of Proceedings: 34th Annual Conference ATLA* (Philadelphia: ATLA, 1980), p. 79.

3. *Reader's Digest*, June 1982, p. 120.

4. Leo Rosten, "I Remember Groucho," *Reader's Digest*, Nov. 1982, pp. 105-106.

5. Richard Schnickel, "Sellers Strikes Again," *Time* 3 Mar. 1980, pp. 66-67.

6. Maurice Bozarth, "Those Who Shun Solemnity for a Laugh Find Comedy a Religious Experience," *Baptist Messenger*, 5 July 1984, p. 13.

7. Maury M. Breecher, "10 Keys to Happiness," *Columbus Dispatch*, 5 Nov. 1982, p. D1.

8. Harvey Potthoff, "Humor and Religious Faith," in *Summary of Proceedings: 34th Annual Conference ATLA* (Philadelphia: ATLA, 1980), p. 75.

9. Ibid.

10. Frank S. Mead, ed. and comp., *Encyclopedia of Religious Quotations* (Westwind: Fleming H. Revell, 1965), p. 158.

11. Eleanor Doan, *Sourcebook for Speakers* (Grand Rapids: Zondervan, 1965), p. 224.

12. David Augsburger, *Medicine of Laughter* (Harrisonburg, Virginia: Mennonite Hour, No. 113), p. 4.

13. Kenneth Hamilton and Robert T. Haverluck, "Laughter and Vision," *Soundings*, 55 (Summer 1972), p. 177.

14. Fred D. Layman, "Theology and Humor," *Asbury Seminarian*, 38 (Winter 1982-83), p. 20.

15. Elton Trueblood, *The Humor of Christ* (San Francisco: Harper & Row, 1964), p. 64.

16. Fred D. Layman, "Theology and Humor," p. 21.

17. Eleanor Doan, *Sourcebook for Speakers*, p. 224.

18. Nelvin Vos, *For God's Sake Laugh!* (Richmond, Va.: John Knox Press, 1967), p. 25.

19. Henri Cormier, *Humor of Jesus* (New York: Alba House, 1977), p. 150.

20. Rusty Wright and Linda R. Wright, *Secrets of Successful Humor* (San Bernardino, Calif.: Here's Life Publishers, 1985), p. 123.

21. Ibid., pp. 123-126.

22. Ibid., p. 139.

23. Conrad Hyers, ed., *Holy Laughter* (New York: Seabury Press, 1969), p. 208.

24. Tal D. Bonham, "An Interview with Jerry Clower," *L.I.G.H.T.*, 1 (Fall 1984), p. 20.

25. Jack Gulledge, "Humor in the Pulpit: An Exclusive Interview with Jerry Clower," *Proclaim*, 9, Apr. 1979, p. 6.

26. Rusty Wright and Linda R. Wright, *Secrets*, p. 139.

27. James C. Coleman, *Abnormal Psychology and Modern Life* (Glenview, Ill.: Scott, Foresman Co., 1964), p. 72.

28. Tal. D. Bonham, "We Sure Could Use a Little Good News," *Ohio Baptist Messenger*, 12 Jan. 1984, p. 9.

29. Paul Burleson, "The Voice," newsletter of Vital Truth Ministries (Summer 1986), p. 2.

Chapter Seven

1. Cal Samra, *The Joyful Christ: The Healing Power of Humor* (San Francisco: Harper & Row, 1986), p. 193.

2. William J. Tobin, "Your Sense of Humor," *Talent* (Summer 1983), pp. 15-16.

3. Stewart Harral, *When It's Laughter You're After* (Norman, Okla.: University of Oklahoma Press, 1962), p. 113.

4. David Gelman with George Hackett. "Making Fun for Profit," *Newsweek*, Apr. 20, 1983, p. 70.

5. Esther Blumenfeld and Lynne Alpern, *The Smile Connection* (Englewood Cliffs, N.J.: Prentice-Hall, 1986), pp. 41-42.

6. Tom Mullen, *Laughing Out Loud and Other Religious Experiences* (Waco, Texas: Word Books, 1983), p. 70.

7. Ibid.

8. Ibid., p. 73.

9. Robert E. Burns, "Some Humor Is Out of Bounds," *U. S. Catholic*, Jan. 1979, p. 2.

10. Ibid.

11. Tal D. Bonham, *The Treasury of Clean Church Jokes* (Nashville: Broadman Press, 1986), p. 21 *ff.*

12. Blumenfeld and Alpern, *The Smile Connection*, p. 79.

13. Mike Harden, "Sick Humor Nothing to Laugh About," *Columbus Dispatch*, 2 Feb. 1986), p. B1.

14. Ibid.

15. Ibid.

16. Mullen, *Laughing Out Loud*, p. 90.

17. Frederic B. Hill, "We Dare Not Lose the Will to Laugh," *Columbus Dispatch*, 14 Jan. 1983, p. B3.

18. Ibid.

19. "This Is What You Thought about Tasteless Jokes," *Glamour*, 82, Mar. 1984, p. 47.

20. Blumenfeld and Alpern, *The Smile Connection*, p. 44.

21. Ibid., pp. 44-45.

22. "Something Funny's Going On . . . eh, Mr. President?" *The Sunday Tennessean*, 17 Aug. 1981, p. A1. And John Bussey, "U.S. Presidents are Very Funny Fellows, Often on Purpose," *The Wall Street Journal*, 17 Sept. 1986, pp. 1 & 27.

23. Gaines S. Dobbins, "Is It Folly to be Jolly?" *Baptist Messenger*, 14 Dec. 1972.

Chapter Eight

1. Eivind Berggrav, "Humor and Seriousness," *Dialog* 22 (Summer 1983), p. 209.

2. *International Dictionary of Thoughts* (Chicago: J.G. Ferguson Publishing Co., 1969), p. 372.

3. "Use of Humor Lauded," *Columbus Dispatch*, 27 Nov. 1980, p. F1.

4. Fred D. Layman, "Theology and Humor," *Asbury Seminarian* 38 (Winter 1982-83), p. 14.

5. Jim Hassett and Gary E. Schwartz, "Why Can't People Take Humor Seriously?" *New York Times Magazine* 6 Feb. 1977, p. 103.

6. Lorenz Nieting, "Humor in the New Testament," *Dialog* 22 (Summer 1983), p. 170.

7. *International Dictionary of Thoughts* (Chicago: J.G. Ferguson Publishing Co., 1969), p. 427.

8. Laurence J. Peter and Bill Dana, *Laughter Prescription* (New York: Ballantine Books, 1982), p. 45.

9. Fred D. Layman, "Theology and Humor," p. 14.

10. Tom Mullen, *Laughing Out Loud and Other Religious Experiences* (Waco, Texas: Word Books, 1983), p. 54.

11. Eugene J. Fisher, "Divine Comedy: Humor in the Bible," *Religious Education*, Nov. 1977, p. 574.

12. Bernard Ramm, *After Fundamentalism* (San Francisco: Harper & Row, 1983), p. 193.

13. Cal Samra, *The Joyful Christ: The Healing Power of Humor* (San Francisco: Harper and Row, 1986), p. 19.

14. Ruth McRoberts Ward, *Self-Esteem: Gift from God* (Grand Rapids: Baker Book House, 1984), p. 224.

15. Joe Johnson, *"Preacher You're the Best Pasture We've Ever Had!"* (Nashville: Broadman Press, 1972), p. 96.

16. Eleanor Doan, *Sourcebook for Speakers* (Grand Rapids: Zondervan, 1965), p. 230.

17. Desiderius Erasmus, *Praise and Folly* (Chicago: Packard & Co., 1946), p. 33.

18. Julius Gordon, *Your Sense of Humor* (New York: Didier, 1950), p. 26.

19. Francine Klagburn, *Married People Staying Together in the Age of Divorce* (Bantam Book Publishing Co., 1985).

20. "Laughter Instead of Violence," *USA Today*, Apr. 1982, pp. 2-3.

21. Jacob M. Brande, *Brande's Handbook of Humor for all Occasions* (Englewood Cliffs, N.J.: Prentice-Hall, 1958), p. 4.

22. Mullen, *Laughing Out Loud*, p. 43.

23. Grady Nutt, "Gift of Laughter" (Louisville: Oakriver Productions), sound cassette. p. 3.

24. Phylis C. Dryden, "Families Need a Sense of Humor," *Home Life*, July 1981, p. 33.

25. Julius Gordon, *Your Sense of Humor* (New York: Didier, 1950), p. 237.

26. Esther Blumenfeld and Lynne Alpern, *The Smile Connection* (Englewood Cliffs, N.J.: Prentice-Hall, 1986), p. 170.

27. Tom Mullen, *Laughing Out Loud*, p. 118.

28. Byron W. Arledge, *Laugh with Your Teenager* (Wheaton: Tyndale House, 1985), p. 89.

29. Tom Mullen, *Laughing Out Loud*, p. 119.

30. Julia Keller, "Yukking It Up the Corporate Ladder," *Columbus Dispatch*, 27 April 1986, p. C2.

31. Susan Dentzer, "A Cure for Job Stress," *Newsweek*, 2 June 1986, p. 46.

32. Keller, "Yukking It Up the Corporate Ladder," p. C2.

33. Blumenfeld and Alpern, *The Smile Connection*, p. 45.

34. Mike McCormack, *What They Don't Teach You at Harvard Business School* (New York: Bantam Books, 1986), pp. 46-47.

35. Ibid.

36. John D. Yeck, from newsletter of "Let's Have Better Mottoes Association, Inc." Dayton, Oh. Used by permission.

37. Blumenfeld and Alpern, *The Smile Connection*, p. 176.

38. William J. Tobin, "Your Sense of Humor," *Talent* (Summer 1983), pp. 15-16.

39. Blumenfeld and Alpern, *The Smile Connection*, pp. 178-184.

Chapter Nine

1. Stewart Harral, *When It's Laughter You're After* (Norman: University of Oklahoma Press, 1962), p. ix.

2. Josh Lee, *How to Hold an Audience without a Rope* (Chicago: Ziff David, 1947), p. 100.

3. Roger C. Palms, "Punch Lines from the Pulpit," *Christianity Today*, 20 Apr. 1979, p. 28.

4. Laurence J. Peter and Bill Dana, *Laughter Prescription* (New York: Ballantine Books, 1982), p. 140.

5. Stewart Harral, *When It's Laughter You're After* (Norman, Okla.: University of Oklahoma Press, 1962), p. ix.

6. Tom Mullen, *Mountaintops and Molehills* (Waco, Texas: Word Books, 1978), p. 58.

7. Jim Savage, "What to do Before You Step Behind a Podium," *News At the Top*, Oct. 1985, p. 1.

8. Cal Samra, *The Joyful Christ: The Healing Power of Humor* (San Francisco: Harper & Row, 1986), p. 138.

9. Rusty Wright and Linda R. Wright, *Secrets of Successful Humor* (San Bernardino, Calif.: Here's Life Publishers, 1985), p. 89.

10. Allen James, comp., *Keep Smiling and Have a Happy Day* (New York: Random House, 1972), p. 19.

11. Samra, *The Joyful Christ*, p. 137.

12. Allen F. Harrod, "High Use of Humor," *Proclaim*, Jan. 1976, p. 44.

13. The material that I have shared by Vance Havner were statements that I heard him say in person. Recently, a new book which contains an array of such quotations has been published: Dennis J. Hester, comp., *The Vance Havner Quote Book* (Grand Rapids, 1986 Baker Book House.)

14. "Use of Humor Lauded," *Columbus Dispatch*, 27 Nov. 1980, p. F1.

15. Ronald Alsop, "Humor and Subtlety Supplant Hard-Selling Retailers' TV Ads," *Wall Street Journal*, 30 Jan. 1986, p. 27.

16. Mike Harden, "Ugly Is in the Mouth of the Beholder," *Columbus Dispatch Capitol Magazine*, 23 Feb. 1986, p. 4.

17. Bennett Cerf, *Laugh's on Me* (Garden City, N.Y.: Doubleday & Co., 1959), p. 11.

18. James, comp., *Keep Smiling*, p. 50.

19. JoAnne Kaufman, "Milton Berle: At 77, Wise and Still Cracking," *USA Today*, 12 Dec. 1985, p. D2.

20. Ibid.

21. Cerf, *Laugh's on Me*, p. 15

22. "Parodies Called Not a Good Sign," *Columbus Dispatch*, 28 Sept. 1986, p. A16.

23. Martin Ragaway, comp., *Funny, Funny Signs* (Los Angeles: Price/Stern/Sloan 1979).

24. Wright and Wright, *Secrets of Successful Humor*, p. 22.

25. Esther Blumenfeld and Lynne Alpern, *The Smile Connection* (Englewood Cliffs, N.J.: Prentice-Hall, 1986), p. 104.

26. Peter and Dana, *Laughter*, p. 127.

27. William J. Tobin, "Your Sense of Humor," *Talent* (Summer 1983), p. 16.

28. Peter and Dana, *Laughter*, p. 133.

29. Millard Bennett and John D. Corrigan, *Successful Communications and Effective Speaking* (West Nyack, N.Y.: Parker Publishing Co., 1972), p. 108.

30. Leonard Spinrad and Thelma Spinrad, *Speaker's Lifetime Library* (West Nyack, N.Y.: Parker Publishing Co., 1979), p. 129.

31. "Laughter Instead of Violence," *USA Today*, 110, Apr. 1982, pp. 2-3.

32. Tal D. Bonham, "An Interview with Jerry Clower," *L.I.G.H.T.* 1 (Fall 1984), p. 20.

33. Lee, *How to Hold an Audience*, p. 109.

34. Blumenfeld and Alpern, *The Smile Connection*, pp. 9-10.

35. Nancy Seaman, "Phenomena, Comment and Notes," *Smithsonian*, Nov. 1982, p. 40.

36. Jacob M. Brande, *Brande's Handbook of Humor for all Occasions* (Englewood Cliffs, N.J.: Prentice-Hall, 1958), p. 3.

37. Allen F. Harrod, "High Use of Humor," *Proclaim*, Jan. 1976, p. 43.

38. Josh Lee, *How to Hold an Audience*, p. 112.

39. Ibid.

40. Ibid., p. 109.

41. Jacob M. Brande, *Brande's Handbook of Humor*, p. 3.

Chapter Ten

1. Grady Nutt, "More on the Humor of Christ," *The Student*, 53, Feb. 1974, p. 22.

2. "Joking Helped Men Hang On," *Fort Worth Star-Telegram*, 28 Nov. 1983, p. A8.

3. Harvey Potthoff, "Humor and Religious Faith," in *Summary of Proceedings: 34th Annual Conference ATLA* (Philadelphia: ATLA, 1980), p. 77.

4. James Thurber, *Lanterns and Lances* (New York: Harper, 1955), p. 61.

5. Julius Gordon, *Your Sense of Humor* (New York: Didier, 1950), p. 23.

6. Tom Mullen, *Laughing Out Loud and Other Religious Experiences* (Waco, Texas: Word Books, 1983), p. 64.

7. Laurence J. Peter and Bill Dana, *Laughter Prescription* (New York: Ballantine Books, 1982), p. 64.

8. Allen James, comp., *Keep Smiling and Have a Happy Day* (New York: Random House, 1972), p. 43.

9. Ibid., p. 15.

10. Gaines S. Dobbins, "Is It Folly to be Jolly?" *Baptist Messenger*, 14 Dec. 1972, p. 3.

11. James, comp., *Keep Smiling*, p. 39.

12. Laurence J. Peter and Bill Dana, *Laughter*, p. 221.

13. Bryon W. Arledge, *Laugh with Your Teenager* (Wheaton, Ill.: Tyndale House, 1985), p. 23.

14. Ibid., p. 103 *ff*.

15. Dale M. Baughman, *Handbook of Humor in Education* (West Nyack, N.Y.: Parker Publishing Co., 1974), p. 129.

16. Fred D. Layman, "Theology and Humor," *Asbury Seminarian*, 38 (Winter 1982-83), p. 17 *ff*.

17. Ibid., p. 5.

18. Erma Bombeck, *At Wit's End* (New York: Fawcett Crest, 1965).

19. Jan S. Doward, "Even the Angels Must Laugh Sometimes," *These Times*, Feb. 1983, p. 26.

20. Grady Wilson, *Count It All Joy* (Nashville: Broadman Press, 1984), p. 244.

21. Tal D. Bonham, *The Treasury of Clean Church Jokes* (Nashville: Broadman Press, 1986), pp. 72-74.

22. Cal Samra, *The Joyful Christ: The Healing Power of Humor* (San Francisco: Harper & Row, 1986), p. 27.

23. Tom Mullen, *Laughing Out Loud*, p. 34.

24. Maurice Bozarth, "Those Who Shun Solemnity for a Laugh Find Comedy a Religious Experience," *Baptist Messenger*, 5 July 1984, p. 13.

25. *The Joyful Noiseletter*, Nov.-Dec. 1986, p. 3.

26. Mike Harden, "Sailing into Life's Sunset Can be Hazardous to the Health," *Columbus Dispatch*, 2 Feb. 1986, p. 4.

27. Nelvin Vos, *For God's Sake Laugh!* (Richmond, Va.: John Knox Press,

1967), p. 32. For an interesting array of such epitaphs, see Thomas C. Mann and Janet Greene, eds., *Over Their Dead Bodies,* (New York: Stephen Greene Press, 1961.)

28. Nelvin Vos, *For God's Sake Laugh!* p. 71.

29. Conrad Hyers, "Christian Humor: Uses and Abuses of Laughter," *Dialog,* 22 (Summer 1983), p. 203.

30. Mullen, *Laughing Out Loud,* p. 126.

31. Ibid., p. 19.

32. Potthoff, "Humor and Religious Faith," p. 80.

Notes on Quotable Quotations

1. Laurence J. Peter and Bill Dana, *Laughter Prescription* (New York: Ballantine Books, 1982), p. 73.

2. Allen James, comp., *Keep Smiling and Have a Happy Day* (New York: Random House, 1972), p. 14.

3. Jacob M. Brande, *Brande's Handbook of Humor for all Occasions* (Englewood Cliffs, N.J.: Prentice-Hall, 1958), p 11.

4. Esther Blumenfeld and Lynne Alpern, *The Smile Connection* (Englewood Cliffs, N.J.: Prentice-Hall, 1986), p. 155.

5. Kenneth Hamilton and Robert T. Haverluck, "Laughter and Vision," *Soundings* 55 (Summer 1972), p. 168.

6. *International Dictionary of Thoughts* (Chicago: J.G. Ferguson Publishing Company, 1969), p. 428.

7. Farrell Cross and Wilbur Cross, "Cheers! A Belly Laugh Can Help You Stay Well," *Science Digest*, (Nov. 1977), p. 16.

8. Blumenfeld and Alpern, *The Smile Connection*, p. 39.

9. Robert McAffee Brown, "Spirit's Eighth Gift," *Christianity & Crisis*, 4 Feb. 1980, p. 8.

10. Leonard Spinrad and Thelma Spinrad, *Speaker's Lifetime Library* (West Nyack, N.Y.: Parker Publishing Company, 1979), p. 129.

11. Eleanor Doan, *Sourcebook for Speakers* (Grand Rapids: Zondervan, 1965), p. 230.

12. James, *Keep Smiling and Have a Happy Day*, p. 36.

13. *International Dictionary of Thoughts*, p. 428.

14. Peter and Dana, *The Laughter Prescription*, p. 8.

15. Fred D. Layman, "Theology and Humor," *Asbury Seminarian*, 38 (Winter 1982-83), p. 18.

16. Grady Nutt, "Humortality," *The Student*, Feb. 1974, p. 6.

17. Tom Mullen, *Laughing Out Loud and Other Religious Experiences* (Waco, Texas: Word Books, 1983), p. 35.

18. Stewart Harral, *When It's Laughter You're After* (Norman, Okla.: University of Oklahoma Press, 1962), p. 123.

19. Cal Samra, *The Joyful Christ: The Healing Power of Humor* (San Francisco: Harper & Row, 1986), p. 9.

20. Mullen, *Laughing Out Loud*, p. 89.

21. Conrad Hyers, "Christian Humor: Uses and Abuses of Laughter," *Dialog*, 22 (Summer 1983), p. 201.

22. Blumenfeld and Alpern, *The Smile Connection*, p. 41.

23. Paul K. Jewett, "Wit and Humor of Life," *Christianity Today*, 8 June 1959, p. 9.

24. Mullen, *Laughing Out Loud*, p. 103.

25. Blumfeld and Alpern, *The Smile Connection*, p. 45.

26. J. Oswald Sanders, *Spiritual Leadership*, rev. ed. (Chicago: Moody Press, 1980), p. 36.

27. Rusty Wright and Linda R. Wright, *Secrets of Successful Humor* (San Bernardino, Calif.: Here's Life Publishers, 1985), p. 19.

28. Blumenfeld and Alpern, *The Smile Connection*, p. 40.

29. Conrad Hyers, "Comic Vision in a Tragic World," *Christian Century*, 20 Apr. 1983, p. 363.

30. Blumenfeld and Alpern, *The Smile Connection*, p. 47.

31. "Use of Humor Lauded," *Columbus Dispatch*, 27 Nov. 1980, p. F1.

32. Blumenfeld and Alpern, *The Smile Connection*, p. 43.

33. John W. Drakeford, *Humor in Preaching* (Grand Rapids: Zondervan Publishing House, 1986), p. 40.

34. Eugene J. Fisher, "Divine Comedy: Humor in the Bible," *Religious Education*, Nov. 1977, p. 579.

35. Frederick W. Danker, "Laughing with God," *Christianity Today*, 6 Jan. 1967, p. 11.

36. Conrad Hyers, "The Day that Jonah Swallowed the Whale," *L.I.G.H.T.*, 1 (Fall 1984), p. 13.

37. Fisher, "Divine Comedy: Humor in the Bible," p. 571.

38. John Vannorsdall, "Humor as Content and Device in Preaching," *Dialog*, 22 (Summer 1983), p. 190.

39. Conrad Hyers, *And God Created Laughter* (Atlanta: John Knox Press, 1987), p. 6.

40. Herb Barks, "Laughter: Sanity's Hope," *The Student*, Apr. 1976, p. 19.

41. Samra, *The Joyful Christ*, p. 203.

42. Ibid., p. 37.

43. Larry M. Taylor, "In Celebration of Humor," *The Student*, Apr. 1984, p. 16.

44. Grady Nutt, "More on the Humor of Christ," *The Student*, Feb. 1974, p. 23.

45. Samra, *The Joyful Christ*, p. 203.

46. Ibid., p. 11.

47. Ibid., p. 36.

48. Thomas B. Maston, *Real Life in Christ* (Nashville: Broadman Press, 1974), p. 111.

49. Meyer Friedman, MD, and Ray H. Rosenman, MD, *Treating Type A Behavior—and Your Heart* (New York: Fawcett Crest, 1984), p. 120.

50. Joe Johnson, *"Preacher, You're the Best Pasture We've Ever Had!"* (Nashville: Broadman Press, 1972), p. 11.

51. Robert Schuller, *The Be-Happy Attitudes* (Waco: Word Books, 1985), p. 20.

52. Larry M. Taylor, "In Celebration of Humor," *The Student*, Apr. 1984, p. 15.

53. Gary Webster, *Laughter in the Bible* (St. Louis: The Bethany Press, 1960), p. 106.

54. Humphrey Palmer, "Just Married, Cannot Come," *Novum Testamentum*, Oct. 1976.

55. Joseph K. Neumann, "Last Laugh the Best?" *Journal of Pastoral Practice*, 6 (1983), p. 43.

56. Maston, *Real Life in Christ*, p. 120.

57. Delos Miles, *Master Principles of Evangelism* (Nashville: Broadman Press, 1982), p. 76.

58. George A. Buttrick, *Sermons Preached in a University Church* (New York: Abingdon Press, 1959), p. 57.

59. Minnie Pearl with Joan Dew, *Minnie Pearl: an Autobiography* (New York: Simon & Schuster, 1980), p. 249.

60. Drakeford, *Humor in Preaching*, p. 101.

61. Kenneth Hamilton and Robert T. Haverluck, "Laughter and Vision," *Soundings*, 55 (Summer 1972), p. 176.

62. Larry M. Taylor, "In Celebration of Humor," *The Student*, Apr. 1984, p. 16.

63. Bernard Ramm, *After Fundamentalism* (San Francisco: Harper & Row, 1983), p. 197.

64. Samra, *The Joyful Christ*, p. 20.

65. *International Encyclopedia of the Social Sciences*, s.v. "Humor," by Jacob Levine, p. 7.

66. Samra, *The Joyful Christ*, p. 33.

67. Marcian Strange, "God and Laughter," *Worship*, Jan. 1971, p. 7.

68. Drakeford, *Humor in Preaching*, p. 74

69. Mullen, *Laughing Out Loud*, p. 125.

70. Ibid., p. 99.

71. Mike Harden, "Sick Humor Nothing to Laugh About," *Columbus Dispatch*, 2 Feb. 1986, p. 1B.

72. Jean Strange, "Famous Last Words," *Time*, 1 Aug. 1983, p. 69.

73. Tom Mullen, *Seriously, Life Is a Laughing Matter* (Waco, Texas: Word Books, 1978), p. 98.

74. Julius Gordon, *Your Sense of Humor* (New York: Didier, 1950), p. 213.

75. Betty Rogers, *Will Rogers: His Wife's Story* (Norman, Okla.: University of Oklahoma Press, 1979), p. 179.

76. Jean Strange, "Famous Last Words," *Time,* 1 Aug. 1983, p. 69.

77. Tom Mullen, *Laughing Out Loud,* p. 126.

78. Mullen, *Life Is a Laughing Matter,* p. 98.

79. Sharon Begley and John Carey, "A Healthy Dose of Laughter," *Newsweek,* 4 Oct. 1982, p. 74.

80. Raymond A. Moody, *Laugh after Laugh* (Jacksonville, Fla.: Headwaters Press, 1978), p. 27.

81. Conrad Hyers, "Time to Laugh," *Presbyterian Survey,* Apr. 1982, p. 15.

82. _____, ed., *Holy Laughter* (New York: Seabury Press, 1969), p. 133.

83. Nelvin Vos, "Religious Meaning of Comedy," *Christian Imagination* (Grand Rapids: Baker Book House, 1981), p. 253.

84. Hyers, *Holy Laughter,* p. 245.

85. Grady Nutt, *So Good. So Far* (Nashville: Impact Books, 1979), p. 143.

86. Hyers, "Christian Humor: Uses and Abuses of Laughter," p. 202.

87. Samra, *The Joyful Christ,* p. 197.

88. *International Dictionary of Thoughts,* p. 428.

89. Moody, *Laugh after Laugh,* p. 19.

90. Vos, *Christian Imagination,* p. 243.

91. Paul E. McGhee and Jeffrey H. Goldstein, eds., *Psychology of Humor* (New York: Academic Press, 1972), p. 43.

92. Jewett, "Wit and Humor of Life," p. 8.

93. Bryon W. Arledge, *Laugh with Your Teenager* (Wheaton: Tyndale House, 1985), p. 103.

94. Samra, *The Joyful Christ,* p. 32.

95. Spinrad and Spinrad, *Speaker's Lifetime Library,* p. 130.

96. Moody, *Laugh after Laugh,* pp. 38-39.

97. Conrad Hyers, "Christian Humor: Uses and Abuses of Laughter," *Dialog,* 22 (Summer 1983), p. 200.

98. Vos, *For God's Sake Laugh!* (Richmond, Va.: John Knox Press, 1987), p. 68.

99. Moody, *Laugh after Laugh,* p. 75.

100. Farrell Cross and Wilbur Cross, "Cheers! A Belly Laugh Can Help You Stay Well," *Science Digest,* Nov. 1977, p. 18.

101. Samra, *The Joyful Christ,* p. 22.

102. Ibid., p. 22.

103. "Face It: Smiles, Frowns Reveal Emotional Health," *Dallas Times Herald,* 24 Apr. 1982.

104. Moody, *Laugh after Laugh,* pp. 11-12.

105. Cross and Cross, "Cheers! A Belly Laugh Can Help You Stay Well," p. 18.

106. Dudley Zuver, *Salvation by Laughter* (New York: Harper & Brothers, 1933), p. 6.

107. Julia Keller, "Yukking It Up the Corporate Ladder," *Columbus Dispatch*, 27 Apr. 1986, p. G2.

108. Blumenfeld and Alpern, *The Smile Connection*, p. 92.

109. Keller, "Yukking It Up the Corporate Ladder," p. G2.

110. Wright and Wright, *Secrets of Successful Humor*, p. 36.

111. Peter and Dana, *Laughter Prescription*, p. 45.

112. Blumenfeld and Alpern, *The Smile Connection*, p. 90.

113. Doan, *Sourcebook for Speakers*, p. 230.

114. Schuller, *The Be-Happy Attitudes*, p. 61.

115. Blumenfeld and Alpern, *The Smile Connection*, p. 7.

116. Avner Ziv, *Personality and Sense of Humor* (New York: Springer Publishing Co., 1984), p. 3.

117. Samra, *The Joyful Christ*, p. 31.

118. Spinrad and Spinrad, *Speaker's Lifetime Library*, p. 129.

119. Louis Untermeyer, *Treasury of Laughter* (New York: Simon & Schuster, 1946), p. xviii.

120. Blumenfeld and Alpern, *The Smile Connection*, p. 85.

121. "Laughter Instead of Violence," *USA Today*, Apr. 1982.

122. Mullen, *Laughing Out Loud*, p. 46.

123. Jewett, "Wit and Humor of Life," p. 8.

124. Samra, *The Joyful Christ*, p. 9.

125. Penrose Saint Amant, "Church: A Community of Celebration Psalm 150, Luke 4:31," pp. 27-31, in *1980 ACPE Conference: Fantasy and Festivity in the Church* (New York: Association for Clinical Pastoral Education, 1980), p. 30.

126. Taylor, "In Celebration of Humor," p. 16.

127. Samra, *The Joyful Christ*, pp. 31-32.

128. Grady Nutt, "More on the Humor of Christ," p. 23.

129. James I. McCord, "On Getting and Keeping a Sense of Humor," *Princeton Seminary Bulletin*, 67 (Winter 1975), p. 49.

130. Wilbur H. Mullen, "Toward a Theology of Humor," *Christian Scholar's Review*, 3 (1973), p. 4.

131. Mullen, *Laughing Out Loud*, p. 19.

132. Marcian Strange, "God and Laughter," *Worship*, Jan. 1971, p. 11.

133. Layman, "Theology and Humor," p. 19.

134. "Humor, an Effective Tool in Therapy for Disturbed," *Florida Baptist Witness*, 10 June 1982, p. 8.

135. Goodman Ace, "Top of My Head," *Saturday Review*, 18 Dec. 1973, p. 8.

136. Gaines S. Dobbins, "Is It Folly to be Jolly?" *Baptist Messenger*, 14 Dec. 1972, p. 3.

137. Samra, *The Joyful Christ*, p. 37.

138. Grady Nutt, "Gift of Laughter" (Louisville: Oakriver Productions), audio recording.

139. James, *Keep Smiling*, p. 19.

140. Mullen, *Laughing Out Loud*, p. 26.

141. Layman, "Theology and Humor," p. 19.

142. G. Roger Schoehals, "Go Ahead, Laugh," *Herald of Holiness*, 15 March 1984, p. 5.

143. Wright and Wright, *Secrets of Successful Humor*, p. 44.

144. James, *Keep Smiling*, p. 9.

145. Mullen, *Laughing Out Loud*, p. 31.

146. Schuller, *The Be Happy Attitudes*, p. 231.

147. Mullen, *Life Is a Laughing Matter*, p. 92.

148. Frank B. Minirth and Paul D. Mier, *Happiness Is a Choice* (Grand Rapids: Baker Book House, 1978), p. 12.

149. Jack Gulledge, "Humor in the Pulpit: an Exclusive Interview with Jerry Clower," *Proclaim*, Apr. 1979, p. 5.

150. Moody, *Laugh after Laugh*, p. xiii.

151. Friedman and Roseman, *Type A Behavior and Your Heart*, p. 3.

152. Mullen, *Laughing Out Loud*, p. 28.

153. Steve Allen, *Funny People* (Briarcliffe Manor, N.Y.: Stein and Day Publishers, 1982), p. 4.

154. Wright and Wright, *Secrets of Successful Humor*, p. 35.

155. Blumenfeld and Alpern, *The Smile Connection*, p. 172.

156. Mullen, *Laughing Out Loud*, p. 117.

156. Bryon W. Arledge, *Laugh with Your Teenager* (Wheaton: Tyndale House, 1985), p. 42.

158. Phylis C. Dryden, "Families Need a Sense of Humor," *Home Life*, July 1981, p. 33.

159. Samra, *The Joyful Christ*, p. 142.

160. Yuri B. Boryev, "The World Will Never Die if It Dies Laughing," *UNESCO Courier*, Apr. 1976, p. 24.

161. Samra, *The Joyful Christ*, p. 24.

162. Friedman and Roseman, *Type A Behavior and Your Heart*, p. 218.

163. Hamilton and Haverluck, "Laughter and Vision," p. 168.

164. Belden C. Lane, "Spirituality and Politics of Holy Folly," *Christian Century* 15 Dec. 1982, p. 1282.

165. Hyers, "Christian Humor: Uses and Abuses of Laughter," p. 202.

166. Allen, *Funny People*, p. 2.

167. Peter and Dana, *Laughter Prescription*, p. 206.

168. Layman, "Theology and Humor," p. 17.

169. Peter and Dana, *Laughter Prescription*, p. 191.

170. Mullen, "Toward a Theology of Humor," p. 12.

171. Harral, *When It's Laughter You're After*, p. 123.

172. Nancy Seaman, "Phenomena, Comment and Notes," *Smithsonian*, Nov. 1982, p. 47.

173. Samra, *The Joyful Christ*, p. 4.

174. *International Dictionary of Thoughts*, p. 372.

175. Roger C. Palms, "Punch Lines from the Pulpit," *Christianity Today*, 20 Apr., p. 29.

176. Layman, "Theology and Humor," p. 16.

177. Mullen, *Laughing Out Loud*, p. 125.

178. *The Encyclopedia of Religious Quotations*, ed. and comp. Frank S. Mead (Westwind: Fleming H. Revell, 1965), p. 258.

179. Samra, *The Joyful Christ*, p. 101.

180. Doan, *Sourcebook for Speakers*, p. 224.

181. Moody, *Laugh after Laugh*, p. 29.

182. Doan, *Sourcebook for Speakers*, p. 224.

183. Mullen, *Laughing Out Loud*, p. 28.

184. Doan, *Sourcebook for Speakers*, p. 224.

185. Ibid.

186. Mead, *The Encyclopedia of Religious Quotations*, p. 258.

187. Doan, *Sourcebook for Speakers*, p. 224.

188. Mead, *The Encyclopedia of Religious Quotations*, p. 258.

189. Tom Mullen, *Mountaintops and Molehills* (Waco, Texas: Word Books, 1981), p. 17.

190. Doan, *Sourcebook for Speakers*, p. 224.

191. James, *Keep Smiling*, p. 37.

192. Harvey Potthoff, "Humor and Religious Faith," in *Summary of Proceedings: 34th Annual Conference ATLA*, (Philadelphia: ATLA, 1980), p. 78.

193. "Laughter Instead of Violence," *USA Today*, Apr. 1982.

194. Harral, *When It's Laughter You're After*, p. 123.

195. *International Dictionary of Thoughts*, p. 427.

196. Boryev, "The World Will Never Die if It Dies Laughing," p. 22.

197. "Laughter Instead of Violence," *USA Today*, Apr. 1982.

198. James, *Keep Smiling*, p. 53.

199. Spinrad and Spinrad, *Speaker's Lifetime Library*, p. 128.

200. Hyers, *And God Created Laughter*, p. 14.

201. Gordon, *Your Sense of Humor*, p. 219.

202. Nutt, "Humortality," p. 6.

203. Potthoff, "Humor and Religious Faith," p. 79.

204. Conrad Hyers, ed., *Holy Laughter* (New York: Seabury Press, 1969), p. 10.

205. Blumenfeld and Alpern, *The Smile Connection*, p. 39.

206. Samra, *The Joyful Christ*, p. 22.

207. Zuver, *Salvation By Laughter*, p. 259.

208. Buttrick, *Sermons Preached in a University Church*, p. 57.

209. Samra, *The Joyful Christ*, p. 22.

210. Mullen, *Laughing Out Loud*, p. 57.

211. Spinrad and Spinrad, *Speaker's Lifetime Library*, p. 129.

212. Mullen, *Laughing Out Loud*, p. 61.

213. Peter and Dana, *Laughter Prescription*, p. 74.

214. Samra, *The Joyful Christ*, p. 74.

215. Mullen, *Laughing Out Loud*, p. 43.

216. Zuver, *Salvation By Laughter*, p. 14.

217. Blumenfeld and Alpern, *The Smile Connection*, p. 43.

218. Gulledge, "Humor in the Pulpit," p. 6.

219. *International Dictionary of Thoughts*, p. 410.

220. Mullen, *Laughing Out Loud*, p. 81.

221. Peter and Dana, *Laughter Prescription*, p. 207.

222. *International Dictionary of Thoughts*, p. 410.

223. Drakeford, *Humor in Preaching*, p. 66.

224. Ibid. p. 74.

225. Moody, *Laugh after Laugh*, p. 118.

226. Samra, *The Joyful Christ*, p. 32.

227. Ibid., p. 29.

228. Ibid., p. 21.

229. "Why Laughing Is Good for You," *Science Digest*, June 1981, p. 17.

230. Norman Cousins, *Healing Heart* (New York: W. W. Norton, 1983), p. 202.

231. Claudia M. Dewane, "Humor in Theology," *Social Work*, Nov. 1978, p. 509.

232. Moody, *Laugh after Laugh*, pp. 33-34.

233. Samra, *The Joyful Christ*, p. 24.

234. Moody, *Laugh after Laugh*, p. 28.

235. Samra, *The Joyful Christ*, p. 25.

236. Doan, *Sourcebook for Speakers*, p. 230.

237. Antonia Van der Meer, "So This Is Fitness?" *Health*, Mar. 1983, p. 19.

238. Ibid.

239. Blumenfeld and Alpern, *The Smile Connection*, p. 21.

240. Schoenhals, "Go Ahead, Laugh," p. 5.

241. Samra, *The Joyful Christ*, p. 31.

242. Ibid., p. 18.

243. Wright and Wright, *Secrets of Successful Humor*, p. 23.

244. Samra, *The Joyful Christ: The Healing Power of Humor* (San Francisco: Harper and Row, 1986), p. 17.

245. Blumenfeld and Alpern, *The Smile Connection*, p. 39.

246. Moody, *Laugh after Laugh*, p. 37.

247. Friedman and Roseman, *Type A Behavior and Your Heart*, p. 3.

248. "Laughter Stressed at Meeting," *The Columbus Dispatch*, 21 Mar. 1987, p. 4A.

249. Wright and Wright, *Secrets of Successful Humor*, p. 21.

250. "Laughter Stressed at Meeting," p. 4A.

251. Maurice Bozarth, "Those Who Shun Solemnity for a Laugh Find Comedy a Religious Experience," *Baptist Messenger*, 73 5 July 1984, p. 13.

252. Zuver, *Salvation by Laughter* (New York: Harper & Brothers, 1933), p. 2.

253. Taylor, "In Celebration of Humor," p. 15.

254. Reinhold Niebuhr, "Humour and Faith," *20 Centuries of Great Preaching*, Vol. 10, comp. Clyde E. Fant, Jr., and William M. Pinson, Jr. (Waco, Texas: Word Books, 1971), p. 377.

255. John E. Benson, "Divine Sense of Humor" *Dialog*, 22 (New York: Doubleday and Co., 1961), p. 101.

256. Hyers, *Holy Laughter*, p. 27.

257. Bernard Ramm, *After Fundamentalism* (San Francisco: Harper & Row, 1983), p. 196.

258. Potthoff, "Humor and Religious Faith," p. 77.

259. Vannorsdall, "Humor as Content and Device in Preaching," p. 188.

260. Hyers, *Holy Laughter*, p. 244.

261. Jackson Lee Ice, "Notes Toward a Theology of Humor," *Religion in Life*, 42 (Autumn 1973), p. 391.

262. Taylor, "In Celebration of Humor," p. 15.

263. Vos, "Religious Meaning of Comedy," pp. 241-253.

264. Potthoff, "Humor and Religious Faith," p. 76.

265. Sanders, *Spiritual Leadership*, rev. ed., p. 94.

266. Doan, *Sourcebook for Speakers*, p. 224.

267. Fisher, "Divine Comedy: Humor in the Bible," p. 572.

268. Saint Amant, "Church: A Community of Celebration Psalm 150, Luke 4:31," pp. 27-31.

269. "Eutychus and His Kin," *Christianity Today*, 16 March 1959, p. 17.

270. Hyers, *Holy Laughter*, p. 243.

271. Samra, *The Joyful Christ*, p. 4.

272. Mullen, "Toward a Theology of Humor," p. 11.

273. Niebuhr, *20 Centuries of Great Preaching*, p. 373.

274. Hyers, "Time to Laugh," p. 14.

275. Ice, "Notes Toward a Theology of Humor," p. 399.

276. Ramm, *After Fundamentalism*, p. 195.

277. Vos, "Religious Meaning of Comedy," pp. 241-253.

278. James Masters, "Researchers Say Laughter Is a Serious Subject," *Fort Worth Star-Telegram*, 23-24 Nov. 1983, p. 7.

279. Saint Amant, "Church: A Community of Celebration Psalm 150, Luke 4:31," pp. 27-31.

280. *International Dictionary of Thoughts*, p. 427.

281. Brown, "Spirit's Eighth Gift," p. 9.

282. Mullen, "Toward a Theology of Humor," p. 9.

283. Jan S. Doward, "Even the Angels Laugh Sometimes," *These Times*, Feb. 1983, p. 25.

284. Ramm, *After Fundamentalism*, p. 194.

285. Mullen, "Toward a Theology of Humor," p. 12.

286. Barks, "Laughter: Sanity's Hope," p. 19.

287. Drakeford, *Humor in Preaching*, p. 23.

288. Hyers, *And God Created Laughter,* p. 13.

289. Kenneth Chafin, "Is Humor Holy?" *Baptist Record* (16 Nov. 1968).

290. Henri Cormier, *Humor of Jesus* (New York: Alba House, 1977).

291. Drakeford, *Humor in Preaching,* p. 72.

292. Mullen, *Laughing Out Loud,* p. 54.

293. Dewane, "Humor in Theology," p. 508.

294. "Laughter Instead of Violence," *USA Today,* Apr. 1982.

295. Anthony J. Chapman and Hugh C. Foot, *Humour and Laughter: Theory, Research and Application* (Chichester, Eng.: Wiley & Sons, Ltd., 1976), p. 1).

296. Blumenfeld and Alpern, *The Smile Connection,* p. 42.

297. Potthoff, "Humor and Religious Faith," p. 60.

298. Mullen, *Laughing Out Loud,* p. 49.

299. Ibid., p. 33.

300. Peter L. Berger, *Precarious Vision* (Garden City, N.Y.: Doubleday & Co., 1961), p. 209.

301. Mullen, *Laughing Out Loud,* p. 51.

302. Samra, *The Joyful Christ,* p. 35.

303. Mullen, *Laughing Out Loud,* p. 34.

304. Blumenfeld and Alpern, *The Smile Connection,* p. 27.

305. Allen, *Funny People,* p. 1.

306. Eivind Berggrav, "Humor and Seriousness," *Dialog,* 22 (Summer 1983), p. 206.

307. *International Dictionary of Thoughts,* p. 427.

308. Hyers, *Holy Laughter,* p. 216.

309. Vos, "Religious Meaning of Comedy," pp. 253.

310. Sanders, *Spiritual Leadership,* p. 19.

311. Ice, "Notes Toward a Theology of Humor," p. 392.

312. Vannorsdall, "Humor as Content and Device in Preaching," p. 188.

313. Mullen, *Laughing Out Loud and Other Religious Experiences,* p. 41.

314. Ann Landers, "Funeral Prompts Laughter and Tears," *Columbus Dispatch,* 23 Nov. 1984, p. H2.

315. Samra, *The Joyful Christ,* p. 24.

316. Drakeford, *Humor in Preaching,* p. 22.

317. Harral, *When It's Laughter You're After,* p. xi.

318. *International Dictionary of Thoughts,* p. 372.

319. James, *Keep Smiling,* p. 48.

320. Samra, *The Joyful Christ,* p. 21.

321. James, *Keep Smiling,* p. 13.

322. William Barclay, *The Mind of Jesus* (New York: Harper & Brothers, 1960), p. 93.

323. James, *Keep Smiling,* p. 60.

324. Drakeford, *Humor in Preaching,* p. 90.

325. Carol Kivo, "Universal Remedy," *Home Life,* Sept. 1977, p. 43.

326. Brande, *Handbook of Humor,* p. 2.

327. *International Dictionary of Thoughts*, p. 410.

328. Drakeford, *Humor in Preaching*, p. 93.

329. Allen F. Harrod, "High Use of Humor," *Proclaim*, Jan. 1976, p. 44.

330. Anonymous.

331. Harrod, "High Use of Humor," p. 44

332. Drakeford, *Humor in Preaching*, p. 96.

333. Blumenfeld and Alpern, *The Smile Connection*, p. 107.

334. Sanders, *Spiritual Leadership*, p. 95.

335. Charles Haddon Spurgeon, *Lectures to My Students*, rev. ed. (Grand Rapids: Zondervan, 1954), p. 362.

336. Mullen, *Mountaintops and Molehills*, p. 57.

337. Vannorsdall, "Humor as Content and Device in Preaching," p. 188.

338. Drakeford, *Humor in Preaching*, p. 101.

339. Hyers, "Christian Humor: Uses and Abuses of Laughter," p. 200.

340. *International Dictionary of Thoughts*, p. 410.

341. Ice, "Notes Toward a Theology of Humor," p. 397.

342. Jim Hassett and Gary E. Schwartz, "Why Can't People Take Humor Seriously?" *New York Times Magazine*, 6 Feb. 1977, p. 103.

343. Blumenfeld and Alpern, *The Smile Connection*, p. 46.

344. Wright and Wright, *Secrets of Successful Humor*, p. 34.

345. Ziv, *Personality and Sense of Humor*, p. 29.

346. Ibid.

347. Blumenfeld and Alpern, *The Smile Connection*, p. 52.

348. Johnson, *"Preacher, You're the Best,"* p. 11.

349. Blumenfeld and Alpern, *The Smile Connection*, p. 5.

350. Harrod, "High Use of Humor," p. 44.

351. Blumenfeld and Alpern, *The Smile Connection*, p. 50.

352. Samra, *The Joyful Christ The Healing Power of Humor* p. 5.

353. Drakeford, *Humor in Preaching*, p. 49.

354. Bozarth, "Those Who Shun Solemnity for a Laugh Find Comedy a Religious Experience," p. 13.

355. Peter and Dana, *Laughter Prescription*, p. 45.

356. Blumenfeld and Alpern, *The Smile Connection*, p. 52.

357. Drakeford, *Humor in Preaching*, p. 49.

358. Cross and Cross, "Cheers! A Belly Laugh Can Help You Stay Well," p. 20.

359. Vannorsdall, "Humor as Content and Device in Preaching," p. 187.

360. Brande, *Handbook of Humor for all Occasions*, p. 6.

361. Drakeford, *Humor in Preaching*, p. 43.

362. William J. Tobin, "Your Sense of Humor," *Talent* (Summer 1983), p. 16.

363. Drakeford, *Humor in Preaching*, p. 12.

364. Hassett and Schwartz, "Why Can't People Take Humor Seriously?" p. 103.

365. John Bussey, "U.S. Presidents are Very Funny Fellows, Often on Purpose," *The Wall Street Journal*, 17 Sept. 1986, p.1.

366. James, *Keep Smiling*, p. 44.

367. Ibid., p. 59.

368. Mullen, *Laughing Out Loud*, p. 33.

369. Peter and Dana, *Laughter Prescription*, p. 145.

370. Untermeyer, *Treasury of Laughter*, p. xviii.

371. Spinrad and Spinrad, *Speaker's Lifetime Library*, p. 128.

Bibliography

Ace, Goodman. "Top of My Head," *Saturday Review*, 18 Dec. 1973, p. 8.

Allen, Nancy, M.P.H., and Peck, Michael L., Ph.D. "Suicide in Young People." Pamphlet. West Point, Pa.: Merek, Sharp and Dohme, n.d.

Allen, Steve. *Funny People*. Briarcliffe Manor, N.Y.: Stein and Day Publishers, 1982.

———. *More Funny People*. Briarcliffe Manor, N.Y.: Stein and Day Publishers, 1982.

Alsop, Ronald. "Humor and Subtlety Supplant Hard Selling Retailers' TV Ads." *Wall Street Journal*, 30 January 1986, p. 27.

Arledge, Byron W. *Laugh with Your Teenager*. Wheaton, Ill.: Tyndale House, 1985.

Augsburger, David. "Medicine of Laughter." Harrisonburg, Va.: Mennonite Hour, No. 113.

"Baby Boom Suicide Wave." *Columbus Dispatch*, 8 September 1986, p. 1.

Barclay, William. *The Mind of Jesus*. New York: Harper and Brothers, 1960.

Barks, Herb. "Laughter: Sanity's Hope." *The Student*, April 1976, pp. 16-19.

Baughman, M. Dale. *Handbook of Humor in Education*. West Nyack, N.Y.: Parker Publishing Co., 1974.

Begley, Sharon, and Carey, John. "A Healthy Dose of Laughter." *Newsweek,* 4 October 1982, p. 74.

"Behavior: Killing Laughter." *Time,* 2 August 1976, p. 58.

Bennett, Millard, and Corrigan, John D. *Successful Communications and Effective Speaking.* West Nyack, N.Y.: Parker Publishing Co., 1972.

Benson, John E. "Divine Sense of Humor." *Dialog,* No. 22 (Summer 1983), pp. 191-197.

Berger, Peter L. *Precarious Vision.* Garden City, N.Y.: Doubleday and Co., 1961.

Berggrav, Eivind. "Humor and Seriousness." *Dialog,* No. 22 (Summer 1983), pp. 206-210.

Blumenfeld, Esther, and Alpern, Lynne. *The Smile Connection.* Englewood Cliffs, N.J.: Prentice-Hall, 1986.

Bombeck, Erma. *At Wit's End.* New York: Fawcett Crest, 1965.

Bonham, Tal D. *Another Treasury of Clean Jokes.* Nashville: Broadman Press, 1983.

————. "An Interview with Jerry Clower." *L.I.G.H.T.,* 1 (Fall 1984), pp. 19-21.

————. "Living the Love Life." *Ohio Baptist Messenger,* 12 February 1981, p. 8.

————. "We Sure Could Use a Little Good News." *Ohio Baptist Messenger,* 12 January 1984, p. 9.

————. "Easter—Our Blessed Assurance."*Ohio Baptist Messenger,* 9 April 1981, p. 8.

————. "Suggestions for Stress." *Ohio Baptist Messenger,* 26 July 1984, p. 8.

————. *The Demands of Discipleship.* Pine Bluff, Ark.: Discipleship Book Company, 1967.

————. "The Influence of the Bible." *Ohio Baptist Messenger,* 28 June 1984.

————. *Treasury of Clean Business Jokes.* Nashville: Broadman Press, 1985.

———. *Treasury of Clean Church Jokes*. Nashville: Broadman Press, 1986.

———. *Treasury of Clean Country Jokes*. Nashville: Broadman Press, 1986.

———. *Treasury of Clean Jokes*. Nashville: Broadman Press, 1981.

———. *Treasury of Clean Sports Jokes*. Nashville: Broadman Press, 1986.

———. *Treasury of Clean Teenage Jokes*. Nashville: Broadman Press, 1985.

Boryev, Yuri B. "The World Will Never Die if It Dies Laughing." *UNESCO Courier*, April 1976, pp. 22-24.

Bozarth, Maurice. "Those Who Shun Solemnity for a Laugh Find Comedy a Religious Experience." *Baptist Messenger*, 5 July 1984, p. 13.

Breecher, Maury M. "10 Keys to Happiness." *Columbus Dispatch*, 5 November 1982, p. 1D.

Brande, Jacob M. *Brande's Handbook of Humor for all Occasions*. Englewood Cliffs, N.J.: Prentice Hall, 1958.

Brown, Robert McAffee. "Spirit's Eighth Gift." *Christianity & Crisis*, 4 February 1980, pp. 8-10.

Burleson, Paul. "The Voice." Newsletter. Vital Truth Ministries (Summer 1986, p. 2.

Burns, Robert E. "Some Humor is Out of Bounds." *U.S. Catholic*, January 1979, p. 2.

Bussey, John. "U.S. Presidents are Very Funny Fellows, Often on Purpose." *The Wall Street Journal*, 17 September 1986, p. 1 & 27.

Buttrick, George A. *Sermons Preached in a University Church*. New York: Abingdon Press, 1959.

Byron, Christopher. "Killing Laughter." *Time*, 2 August 1976, p. 58.

Cameron, James R. *God, The Christlike*. Nashville: Cokesbury Press, 1935.

Carter, James E. *Facing the Final Foe.* Nashville: Broadman Press, 1986.

Cerf, Bennett. *Laugh's on Me.* Garden City, N.Y.: Doubleday and Co., 1959.

Chapman, Anthony J., and Foot, Hugh C., eds. *Humour and Laughter, International Conference on Research Into: "It's a Funny Thing Humour."* Oxford, Eng.: Pergamon Press, 1976.

_____. *Humour and Laughter: Theory, Research and Application.* Chichester, Eng.: Wiley & Sons, Ltd., 1976.

Churchill, Ralph D. "Your 'Blu-Oops' Are Showing" *Fort Worth Tribune,* 31 May 1963.

Clower, Jerry. *Let the Hammer Down!* Waco, Texas: Word Books, 1978.

Coleman, James C. *Abnormal Psychology and Modern Life.* Glenview, Ill.: Scott, Foresman & Co., 1964.

Cooper, Edgar R. "Be Happy." *Florida Baptist Witness* (1979):4.

Cormier, Henri. *Humor of Jesus.* New York: Alba House, 1977.

Cousins, Norman. *Anatomy of an Illness.* New York: W. W. Norton, 1979.

_____. "Anatomy of an Illness." *Reader's Digest,* June 1977, pp. 130-134.

_____. "Anatomy of an Illness." *New England Journal of Medicine,* 23 December 1976, pp. 1458-1463.

_____. "Anatomy of an Illness." *Saturday Review,* 28 May 1977, p. 4 *ff.*

_____. *Healing Heart.* New York: W.W. Norton, 1983.

_____. "Healing Heart." *Ladies' Home Journal,* October 1983, p. 42 *ff.*

Cross, Farrell, and Cross, Wilbur. "Cheers! A Belly Laugh Can Help You Stay Well." *Science Digest,* November 1977, pp. 15-21.

Danker, Frederick W. "Laughing with God." *Christianity Today,* 6 January 1967, pp. 16-18.

Dean, Lou. "A Letter for Later to My Son." *McCall's,* May 1986, p. 162.

Deedy, John. "Church in the World: Sober Surveys and Religious Humor." *Theology Today,* October 1977, pp. 299-302.

Dentzer, Susan. "A Cure for Job Stress." *Newsweek,* 2 June 1986, pp. 46-47.

Dewane, Claudia M. "Humor in Therapy." *Social Work,* November 1978, pp. 508-510.

Doan, Eleanor. *Sourcebook for Speakers.* Grand Rapids: Zondervan, 1965.

Dobbins, Gaines S. "Is It Folly to be Jolly?" *Baptist Messenger,* 14 December 1972, p. 2 *ff.*

Doward, Jan. S "Even the Angels Must Laugh Sometimes." *These Times,* February 1983, pp. 24-27.

Dryden, Phylis C. "Families Need a Sense of Humor." *Home Life,* July 1981, pp. 31-33.

Duddington, John W. "Conclusive Laughter of God." *Christianity Today,* 16 March 1959, pp. 13-15.

Eastman, Max. *Sense of Humor.* New York: Charles Scribner's Sons, 1921.

Encyclopedia of Religion and Ethics. S.v. "Humour," by John Reid; "Laughter," by C. Lloyd Morgan.

Erasmus, Desideririus. *Praise and Folly.* Chicago: Packard and Co., 1946.

"Eutychus and His Kin." *Christianity Today,* 16 March 1959, pp. 17-18.

"Face It: Smiles, Frowns Reveal Emotional Health." *Dallas Times Herald,* 24 April 1982.

Fields, W.C. "It Only Hurts When I Don't Laugh." *The Student,* February 1974, pp. 8-11.

Fisher, Eugene J. "Divine Comedy: Humor in the Bible."
    Religious Education November 1977, pp. 571-579.
Flugel, J.C. "Humor and Laughter." In *Handbook of So-
    cial Psychology.* 2 vols. pp. 709-734. Edited by Gardner
    Lindzay. Cambridge, Mass.: Addison-Wesley, 1954.
Flynn, Leslie B. *Serve Him with Joy.* Wheaton, Ill.: Key
    Publishers, 1960.
_____. *Serve Him with Mirth—The Place of Humor in the
    Christian Life.* Grand Rapids: Zondervan, 1960.
Friedman, Meyer, M.D., and Rosenman, Ray H., M.D.
    Type A Behavior and Your Heart. New York: Fawcett
    Crest, 1974.
Friedman, Meyer, MD, and Rosenman, Ray H., MD,
    Treating Type A Behavior—and Your Heart. New York:
    Fawcett Crest, 1984.
Garrett, Graeme. " 'My Brother Esau is an Hairy Man': An
    Encounter Between the Comedian and the Preacher."
    Scottish Journal of Theology 33 (1980) 239-256.
Gelman, David, with George Hackett. "Making Fun for
    Profit." *Newsweek,* 20 April 1983, p. 70.
Gevirtz, Stanley. "Of Patriarchs and Puns: Joseph at the
    Fountain, Jacob at the Ford." *Hebrew Union College
    Annual* 46 (1976):33-55.
Gordon, Julius. *Your Sense of Humor.* New York: Didier,
    1950.
Gorney, Cynthia. "Everyday Therapy Helps Type A's
    Calm Down." *Columbus Dispatch* 19 September 1984,
    p. G5.
Gruner, Charles R. *Understanding Laughter: The Work-
    ings of Wit and Humor.* Chicago: Nelson Hall, 1978.
Gulledge, Jack. "Humor in the Pulpit: an Exclusive Inter-
    view with Jerry Clower." *Proclaim,* April 1979, pp. 4-7.
Hamilton, Kenneth, and Haverluck, Robert T. "Laughter

and Vision." *Soundings,* no. 55 (Summer 1972), pp. 163-177.

Harden, Mike. "Aunt Gracie Didn't Tell Us if Mama Still Wears Bangs." *Columbus Dispatch,* 26 May 1985, p. 5.

———. "There's Noah Way He'll Get It Built." *Columbus Dispatch,* 20 November 1985, p. 2F.

———. "Sailing Into Life's Sunset Can Be Hazardous to the Health." *Columbus Dispatch,* 2 February 1986, p. 4.

———. "Sick Humor Nothing to Laugh About." *Columbus Dispatch,* 2 February 1986, p. 1B.

———. "Ugly Is in the Mouth of the Beholder." *Columbus Dispatch* "Capitol Magazine," 23 February 1986, p. 4.

Harral, Stewart. *When It's Laughter You're After.* Norman, Okla.: University of Oklahoma Press, 1962.

Harrod, Allen F. "High Use of Humor." *Proclaim,* January 1976, p. 43-44.

Hassett, Jim, and Schwartz, Gary E. "Why Can't People Take Humor Seriously?" *New York Times Magazine,* 6 February 1977, pp. 102-103.

Helitzer, Melvin. *Comedy Techniques for Writers and Performers.* Athens, Ohio: Lawhead Press, 1984.

Henry, Carl F.H. *Christian Personal Ethics.* Grand Rapids: Wm. B. Eerdmans Publishing Co., 1957.

Hertzler, Joyce O. *Laughter: A Socio-scientific Analysis.* New York: Exposition Press, 1970.

Hester, Dennis J. "Vance Havner: Enjoying the Desires of His Heart." *Proclaim,* October 1982, pp. 4-5.

———, comp. *Vance Havner Quote Book.* Grand Rapids: Baker Book House, 1986.

Hill, Frederic B. "We Dare Not Lose the Will to Laugh." *Columbus Dispatch,* 14 January 1983, p. 3B.

Hill, Rick. *Don't Trip Into the Podium.* Boca Raton, Fla.: Hill Publishing, 1981.

Holland, Norman N. *Laughing, a Psychology of Humor.* Ithaca, N.Y.: Cornell University Press, 1982.

Hood, Marshall. "Laugh: Going for the Giggle May be the Best Medicine." *Columbus Dispatch,* 2 February 1983, p. 1C.

Horst, P. W. van der. "Is Wittiness Unchristian?" In *Miscellanea Neotestamentica.* 2 vols. Edited by T. Baarda. supplements to *Novum Testamentum,* vol. 48. Leiden: E.J. Brill, 1978.

How's Your Sense of Humor? New York: Good Reading Rack Service Division, Koster-Dana Corporation, 1962.

Hughey, J.D. "How to Praise God When It Is Difficult." *Baptist Program,* June 1983, p. 5-8.

"Humor, an Effective Tool in Therapy for Disturbed." *Florida Baptist Witness,* 10 June 1982, p. 8.

Hvidberg, Flemming F. *Weeping and Laughing in the Old Testament.* Leiden: E.J. Brill, 1962.

Hyers, Conrad. "Christian Humor: Uses and Abuses of Laughter." *Dialog,* no. 22 (Summer 1983, pp. 98-205.

_____. "Comedy and Creation." *Theology Today,* April 1982, pp. 17-26.

_____. "Comic Vision in a Tragic World." *Christian Century,* 20 April 1983, p. 363-367.

_____. "The Day that Jonah Swallowed the Whale." *L.I.G.H.T.,* 1 (Fall 1984), pp. 13-18.

_____. "Funny Faith." *One World,* July 1982, pp. 10-11.

_____, ed. *Holy Laughter.* New York: Seabury Press, 1969.

_____. "Time to Laugh." *Presbyterian Survey,* April 1982, pp. 14-15.

Ice, Jackson L. "Notes Toward a Theology of Humor." *Religion in Life,* no. 42 (Autumn 1973, pp. 388-400.

Ingram, Joe L., "Viewpoint." *Baptist Messenger,* 1 June 1980, p. 7.

International Dictionary of Thoughts. Chicago: J.G. Ferguson Publishing Co., 1969.

International Dictionary of New Testament Theology. Grand Rapids, Michigan: Zondervan Publishing House, 1971.

International Encyclopedia of the Social Sciences. S.v. "Humor," by Jacob Levine.

International Standard Bible Encyclopedia. S.v. "Humor in the Bible," by C.D. Linton.

James, Allen, ed. *Keep Smiling and Have a Happy Day.* New York: Random House, 1972.

Jeter, Jeremiah Bell. *The Recollections of a Long Life.* Richmond: The Religious Herald Co., 1891.

Jewett, Paul K. "Wit and Humor of Life." *Christianity Today,* 8 June 1959, pp. 5-9.

Johnson, Joe. *"Preacher, You're the Best Pasture We've Ever Had!"* Nashville: Broadman Press, 1972.

"Joking Helped Men Hang On." *Fort Worth Star-Telegram* 28 November 1983, p. 8A.

Jonsson, Jakob. *Humour and Irony in the New Testament.* Reykjavik, Ice.: Bokatgafa Menningarsjod, 1965.

Joubert, Laurent. *Treatise on Laughter.* Translated by George D. de Rocher. Tuscaloosa, Ala.: University of Alabama Press, 1980.

The Joyful Noiseletter (Nov.-Dec., 1986).

Kaufman, JoAnne. "Milton Berle: At 77, Wise and Still Cracking." *USA Today,* 12 Dec. 1985, p. 2D.

Keller, Julia. "Yukking It Up the Corporate Ladder." *Columbus Dispatch,* 27 April 1986, p. G2.

King, Robbie W. "Humor Holds Untapped Healing." *SBC Today,* April 1985, p. 5.

Kivo, Carol. "Universal Remedy." *Home Life,* September 1977, p. 43.

Klagburn, Francine. *Married People Staying Together in the Age of Divorce*. Bantam Book Publishing Co., 1985.

Loenig, John. "St. Mark 'On Stage: Laughing All the Way to the Cross.' " *Theology Today*, April 1979, pp. 84-86.

Korda, Michael. "The New Pessimism." *Newsweek*, 14 June 1982, p. 20.

Landers, Ann. "Funeral Prompts Laughter and Tears." *Columbus Dispatch*, 23 November 1984, p. H2.

Lane, Belden C. "Spirituality and Politics of Holy Folly." *Christian Century*, 15 December 1982, pp. 1281-1286.

"Laughter Instead of Violence." *USA Today*, April 1982, pp. 2-3.

Layman, Fred D. "Theology and Humor." *Asbury Seminarian*, (Winter 1982-83, pp. 3-25.

Lee, Josh. *How to Hold an Audience without a Rope*. Chicago: Ziff David, 1947.

Lee, A. Russell, M.D.; Costa, Contra; and Ross, Charlotte P. "Suicide in Youth and What You Can Do about It." Pamphlet. San Mateo County, Calif.: Suicide Prevention and Crisis Center.

Lehmann, P. E. "Laughter: Mind/Body Restorer." *Vogue*, October 1979, p. 331 *ff*.

Levine, Jacob. *Motivation in Humor*. New York: Atherton Press, 1969.

Lloyd-Jones, D. Martyn. *Preaching and Preachers*. Grand Rapids: Zondervan, 1971.

Ludovici, Anthony M. *Secret of Laughter*. London: Constable and Son, 1932.

McCollum, Evelyn. "Humor Holds Our Home Together." *Home Life*, July 1977, pp. 38-39.

McCord, James I. "On Getting and Keeping a Sense of Humor." *Princeton Seminary Bulletin*, no. 67 (Winter 1975, pp. 48-51.

McCormack, Mike. *What They Don't Teach You at Harvard Business School.* New York: Bantam Books, 1986.

McDowell, Josh. *Evidence that Demands a Verdict.* San Bernardino, Calif.: Campus Crusade for Christ, 1972.

————. *More Than a Carpenter.* Wheaton, Ill.: Tyndale House, 1977.

McGhee, Paul E., and Goldstein, Jeffrey H., eds. *Psychology of Humor.* New York: Academic Press, 1972.

Mamchak, P. Susan, and Mamchak, Steven R. *Educator's Lifetime Library of Stories, Quotes, Anecdotes, Wit and Humor.* West Nyack, N.Y.: Parker Publishing Co., 1979.

Masters, James. "Researchers Say Laughter Is a Serious Subject." *Fort Worth Star-Telegram* (November 23-24, 1983):7.

Maston, T. B. *Real Life in Christ.* Nashville: Broadman Press, 1974.

Mead, Frank S., ed. and comp. *Encyclopedia of Religious Quotations.* Westwind: Fleming H. Revell, 1965, p. 158.

Meer, Antonia van der. "So This is Fitness?" *Health,* March 1983, p. 19.

Miles, Delos. *Master Principles of Evangelism.* Nashville: Broadman Press, 1982.

Minirth, Frank B., and Mier, Paul D. *Happiness Is a Choice.* Grand Rapids: Baker Book House, 1978.

Monro, D. H. *Argument of Laughter.* South Bend, Ind.: University of Notre Dame Press, 1963.

Moody, Raymond A. *Laugh after Laugh.* Jacksonville, Fla.: Headwaters Press, 1978.

Moore, W. Levon. "Let's Reverse This Trend." *Baptist Record,* 11 November 1982.

Morreall, John. *Taking Laughter Seriously.* Albany, N.Y.: State University of New York, 1983.

Mullen, Tom. *Laughing Out Loud and Other Religious Experiences.* Waco, Texas: Word Books, 1983.

_____. *Mountaintops and Molehills.* Waco, Texas: Word Books, 1981.

_____. *Seriously, Life Is a Laughing Matter.* Waco: Word Books, 1978.

_____. *Where 2 or 3 are Gathered Together, Someone Spills His Milk.* Waco, Texas: Word Books, 1973.

Mullen, Wilbur H. "Toward a Theology of Humor." *Christian Scholar's Review,* no. 3 (1973), pp. 3-12.

Neumann, Joseph K. "Last Laugh the Best?" *Journal of Pastoral Practice* 6 (1983):42-47.

New International Dictionary of New Testament Theology. S.v. "Laugh," by E. M. Embry.

Newsweek. 4 October 1982, p. 74; see also Maria Harris, "Religious Education and the Comic Vision." *Religious Education,* no. 75 (1980), p. 427.

Nicholas, Tim. "Humor in Home Missions." *Missions USA,* January 1986, p. 33 *ff.*

Niebuhr, Reinhold. "Humour and Faith." In *20 Centuries of Great Preaching* 10:373-382. Compiled by Clyde E. Fant, Jr. and William M. Pinson, Jr. Waco, Texas: Word Books, 1971.

Nieting, Lorenz. "Humor in the New Testament." *Dialog,* no. 22 (Summer 1983), pp. 168-170.

Nutt, Grady. "Gift of Laughter." Louisville: Oakriver Productions, 1987. Audio cassette.

_____. "Humor, Story, and Communication." Vol. 8. Tape 1, Catalyst Cassettes. (January 1976).

_____. "Humortality." *The Student,* February 1974, pp. 2-6.

_____. "More on the Humor of Christ." *The Student,* February 1974, pp. 22-24.

_____. *So Good, So Far.* Nashville: Impact Books, 1979.

O'Neill, Eugene. *Lazarus Laughed.* New York: Random House, 1941.

Palmer, Humphrey. "Just Married, Cannot Come." *Novum Testamentum,* October 1976, pp. 241-257.

Palms, Roger C. "Punch Lines from the Pulpit." *Christianity Today,* 20 April 1979, pp. 28-29.

"Parodies Called Not a Good Sign." *Columbus Dispatch,* 28 September 1986, p. 16A.

Patterson, Ben. "Dirty Jokes." *Wittenburg Door,* April 1981, pp. 3-4.

Pearl, Minnie, with Dew, Joan. *Minnie Pearl: an Autobiography.* New York: Simon & Schuster, 1980.

Peale, Norman Vincent. *The Positive Power of Jesus Christ.* Wheaton: Tyndale House Publishing, 1980.

Perret, Gene. *How to Write & Sell Your Sense of Humor.* Cincinnati: Writer's Digest Books, 1982.

Peter, Laurence J., and Dana, Bill. *Laughter Prescription.* New York: Ballantine Books, 1982.

Pierson, Arthur T. *Knowing the Scripture.* New York: Gospel Publishing House, 1910.

Plimpton, George. "How to Make a Speech." *Time,* 14 September 1981, pp. 92-93.

Pollock, John. *Billy Graham: the Authorized Biography.* Grand Rapids, Mich.: Zondervan, 1966.

Potthoff, Harvey. "Humor and Religious Faith." In *Summary of Proceedings: 34th Annual Conference ATLA.* Philadelphia: ATLA, 1980, pp. 74-80.

Ramm, Bernard. *After Fundamentalism.* San Francisco: Harper & Row, 1983.

Rankin, A. H. and Phillip, R. J. *Newsweek,* 26 August 1963, pp. 74-75.

Ragaway, Martin, ed. *Funny Funny Signs.* Los Angeles· Price/Stern/Sloan, 1979.

Rapp, Albert. *The Origins of Wit and Humor.* New York: E.P. Dutton & Co., 1951.

Reader's Digest. *Write Better, Speak Better.* Pleasantville, N.Y.: Reader's Digest Association, 1972.

Reader's Digest, June, 1982.

"Reasons for Teen Suicide Rise Is Focus of New Federal Study." *Columbus Dispatch* 16 March 1984, p. A8.

Redding, David A. *Jesus Makes Me Laugh with Him.* Grand Rapids: Zondervan, 1973.

Rogers, Betty. *Will Rogers: His Wife's Story.* Norman, Okla.: University of Oklahoma Press, 1979.

Rossiter, Al, Jr. "Adapting to Stress by Minimizing Impact." *Daily Reporter,* 11 February 1983, p. 1.

Rosten, Leo. "I Remember Groucho." *Reader's Digest,* November 1982, pp. 105-106.

Safranek, Roma, and Schill, Thomas. "Coping with Stress: Does Humor Help?" *Psychological Reports,* August 1982, p. 222.

Saint Amant, Penrose. "Church: A Community of Celebration Psalm 150, Luke 4:32." pp. 27-31, in *1980 ACPE Conference: Fantasy and Festivity in the Church.* New York: Association for Clinical Pastoral Education, 1980.

Samra, Cal. *The Joyful Christ: The Healing Power of Humor.* San Francisco: Harper and Row, 1986.

_____. "Told He Was Dying, Priest Arranged Own Wake," *Joyful Noisletter,* November-December 1986, p. 3.

Sanders, J. Osward. *Spiritual Leadership.* Rev. ed. Chicago: Moody Press, 1980.

Sapp, W. David. "Sense of Humor Helps?" *The Student,* June 1985, pp. 18-20.

Savage, Jim. "What to do Before You Step Behind a Podium." *News at the Top,* October 1985, p. 2.

Schaeffer, Neil. *Art of Laughter* New York: Columbia University, 1981.

Schnickel, Richard. "Sellers Strikes Again." *Time*, 3 March 1980, pp. 66-67.

Schoenhals, G. Roger. "Go Ahead, Laugh." *Herald of Holiness*, 15 March 1984, p. 5.

Schuller, Robert. *The Be-Happy Attitudes*. Waco, Texas: Word Books, 1985.

Scott, Willard. "Living on the Sunny Side." *Saturday Evening Post*, December 1983, p. 65 *ff*.

Seaman, Nancy. "Phenomena, Comment and Notes." *Smithsonian*, November 1982, pp. 38-47.

Selzer, Richard. "All Right, What Is a Laugh Anyway?" *Esquire*, July 1975, p. 100f.

"Serious Look at Jokes." *Seventeen*, May 1980.

Sheen, Fulton J. *Life is Worth Living*. London: Peter Davies, 1954.

Shelby, Kermit. "Laughter in the Heart." *These Times*, Dec. 1983, p. 5 *ff*.

"Smile Wouldn't Break Your Face." *Daily Oklahoman*, 6 August 1979.

Smith, Frank Hart. "Funny Thing Happened on the Way to Worship." *Church Recreation Magazine* 12:10-11.

"Something Funny's Going On . . . eh, Mr. President?" *The Sunday Tennessean*, 17 August 1986, p. A1.

Spencer, Aida B. "Wise Fool and the Foolish Wise." *Novum Testamentum*, no. 234 (1981), pp. 349-360.

Spinrad, Leonard and Spinrad, Thelma. *Speaker's Lifetime Library*. West Nyack, N.Y.: Parker Publishing Co., 1979.

Spurgeon, Charles Haddon. *Lectures to My Students*. Rev. ed. Grand Rapids: Zondervan, 1954.

Strange, Jean. "Famous Last Words." *Time*, 1 August 1983, p. 69.

Strange, Marcian. "God and Laughter." *Worship*, Jan. 1971, pp. 2-12.

Sully, James. *Essay on Laughter.* New York: Longmans, Green and Co., 1902.

Taylor, Larry M. "In Celebration of Humor." *The Student,* April 1984, pp. 14-16.

Theological Dictionary of the New Testament. S.v. "Gelao," by Karl H. Rengstorf; S.v. "Paizo," by Georg Bertram.

Theological Wordbook of the Old Testament. S.v. "Sahaq," by J. Barton Payne.

"This Is What You Thought About Tasteless Jokes." *Glamour,* March 1984, p. 47.

Thurber, James. *Lanterns and Lances.* New York: Harper, 1955.

Tobin, William J. "Your Sense of Humor." *Talent* (Summer 1983), pp. 15-16.

Trueblood, Elton. *The Humor of Christ.* San Francisco: Harper and Row, 1964.

Untermeyer, Louis. *Treasury of Laughter.* New York: Simon & Schuster, 1946.

"Use of Humor Lauded." *Columbus Dispatch,* 27 November 1980, p. F1.

Van Dyke, Dick. *Faith, Hope and Hilarity.* New York: Doubleday, 1970.

Vannorsdall, John. "Humor as Content and Device in Preaching." *Dialog,* no. 22 (Summer 1983), pp. 187-190.

Vincent, James M., and Jones, John A. "Discovery of Humor in Eulogies as a Positive Persuader." *WHIM Proceedings,* 1 April 1984.

Vos, Nelvin. *For God's Sake Laugh!* Richmond, Va.: John Knox Press, 1967.

_____. "Religious Meaning of Comedy." *Christian Imagination,* pp. 241-253. Grand Rapids: Baker Book House, 1981.

Waddell, Genevieve J. "Meet Jerry Clower." *People*, August 1973, pp. 1-25.

Walsh, J.J. *Laughter and Health*. New York and London: Appleton, 1928.

Ward, Ruth McRoberts. *Self-Esteem: Gift from God*. Grand Rapids: Baker Book House, 1984.

Webster, Gary. *Laughter in the Bible*. St. Louis: The Bethany Press, 1960.

Wellock, Richard M. "Walking with Wisdom." *Table Talk*, Feb. 1984, p. 15.

Whitehead, Alfred North. *Dialogues*. Boston: Little, Brown and Co., 1954.

"Why Laughing Is Good for You." *Science Digest*, June 1981, p. 17.

Wiersbe, Warren W. *Be Joyful: It Beats Being Happy*. Wheaton, Ill.: Victor Books, 1983.

Wilder, Amos N. "The Teaching of Jesus: The Sermons on the Mount." *General Articles on the New Testament, The Gospel According to St. Matthew, The Gospel According to Mark*, by R. H. Strachan, et al, vol. VII of *The Interpreter's Bible*, ed. George A. Buttrick et al (12 vols.;). New York: Abingdon Press, 1951.

Willis, Charles. "Slip of the Tongue Makes Baptist Book Store Life Anything But Dull." *Illinois Baptist*, 9 Aug. 1981, p. 9.

Wilson, Grady. *Count It All Joy*. Nashville: Broadman Press, 1984.

Wolfenstein, Martha. *Children's Humor*. Glencoe, Ill.: Free Press, 1954.

Wright, Rusty and Wright, Linda R. *Secrets of Successful Humor*. San Bernardino, Calif.: Here's Life Publishers, 1985.

Yancy, Philip. "How Dirty Jokes and the Fear of Death

Prove There Is a Heaven." *Christianity Today,* 2 March 1984, p. 78.

Yeck, John. Newsletter of "Let's Have Better Mottoes Association, Inc." P.O. Box 225, Dayton, Ohio.

Young, James Lee. "Psychologist Cites Ways to Be Positive Thinker." *Rocky Mountain Baptist,* 30 August 1979.

Ziglar, Zig. *See You at the Top.* Gretna, La.: Pelican Publishing Co., 1979.

Zinsser, William. "Learning to be Funny Is No Joke." *New York Times Magazine* 2 December 1979, p. 70f.

Ziv, Avner. *Personality and Sense of Humor.* New York: Springer Publishing Co., 1984.

Zuver, Dudley. *Salvation By Laughter.* New York: Harper and Brothers, 1933.

Addenda

Allen, Steve. *How to Be Funny.* New York: McGraw-Hill Book Co., 1987.

Chafin, Kenneth. "Is Humor Holy?" *Baptist Record* (16 Nov. 1968).

Cote, Richard G. *Holy Mirth: A Theology of Laughter.* Natick, Mass: Affirmation Books, 1986.

Hyres, Conrad. *The Comic Vision and the Christian Faith.* New York: Pilgrim Press, 1981.

Index

319